Organizing Leviathan

Why are some countries less corrupt and better governed than others? Challenging conventional explanations on the remarkable differences in quality of government across the globe, this book argues that the organization of bureaucracy is an often overlooked but critical factor. Countries where merit-recruited employees occupy public bureaucracies perform better than those where public employees owe their post to political connections. This book provides a coherent theory of the reasons behind this, and ample evidence showing that meritocratic bureaucracies are conducive to lower levels of corruption, higher government effectiveness, and more flexibility to adopt modernizing reforms. Data comes from both a novel dataset on the bureaucratic structures of over one hundred countries as well as from narratives of particular countries, with a special focus on the relationship between politicians and bureaucrats in Spain and Sweden. This book is a notable contribution to the literature in comparative politics and public policy on good governance, and to corruption studies more widely.

CARL DAHLSTRÖM is a professor at the Department of Political Science, University of Gothenburg, and a research fellow at the Quality of Government Institute. His research is concerned with comparative and historical perspectives on public administration, administrative reforms, and welfare state policymaking.

VICTOR LAPUENTE is an associate professor and research fellow at the Quality of Government Institute in the Department of Political Science at the University of Gothenburg. His research deals with comparative politics and public administration, combining both quantitative and qualitative methods.

Organizing Leviathan

Politicians, Bureaucrats, and the Making of Good Government

CARL DAHLSTRÖM
University of Gothenburg

VICTOR LAPUENTE
University of Gothenburg

CAMBRIDGE
UNIVERSITY PRESS

University Printing House, Cambridge CB2 8BS, United Kingdom

One Liberty Plaza, 20th Floor, New York, NY 10006, USA

477 Williamstown Road, Port Melbourne, VIC 3207, Australia

4843/24, 2nd Floor, Ansari Road, Daryaganj, Delhi – 110002, India

79 Anson Road, #06–04/06, Singapore 079906

Cambridge University Press is part of the University of Cambridge.

It furthers the University's mission by disseminating knowledge in the pursuit of education, learning, and research at the highest international levels of excellence.

www.cambridge.org
Information on this title: www.cambridge.org/9781107177598
DOI: 10.1017/9781316822869

First published 2017

Printed in the United States of America by Sheridan Books, Inc.

A catalogue record for this publication is available from the British Library.

Library of Congress Cataloging-in-Publication Data
Names: Dahlström, Carl, author. | Lapuente Gine, Victor, 1976- author.
Title: Organizing Leviathan : politicians, bureaucrats and the making of good government / Carl Dahlström, Victor Lapuente.
Description: Cambridge, United Kingdon ; New York, NY : Cambridge University Press, 2017. | Includes bibliographical references and index.
Identifiers: LCCN 2017000019| ISBN 9781107177598 (Hardback) | ISBN 9781316630655 (Paperback)
Subjects: LCSH: Bureaucracy–Evaluation. | Administrative agencies–Evaluation. | Executive departments–Evaluation. | Civil service. | Government executives. | Government accountability. | Political corruption. | Comparative government.
Classification: LCC JF1501 .D35 2017 | DDC 320.4–dc23
LC record available at https://lccn.loc.gov/2017000019

ISBN 978-1-107-17759-8 Hardback
ISBN 978-1-316-63065-5 Paperback

Till mina föräldrar, Margareta och Lars
A mis padres, Elisabet y Benjamín

Contents

Acknowledgments

This book project owes a lot to our colleagues, friends, and families. We are particularly grateful to Jan Teorell, with whom we started analyzing how bureaucracy, politics, and corruption are related. It was in dialogue with Jan that we came up with the ideas and saw the empirical patterns that we then developed and examined in this book. Since the three of us began talking about these issues several years ago during a conference on Marstrand, an island on the Swedish west coast, Jan has contributed tremendously to this project – first as co-author and then as a supportive colleague and friend.

Our work with this book has mainly been carried out at the Quality of Government Institute at the Department of Political Science in Gothenburg. It has been a privilege to work at the Quality of Government Institute, not least because of the vibrant research milieu created under the direction of Bo Rothstein. For that, we would like to thank everyone at the Quality of Government Institute. The arguments presented in the book owe a particular intellectual debt to Bo, for which we are very grateful.

We have had the privilege of benefiting from the help of many scholars: Andreas Bergh, Sheri Berman, Philippe Bezes, Rasmus Broms, Andreas Bågenholm, Nicholas Charron, Agnes Cornell, Stefan Dahlberg, Michelle D'Arcy, Gissur Erlingsson, Yadira González de Lara, Marcia Grimes, Sören Holmberg, Phillip Keefer, Edgar Kiser, David Lewis, Per Lægreid, Johannes Lindvall, Martin Lodge, Francisco Longo, Gary Miller, Alina Mungiu-Pippidi, Marina Nistotskaya, Anna Persson, B. Guy Peters, Jon Pierre, Colin Provost, Jan Rovny, David Rueda, Anders Sundell, Ann Towns, Andy Whitford, Sofia Wickberg, Lena Wängnerud, and many others have given invaluable comments on parts of the manuscript or have in other ways been supportive of our work. Three anonymous reviewers for Cambridge University Press offered detailed advice on how to improve the manuscript, and John Haslam – Executive Publisher for Political Science and Sociology at

Cambridge University Press – generously took us onboard and skillfully helped us through the process.

What is more, we have had the opportunity to present our work at many seminars, conferences, and workshops, and we would like to thank the participants in the Comparative Political Economy seminar, Department of Politics and International Relations, University of Oxford; the seminar at Department of Business Administration, Technology and Social Sciences, Luleå University of Technology; the London Public Policy Seminars (co-organized by King's College London, the London School of Economics and Political Science, Queen Mary University of London, and University College London); the Hertie School's Public Management & Governance Research Colloquium; the Political Economy Seminar, Lund University; and the seminar series at the Centre d'études européennes, Sciences Po, Paris. We would also like to thank fellow panelists in the "Societal Consequences of Political and Administrative Relations" panel at the annual meeting of the Council for European Studies, Amsterdam, the Netherlands, 2013, and in the panel on "Political Institutions and the Policy Process in Comparative Perspective" at the 72nd annual Midwest Political Science Association Conference, Chicago, USA, 2014.

We have had vital help from Alice Johansson with preparing the manuscript for submission, and from Richard Svensson, who helped us to prepare the graphs and the data. We would also like to thank Anna Khomenko, Petrus Olander, and Dalila Sabanic for all their help. Janet Vesterlund helped us immensely with language editing.

Moreover, we wouldn't be who we are, intellectually, if it were not for Peter Esaiasson, Mikael Gilljam, and Johannes Lindvall. By questioning our arguments, you made them sharper; by encouraging us, you helped us carry them through.

This book is a part of both the QoG Institute and of ANTICORRP (http://anticorrp.eu/), and we gratefully acknowledge financial support from Riksbankens Jubileumsfond (the Swedish Foundation for Humanities and Social Sciences) and the Seventh Framework Programme for Research and Development of the European Union (project number 290529).

Some of the ideas we present in this book have previously been presented in "The Merit of Meritocratization: Politics, Bureaucracy, and the Institutional Deterrents of Corruption," by Carl Dahlström, Victor Lapuente, and Jan Teorell (*Political Research Quarterly*, 65(3),

2012: 658–670) and in "Explaining Cross-Country Differences in Performance-Related Pay in the Public Sector," by Carl Dahlström and Victor Lapuente (*Journal of Public Administration Research and Theory* 20(3), 2010: 577–600). We are grateful to the publishers and to our co-author for giving permission to publish revised versions in this book.

Finally, Carl thanks Sofia, Isak, and David, and Victor thanks Alvar and Vilgot. Without you, none of this would be really meaningful. Thank you for being there!

1 | *Why Relations between Politicians and Bureaucrats Matter*

Incentives, and Institutions That Shape Them

This book deals with quality of government. In our view, governments of high quality act impartially, are non-corrupt, and use resources efficiently. These might seem to be obvious goals for all governments but, quite the contrary, we observe great variation worldwide. Political leaders, in coalescence with other elite groups, often enrich themselves or in some other way take advantage of their position at the expense of society at large. Corruption, rent-seeking, wasteful spending, and ineffectiveness follow. Conversely, other rulers seem to have the right incentives to provide high quality of government. What explains these differences?

This book shows that elite incentives are shaped by the way political and bureaucratic relations are organized, and that this in turn affects corruption and government effectiveness. Our idea is simple: When groups with known different interests are forced to work together, they monitor each other, which pushes both groups away from self-interest toward the common good. Abuse of power will be more common if everyone at the top has the same interest, because no one will stand in the way of corruption and other self-interests. The problem, of course, is that interests are difficult to observe and are thus not easily organized. We think, however, that the careers of officials provide a useful approximation of their interest, as it is reasonable to assume that most individuals are interested in their own careers. It is therefore vital to maintain a separation between the careers of politicians and the careers of bureaucrats, as they are two significant groups at the top of government.

Specifically, we think that the most important signal of the extent to which the careers of politicians and bureaucrats are separated is sent when recruitments are made. Recruitments *de facto* based on political loyalty signal that bureaucratic careers, regardless of *de jure* regulations, are tied to politicians. In such cases the professional fates of bureaucrats are integrated with those of their political masters. In contrast, when recruitments are based on the merits of the candidate, it signals that it is professional peers, instead of political masters, that influence bureaucratic careers. Institutions guaranteeing a recruitment system based on merit rather than political considerations are consequently important resources for high quality government.

Even though we build on a large literature in comparative politics, economics, and public administration, the suggestion we give here differs from previous research in two ways. First, in most comparative studies in politics and economics, the administrative side of the state is mostly ignored. Incentives are taken into account, to be sure, but only those of the political elite. The incentives of other officials are neglected and, perhaps even more importantly, so is the interplay between bureaucrats and politicians. In turn, the suggested policy implications are almost always on the political side, for example, on the characteristics of election systems. We think that not considering the administrative side of the state misrepresents the dynamics leading to high-quality government and it might make us draw incorrect policy implications.

Second, public administration scholars have indeed studied the bureaucratic side of the state, but the dominant view there differs from ours. The existing literature emphasizes bureaucratic rules, in opposition to managerial discretion, while we highlight the importance of bureaucratic career incentives. This distinction is relevant because the implications of the prevailing view in public administration and our interpretation are very different. The proposition in mainstream public administration is to protect the bureaucracy from political influence by rules, in what can be called a closed Weberian administration. However, the theory and the empirical analyses presented in this book indicate that rules provide only a false hope. When we compare administrations from all over the world, the existence of meritocratic recruitment is, contrary to what is often believed, not correlated with the prevalence of a highly regulated civil service. And, as we will see in a detailed description of countries belonging to the Napoleonic administrative tradition, high levels of closed Weberianism can coexist with high levels of politicization.

In tune with this latter point, we are also skeptical of those who think that formal monitoring through, for example, the establishment of anti-corruption agencies, is effective in the struggle for good government. The reasons are twofold: In comparison with the internal system of mutual monitoring between politicians and bureaucrats that we highlight in this book, an external monitoring mechanism is both costly and less effective, as the opportunities for extracting private benefits from public activities are ubiquitous and external controls can always be circumvented.

Before discussing our theory and previous research in more detail, we will try to illustrate our suggestion concretely and see what happens when a separation between the career incentives of politicians and bureaucrats is missing: that is, how a notable integration of careers contributes to more corruption and less government effectiveness. We provide some narratives of the causal dynamic and how difficult it is for a polity to escape a bad equilibrium of integration of politicians-bureaucrats careers, rent-seeking, waste, and ineffectiveness. For this illustration, we have not chosen a developing country, for which one can suspect that bad governance is a notorious problem, but instead describe how the integration of careers between politicians and bureaucrats creates opportunities for corruption and wasteful spending in an advanced capitalist democracy, namely Spain. While we could expect a longtime OECD and EU member such as Spain to have developed the appropriate social, economic, and cultural barriers against systematic government pathologies, this has not been the case. We argue that the reason in the particular examples we discuss in the following pages lies in the prevailing integration between the career paths of elected officials and bureaucrats in most Spanish public organizations.

Corruption and the Story of *Don Vito*

In the early 1990s, a modest travel agent, Francisco Correa, started to build up relationships with high profile politicians of the ascending conservative Popular Party (Partido Popular). A decade later, Mr. Correa had become a powerful businessman who would claim to be the "master" of administrations across Spain (*El País*, 17-06-2013) and was accordingly nicknamed *Don Vito*. Mr. Correa was able to build a network of firms that, while providing services to the Popular Party, such as the organization of political rallies, was awarded substantial contracts from administrations controlled by this party. A turning point in his career was when the Popular Party won the national elections in 1996, and public tender contracts obtained by Don Vito's numerous companies "multiplied," including a €2.2 million contract with the Airports Authority and hundreds of trips by the Prime Minister's Office (both institutions dependent on the Popular Party-controlled national government), a €6.4 million organization of the Pope's visit in 2006 (dependent on Popular Party-controlled regional governments) and countless contracts from municipal administrations where Mr. Correa gained the confidence of local councilors belonging to the Popular Party (*El País*, 18-04-2010).

The system created by Don Vito was complex. First, he and his collaborators in different areas "convinced" politicians with the help of presents such as organizing birthday parties and trips to Eurodisney for their children (*El País*, 30-05-2013a), €2,000 watches (*El País*, 23-06-2013), a fixed 10 percent of every contract gained to the most valuable political brokers (*El País*, 06-08-2013) and some Christmas presents that led a regional president (in a phone call intercepted by the police) to tell Mr. Correa's collaborator: "Merry Christmas, my soul mate...I love you so much..."[1]

Second, the large network of companies controlled by Mr. Correa managed to overcharge the authorities with prices up to 100 percent above market. In addition, most contracts were fragmented in order not to reach the €12,000 limit that forces public administrations to organize a public offering that must follow a detailed procedure (*El País*, 30-05-2013b). The General Auditing Office reported that, in the regional government of Madrid alone, no less than 104 contracts – amounting to €3.16m – were divided up into different services so that each was under €12,000.

Last, the money generated by this machinery was moved abroad via several figureheads and ghost companies: €24 million to Monaco and Switzerland, and up to €30 million to the United States and many more in tax havens that declined to collaborate with the investigation of this case (*El País*, 02-06-2011). All in all, the charges against Mr. Correa are so numerous that his judicial case occupied over 50,000 pages (*El País*, 07-04-2010), and the money plundered from the public coffers by Mr. Correa and associates is almost impossible to account for, given the large number of shady deals that had taken place simultaneously in different administrations and by diverse individuals, yet it has been estimated at around €449 million (*EL País*, 06-03-2015).

That businessmen and top officials are tempted to carry out selfish acts with the abundant public resources existing in a developed country is not so surprising. What is more disturbing is how the corrupt network can get away with siphoning over €400 million, despite the numerous administrative checks and accountability mechanisms that exist in an advanced democracy. The investigations into this case actually reveal numerous instances where the flow of public money to Mr. Correa's firms could have been stopped, and yet it was not. Going into this level of detail is important for uncovering the micro-foundations of our argument. For instance, let's look at two days in July 2006, when several representatives of Don Vito visited no less than eight departments of the Madrid regional government in order to speed up the payment of hundreds of fragmented public contracts that, under the €12,000 threshold, Mr. Correa's firms had gained (*El País* 26-07-2013). Don Vito's employees carefully recorded the conversations they had with the public officials – some appointed, but many tenured civil servants – during those two days. The notes provide insightful information on how officials – who in most cases had not taken part in the corrupt exchange – reacted in the face of requests to pay a large number of bills that are all suspiciously below €12,000.

Some public officials told Mr. Correa's envoys that they would pay the bills, but it is interesting to observe the behavior of the officials who saw that there was something going on and, nevertheless, did not react. As Mr. Correa's representatives complain in their notes, some public employees "...said that they do not want to pay since one can clearly see there has been a fractioning of the sum" (*El País* 26-07-2013). The responses of these reluctant officials are rather diverse; some opted to delay the payment (e.g., arguing that "they had to talk to their bosses" before ordering the payment); others appealed to existing administrative procedures (e.g., directing Mr. Correa's envoys to another department theoretically responsible for payments); others tried to ignore the payment request (e.g., she "does not want to know anything"); and some even showed disconformity (e.g., "he said he was not very comfortable [with the bills] and since then he does not answer the phone"). Remarkably, despite these officials realizing that they were confronting the payments of a dubious legal exchange, none of them decided to sound the alarm, to report to the corresponding audit authority, to the media, to an opposition party, to the public prosecution office, to a judge, to the police, to whomever. They remained silent.

As a matter of fact, silent acquiescence was the working assumption of Mr. Correa's employees. It was common knowledge to them that, since the political masters of the administration were in the corrupt exchange, no one in the rest of the administrative machinery of government – whether in or out of the particular corrupt exchange – would invest any significant effort in impeding it. Knowing the real rules of the game, Mr. Correa assumed that the great majority of the bureaucratic apparatus was responsive to its political bosses and that there was consequently nothing to worry about.

The case of Ana Garrido, a former municipal employee who dared to unveil Mr. Correa's corrupt network, indicates that this assumption was well-grounded. In her own words, she became a whistleblower "because I have no children" (*El País* 14-02-2016), which was vital since she was expecting a serious disruption in her professional career as a result of revealing the corruption network. In April 2016, before the Spanish Parliament, she summarized the "seven years of Calvary" (*Voz Populi* 09-04-2016) that was the result of starting to speak the truth. First, she was offered a bright professional future if she played along, but, when she refused, she was subject to constant mobbing. One day, when she complained about her working conditions, her superior confessed that he had orders to "make your life impossible" (*Voz Populi* 09-04-2016). She was not only forced to leave her job but had to leave Spain because of the constant psychological pressure she was put under. She spent two years unemployed in Costa Rica and, after returning to Spain, she was unable to resume a career in the public sector, since the mobbing became even more intense. Finally, advised by a medical doctor, she gave up, and today she makes a living selling handmade bracelets.

Effectiveness and the Story of Airports to Nowhere

Carlos Fabra was the president of the provincial government of Castellón, Valencia, when he pushed through what international observers referred to as "a symbol of wasteful spending" in Spain in the 2000s: a $183 million "airport to nowhere" in his hometown. The airport's record was outstanding during its first two years in operation: It had not managed to have a single scheduled flight (*The New York Times* 18-07-2012). But Mr. Fabra is not the only example of the strikingly inefficient ways of spending public money in twenty-first-century Spain. There are other airports that embody the country's "lavish spending on white elephant building projects" (*BBC News* 26-07-2012).

For example, Ciudad Real's international airport has attracted only 100,000 passengers from its opening in 2008 until its closure for lack of activity in 2012, despite having one of the longest runways in Europe and capacity to host 5 million passengers. One year later, the airport was up for auction – and the shocking difference between the starting price (€100 million) and its building cost (€1 billion) can also be seen as indicative of its inefficiency (*The Guardian* 07-08-2013). These examples are part of a larger pattern of airport oversupply. Spain has forty-three international airports, twice as many as Germany, which has almost double the population of Spain.

The same kind of overspending is common in other infrastructure projects in Spain. Not only airports but also trains and highways go nowhere. For instance, Spain has the world's second largest high-speed rail network, after China, ranging over 2,000 kilometers. Yet several economists (Bel 2010) have noted that there is a poor economic rationale behind most public investment decisions in high-speed trains. To start with, the Spanish network also has an extremely low passenger rate (20 percent of that of the French). Further, the location of some high-speed train stations defies economic thought. An inhabitant of Tardienta, a village of 1,000 in the far east corner of Spain, with a high-speed line that only uses 6 percent of its capacity, while admiring the high-speed train, admits that "…to be honest, no one comes here and the people of the village use it very little" (*Público* 27-02-2011). Similarly, the huge investments in highways – Spain built over 5,000 kilometers of motorway in the decade to 2009 (*The New York Times* 18-07-2012) – have also led to a debt of €3,600 million that is seen by observers as the result of an "absurd global design" (*El País* 23-09-2013).

Why were these "white elephants that dragged Spain into the red" (*BBC News* 26-07-2012) not stopped? Digging into the micro-decisions that led to these cases of wasteful spending one finds that, again, a politicized administration seems to be at the root of the problem. The ability of politicians to appoint large numbers of officials has contributed to this proliferation of white elephants all over Spain's territory in two crucial ways. First, political appointments to relevant administrative positions allowed elected officials to disregard technocratic considerations and give priority to short-term goals.

We can see an example of this mechanism in Galicia, in the northwestern corner of Spain. There we have Santiago de Compostela's grandiose City of Culture, with a museum, an opera theater and a library originally devised to host one million books (*El País* 12-11-2011). The longlasting regional president, Manuel Fraga, wanted to leave a legacy as monumental as Santiago de Compostela's world famous cathedral (*Público* 12-01-2011). Nonetheless, years afterwards, the City of Culture remains incomplete after having cost almost four times more than what had initially been planned. One of the members of the jury deciding on the project, the American professor Wilfried Wang, offers an intriguing answer to how this was possible, related to the *de facto* politicization of a policy decision-making that, on paper, was expert based. Professor Wang had been unequivocal on the fact that the real construction costs would skyrocket: "...you only had to compare the plans to realize that it was too big" (*El País* 08-01-2011). And, yet, the project was approved. The reason was crystal clear; among most members of the jury, including several political appointees, there was, literally, a "fear of" the president of the regional government if the most magnificent project was not approved (*El País* 08-01-2011).

A second mechanism would be the following. The clientelistic links between political patrons with the ability to distribute a large portfolio of public sector jobs and their electoral constituencies helped to secure the re-election of the former – almost regardless of their government performance. Mr. Fabra himself acknowledged this, summarizing how he had been able to survive in office for so long despite all the mounting and diverse accusations against him, and was very explicit: "For as the one who wins the elections appoints countless people. And all these people mean safe votes. It gives you so much power in a municipality or in a province. I cannot recall how many individuals I have appointed in 12 years, I don't know" (Sánchez-Cuenca 2009).

The Incentives, Stupid!

What made this extensive corruption and the strikingly inefficient use of public money possible? As we have noted, many people in Spain's public administrations must have known, or at least suspected, that something was wrong. Why did they go along? Why did they keep quiet? Getting to know the incentives of bureaucrats is essential to understanding not only these failures of good government in the Spanish case but also many other similar situations of abuse of public office for private or partisan gain. When there is one single channel of accountability, as was the case in the episodes in Spain related above, no one in a given public organization asks tough questions because they are, for good reason, afraid of being punished. They simply have no incentive to stand up for the common good. Loyalty to the party, your *de facto* employer, quite naturally takes priority over other considerations. It is not only the loyalty of today that determines how public employees act; perhaps even more important is what they think about their situation in the long run. In a system where the career paths of politicians and bureaucrats are integrated, it is common knowledge that how you stand in the eyes of the party is what will define the rest of your career. The actors in the Spanish cases seemed very aware of this.

Generally speaking, integration of politicians' and bureaucrats' careers in public institutions is essential for rent-seeking activities, such as the ones described above, because corrupt deals, favorable treatment of narrow economic interests and other extractive activities are all collective enterprises in modern government. They require the involvement of several public officials, both politicians and bureaucrats, who directly or indirectly, by action or omission of watchdog duties, fail to deter corruption and inefficiencies.

Think of all the interaction on different administrative levels and in different points in time and space that is needed to make rent-extraction from the public coffers possible: for example, when the plan is initially devised between public officials and private actors; when a friendly public tender is written down; when the competing applications are processed and the final winner decided; when money is effectively transferred; and, very importantly, when the losers, or some third parties, start asking uncomfortable questions that must be circumvented. If the careers of all individuals involved in these interactions are directly or indirectly integrated, and they all to a certain extent depend on the electoral fortunes of the ruling party, it is implausible to expect a defection that could ruin the business. On the contrary, when the career interests of public officials are more heterogeneous such that some individuals depend on electoral results and others are completely free of those concerns, then collective action quickly becomes a coordination problem. There is no reason to cover up an illegal activity of your political superior (or your administrative subordinate) when your career prospects are separated and you are confident that your career prospects are independent of the ruling party's electoral performance.

The rest of this book is an attempt, first, to theorize about how and why people with different incentives could and probably should be involved in all major public decisions and, second, empirically investigate some implications of this theory in a large number of countries.

Outline of the Book

In the next chapter, we develop the theoretical idea and its implications. We first situate the argument in relation to previous literature in economics, political science, and public administration and then point out the contributions of our proposal. In short, we argue that a separation of careers between politicians and bureaucrats creates a milieu with low corruption and high effectiveness, which is also favorable for efficiency-enhancing reforms in the public sector. The chapter also discusses the most significant competing explanation. It is relatively common to suggest that bureaucrats should be protected from political influence through what is sometimes referred to as a closed Weberian system. We question this view and argue that a closed Weberian structure and meritocratic recruitment do not necessarily go hand in hand.

We empirically test the closed Weberian hypothesis in Chapter 3 in a cross-country comparison. As it is a competing theory, we try to give it as good a chance as possible and therefore take five steps. First, we map bureaucracies in about 100 countries around the world in two-dimensional space and show that closed Weberianism and meritocratic recruitment are not the same. Second, we look at bivariant correlations between indicators of a closed Weberian bureaucracy and three dependent variables, which we consider to be good indicators of the implications of our theoretical expectations. Third, we include a minimum of controls in the regressions. The controls are specific to each type of dependent variable, as we follow the most influential theories in each field, but they are generally from the cultural, economic, and regime areas. Fourth, we conduct a series of robustness checks in order to exclude the possibility that closed Weberianism only works if several institutions are in place at the same time or in more or less developed parts of the world. The broad comparisons analyzed in this chapter demonstrate that in none of the specifications does the closed Weberian hypothesis have empirical support. Fifth, and finally, we describe the European countries belonging to the Napoleonic administrative tradition and explain why closed Weberianism does not contribute to the expected good outcomes but in fact can rather often be counterproductive.

Chapter 4 tests the impact on corruption of the separation of careers in three analytic steps. We start by demonstrating that there is indeed a strong bivariate correlation between our preferred indicator and low corruption. We then carry on to include the most prevailing prevalent alternative explanations from political science, economics, and sociology. However, our indicator continuously has a statistically significant effect in the predicted direction. We think that the main challenge to our results is the potential endogeneity bias. We therefore make some additional analyses, including an instrumental variable (the structure of bureaucracy in the eighteenth century) and previous levels of corruption on the independent side. Although our results are confirmed in these analyses, we also analyze the historical path from high level to low level corruption in the United Kingdom, the United States, and the Nordic countries to be able to show that administrative reforms were indeed a part of the solution, and not a part of the outcome.

Chapter 5 takes on the challenge of investigating the relationship between bureaucratic institutions creating a separation of careers and effectiveness of government. The chapter starts with a discussion of alternative explanations and the mechanisms we think are at work. Empirically, we employ the same kind of methodology as in Chapter 4, but this time we use indicators of government effectiveness, such as wasteful government spending and management performance on the dependent side. The main result in this chapter is confirmative for our suggestion. A separation of careers does seem to contribute to government effectiveness, even after including several demanding controls.

In Chapter 6, we test whether bureaucratic institutions creating a separation of careers are positively associated with efficiency-enhancing reforms in the public sector. This is important, as it might be an explanation for why countries have such a hard time getting out of vicious circles. The basic message here is that, even if countries identify reforms that could potentially help to improve the quality of government, an integrated career system would probably hamper the reforms. Our theory suggests that public employees should be more willing to make investments that imply an extra effort in systems where the careers of politicians and managers are separated; this should play out in the degree to which incentive systems are used in the public sector. We therefore use the degree of performance-related pay in the public sector as the dependent variable. We see two main problems with the analyses in this chapter. First, we do not like to rely exclusively on analyses with perception measures from the same survey on both sides of the equation, and we therefore present model specifications where we substitute one or both of the indicators with indicators from other sources. Second, we are conscious of a potential omitted variable bias. This problem comes from the fact that it is possible to view both the separation of careers between politicians and bureaucrats and performance-related pay in the public sector as parts of the same reform package. We take two steps to exclude this possibility as far as possible; we use an instrument and study the time sequence of the implementation of performance-related pay in the public sector in Sweden and Spain. Results of this analysis speak against omitted variable bias.

In the final chapter, we describe why we think that the empirical analyses speak in favor of our suggestion and against the closed Weberian hypothesis. We also point at the theoretical implications and discuss potential policy implications from this study.

2 | Theory

On the Importance of Incentives

Widespread corruption and government inefficiencies cause enormous problems in the world today. This chapter presents a theory of how governments should be organized in order to minimize corruption and other malfunctions. Recent scholarship has put quality of government institutions firmly on the agenda. It has given us a better understanding of why some states perform better than others but, even though there are good reasons to believe that bureaucracy is an important part of this story, comparative research has focused mainly on political, economic, and cultural explanations. We want to shift the focus back to bureaucracy and describe why it belongs at the core of a theory on quality of government.

When bureaucracy is left out of the analysis, a possible explanation for the well-documented variance in the quality of government is overlooked. As we illustrated in the first chapter, we think that incentives created by the organization of bureaucratic and political relations are worth special attention. It has been shown that, throughout history, elites have been tempted and have had the opportunity to take advantage of their positions at the expense of society at large (Miller 2000; North, Wallis, and Weingast 2009). It is probably futile to hope for new elites that do not behave in this way, so this problem will always be present, but we suggest that their incentives are formed to some extent by the institutional context in which they work. It is therefore essential to form this context so that it undermines the incentives for greed and opportunism. The main idea in this book is that if the organization of the state apparatus, or the Leviathan in the book's title, divides public officials into two distinct groups, the possibilities for abuse and opportunism by public officials are diminished because these two groups have different career incentives. Consequently, this book argues that if politicians' and bureaucrats' careers are kept separate, corruption will be less attractive and effectiveness will be a more attractive alternative for people at the top.

By separation of careers, we do not refer to the formal, *de jure*, divide via, for example, a Civil Service Act, since it is well documented that such laws are often circumvented (Grindle 2012; Schuster 2014). Instead, we think of the *de facto* separation between the careers of public employees, bureaucrats, and politicians. Such a separation should be well known to everyone working in the administrative and political sphere and is signaled though recruitment and promotions of both bureaucrats and politicians. In a system of that kind, politicians do not colonize the administrative sphere with party loyalists, nor do bureaucrats colonize the political sphere with career civil servants.

The stereotypical example of a separated career system is the United Kingdom, where there are strong limits to politicization of the bureaucracy, as well as to bureaucratization of politics (Rouban 2012; Sausman and Locke 2004). In the late nineteenth century, a "public service bargain" crystallized between civil servants, who renounced having a political career, and politicians, who renounced hiring and firing civil servants (Hood 2000; Schaffer 1973), resulting in a "nonpolitical, permanent civil service, loyal to the government of the day" (Horton 2011, 34). Since then, civil servants in the United Kingdom and Ireland have not been permitted to be active members of political parties; a similar separation of politicians' and bureaucrats' careers is present in countries such as the Netherlands, Denmark, and Norway (Van der Meer, Steen, and Wille 2007).

On the other end of the scale are the "traditional Mexican and Brazilian civil service bargains," where bureaucrats have a person-specific loyalty to the political superior or to the ruling party (Hood 2002, 321). In general, meritocracy is rather weak in Latin American democracies, and even ambitious civil service reforms, like the one in 1991–92 in Argentina, have been "not a serious obstacle to massive political appointments a few years later" (Ferraro 2011, 172; see also Geddes 1994; Zuvanic, Iacoviello, and Rodríguez-Gusta 2010). In these cases, the careers of politicians and bureaucrats are not separated but integrated in the same career system. A similar politicization of the civil service has also been found in post-communist Europe, and cases of bureaucratization of politics can be found in Southern Europe (Grzymala-Busse 2007; Meyer-Sahling and Veen 2012; Parrado 2000; Rouban 2012; Sotiropoulos 2004).

Separation of careers is conducive to good government because it generates an embedded system of mutual checks and balances between officials because they are responsive through different channels of accountability (politicians to electors and bureaucrats to their professional peers). This deters corruption and wasteful spending and creates an environment where the career prospects of public employees do not depend on having a sponsor but instead on job performance, which contributes to government effectiveness. What's more, a separated career system makes innovation and public management reform more probable, which in turn explains why countries with high-quality government institutions continue to be high performers even when they suffer from external shocks. Think, for instance, of the severe budgetary pressures in the Netherlands and the Nordic countries in the 1980s and 1990s and compare these with the crisis in Southern Europe after 2008. High-performing governments can adapt to new situations because they are able to implement wide-ranging reforms, for example strategic decentralization, an introduction of performance reviews and practices of proven efficiency in the private sector, and the like. In contrast, low-performing governments tend to lag behind when it comes to reforms and, as we will see, this is related to the fact that there is an integration of political and bureaucratic careers in those countries that make street-level bureaucrats reluctant to accept changes in the organizational *status quo*. Indeed, as has been noted regarding peripheral economies in the Euro zone, the governments that need to be reformed the most are, a bit paradoxically, those that are reformed the least (Fernández-Villaverde, Garicano, and Santos 2013).

Our suggestion builds heavily on insight from two previous lines of research. First, corruption and government effectiveness are common themes in comparative economics and the political science literature, and these approaches have contributed insightful analyses that allow us to better understand cross-country differences in government performance (see, e.g., Acemoglu and Robinson 2012; North, Wallis, and Weingast 2009; Rauch and Evans 2000; Rothstein 2011). Second, we are building on the public administration literature, following from Max Weber (1978[1921]), Woodrow Wilson (1887), and Frank Goodnow (1900), and the crucial interplay between the political and administrative spheres has also been thoroughly studied (see, e.g., Aberbach, Putnam, and Rockman 1981; Grindle 2012; Hood and Lodge 2006; Lewis 2008; Miller 2000; Peters and Pierre 2004).

In this chapter, we start a dialog between these two lines of research that have thus far not spoken to one another, despite their study of similar problems. The reasons for this unfortunate disconnection are probably both theoretical and methodological, but we try to learn from both approaches. Very generally speaking, we use the way comparative economics has asked questions about corruption and government inefficiencies and combine this with the suggested answer from public administration about the fundamental importance of the relations between politicians and bureaucrats.

We want to contribute to the existing literature by putting these research agendas together, but we also diverge from them in some ways. As most of the comparative literature on corruption and government effectiveness simply ignores the bureaucratic side of the state, this in itself misrepresents reality and can bias conclusions of this literature. Additionally, neglecting the bureaucratic side of the state also increases the risk of deriving the wrong policy implications. And, while the public administration literature has studied political and bureaucratic relations, it puts too much stress on rules and regulations and misses the importance of incentives. Earlier literature developed a specific interpretation of the Weberian legacy, which we question (for earlier critique see Lynn 2001; Svara 1998). Its prediction is that what is often referred to as a closed administration protects the bureaucracy from political influence, which in turn positively affects the quality of government. This hypothesis deserves special attention both theoretically and empirically, and will be discussed at length later in this chapter and in Chapter 3.

It is probably good, however, to now briefly describe a premise for our reasoning. A Weberian bureaucracy is multi-dimensional. Max Weber saw a bureaucratic organization as characterized by: (1) procedures (e.g., standardized and rule based); (2) structure (e.g., hierarchical and specialized); and (3) personnel system (meritocratic, and employment protection) (Barberis 2011). We follow Evans and Rauch (1999) and are only interested in personnel systems. Within this subcategory we distill two dimensions that do not necessarily coincide (Olsen 2005). The first dimension relates to employment protection and cases tend to cluster in so-called closed and open systems. The second dimension relates to the separation of careers between politicians and bureaucrats, and distinguishes between separated and integrated systems. Among other things, this book shows that these dimensions do not correlate with each other. A closed bureaucracy can have both separated careers (e.g., Germany, South Korea) as well as integrated careers (e.g., Spain, Greece). And there are open bureaucracies with separated careers (e.g., Sweden, New Zealand) as well as with integrated careers (e.g., Mexico, Slovakia). Throughout, the empirical analyses show that separation of careers is an important predictor of corruption and misbehavior, while closedness is generally uncorrelated to indicators of good government.

The next section of this chapter describes insight from comparative literature, mainly in economics and political science, tries to pinpoint the way in which it can learn from the public administrative literature, and shows how our approach is different from mainstream public administration. It is important to note at this early point that our discussion of these strains of literature is on a general level. We will therefore return to those studies, and many more, and discuss their details in the coming chapters on closed Weberianism (Chapter 3), corruption (Chapter 4), government effectiveness (Chapter 5), and efficiency-enhancing reforms in the public sector (Chapter 6). Following the discussion of the literature, we turn to our own suggestion, of course informed by both lines of research. We describe the general components of our theory first and then describe the details of the causal mechanism. Finally, we identify three empirical implications of our suggestion, explain how we have designed our empirical study, and give an overview of the data and methods we use.

What Makes Good Governments Tick? Insight in and Limitations of the Existing Research

Social science has benefited much from political economists' ability to address fundamental questions about the relationship between institutions and development, such as "do institutions cause growth?" (Glaser et al. 2004) or "why nations fail" (Acemoglu and Robinson 2012). With all the caution one must exercise in issues that are unavoidably charged with endogeneity problems, it can be argued that scholars have accurately identified a key element for the prosperity of nations: high-quality institutions. Socio-economic development is not so much the result of geography, cultural, or religious values, or a large accumulation of natural, human, or social capital, as has conventionally been held, but of good institutions.[1] What's more, if it is true that historical legacies matter for understanding the hugely diverse fortunes of contemporary countries, this is because the historical experience is transmitted through institutions (Acemoglu, Johnson, and Robinson 2005; Jones 2013; La Porta et al. 1999, 2008). In sum, there is an emerging consensus among political economists that quality of government, as it is currently known in the literature (Rothstein 2011), is a key foundation to understanding the prosperity of nations.

So far, the literature has advanced a great deal in operationalizing quality of government and concepts related to good government, and recent years have seen an explosion of comparative datasets. For example, the World Bank's Governance Indicators, the International Country Risk Guide's Quality of Government indicators, and Transparency International's Corruption Perception Index cover an increasing larger number of countries and years. A quick look at these indicators shows an astonishingly high correlation among them, which leads scholars to conclude that "...it makes sense to talk about the quality of government as a general feature of countries" (Tabellini 2008, 263). But, critically, we still do not know which particular features of government explain why some countries are always at the top (or at the bottom) of those rankings.

One reason for this shortcoming is probably related to the fact that comparative economics and political science have not sufficiently studied the organization of government. Instead, the research agenda has focused on what Rothstein (2009) calls the "input side" of politics (the aggregation of social preferences into policy decisions) while mostly overlooking factors of the "output side" (the transformation of policies into deliverables). Some important examples are studies of government resources (e.g., tax revenue) or of the characteristics of the decision-makers (e.g., democratically elected or not; majoritarian or PR electoral system; presidential or parliamentarian political system). There has indeed been notable progress in understanding the input side, such as Persson and Tabellini's (2003) magisterial *The Economic Effects of Constitutions*. In these studies, however, scholars tend to work with a very simplified view of the state, centered on politics. They thus overlook the importance of the state machinery, and bureaucracy remains, as Terry Moe noted over two decades ago, on the neglected side of the story, while: "[bureaucratic] institutions, more than any others, are characteristic of modern government – indeed, modern government, whether democratic or autocratic, is bureaucratic government" (Moe 1990, 214).

Let's take the brilliant opening of *Why Nations Fail*, where Acemoglu and Robinson (2012) describe the failure of contemporary Egypt to provide quality of government, as an example. There are many references to the rent-seeking behavior of Mubarak and the inner circle, yet not a single one to how the Egyptian state (which employs over five million people) works. It is extremely unlikely that a five million–strong force has not played a major role in the performance of Egyptian government. The implicit assumption in Acemoglu and Robinson (2012), as well as in most conventional accounts, is that bureaucracies are responsive to their rulers, especially if they are autocrats. Yet, what creates incentives for bureaucrats? To what extent are bureaucrats' incentives aligned with those of their political masters? Is it not likely that these incentives may play an important role in explaining differences in quality of government?

Mainstream political science has not done much better in taking the role of bureaucracy into account. Francis Fukuyama (2012, October 2) notes that:

It is curious that, in contemporary American political science, very few people want to study the state, that is, the functioning of executive branches and their bureaucracies. Since the onset of the third wave of democratization, now over a generation ago, the overwhelming emphasis in comparative politics has been on democracy, transitions to democracy, human rights, ethnic conflict, violence, transitional justice and the like... where most people are interested in studying political institutions that limit or check power – democratic accountability and the rule of law – while very few people pay attention to the institution that accumulates and uses power, the state.

This book may be understood partly as a response to Fukuyama, as we hope to contribute to the literature by putting bureaucracies on the agenda of comparative politics, where many scholars and other observers have neglected them. They probably belong there because, as any student of public administration knows, not even the most perfected bureaucracies are machines where a ruler pushes a button and things get done.[2] In addition, public administration scholars have shown once again that the relationship between a politician's order and the outcome from the state apparatus is, at best, conditional on how the bureaucracy is organized (for a review see Dahlström 2012). More specifically, the public administrative research gives us good reason to explore the nature of the relations between politicians and bureaucrats (Aberbach, Putnam, and Rockman 1981; Grindle 2012; Hood and Lodge 2006; Lewis 2008; Miller 2000).

The relevance of the politician-bureaucrat relationship has not historically gone unnoticed by policymakers. Early on, public sector reformers targeted the relations between politicians and bureaucrats, both in Europe and in the United States, in their struggles to achieve better governments. Actually, these reformers tended to give priority to reforms aiming at altering politician-bureaucrat relations over reforms on the input side, such as changes in the electoral formula. For instance, during the nineteenth and early twentieth centuries, corruption and other types of misuse of public resources plagued governance in the British Isles and the United States, as well as in many other parts of Europe and the Americas. Influential reformers, from the British founding fathers of the neutral civil service (Northcote and Trevelyan 1853) to the American entrepreneur of the city managerial government (Richard Childs; see East 1965), thought that a more efficient and reliable administration would be created with professional and meritocratically recruited state officials (Goodnow 1900; Wilson 1887). Many reforms aimed at separating politicians from bureaucrats were also implemented and gave relatively good results (Harling 1995; Kelman 1987; Rubenstein 1983; Schultz and Maranto 1998; Teaford 1993; Van Riper 1958). Simply put, the basic idea in the reform suggestions of that time was to untie the overly close bonds between politicians and bureaucrats by introducing civil service reforms. This insight is fundamental for our suggestion; the incentive structure created by separating careers for politicians and bureaucrats was indeed positive for government performance.

While we take great inspiration from public administration scholars, we see some shortcomings that justify a contribution like the one this book aims to offer. First, most studies in this field have pushed for a return to a more closed Weberian bureaucracy. And there are indeed arguments for this in the literature, for example from the well-known benevolent role played by bureaucracies in numerous state-led economic miracles, such as those of the East Asian "Tigers" (Evans 1995; Pollit and Bouckaert 2011; Rauch and Evans 2000; Suleiman 2003; Wade 1990). We think, however, that it remains unclear what part of the Weberian bureaucracy is important. The problem is that, as Johan P. Olsen (2008; see also Hall 1963) highlighted, such a bureaucracy has many, and even contradictory, elements. For many, a Weberian bureaucracy is defined by the rules and regulations protecting the bureaucracy from political influence. Closing the bureaucracy is in this view positive. For others, it refers to the conditions for those who work in the bureaucracy: in other words, to the staff policy, most clearly expressed in the recruitment system.

A second point at which we part company with the prevailing public administration scholarship is in the excessive faith generally put in bureaucratic agents as guarantors of the common good against short-sighted opportunistic politicians. In short, we do not agree that bureaucrats need always be "above politics," using Gary Miller's (2000, 289) expression. Miller's analysis is probably true for the particular context of the American federal government where "there are probably fewer bribes among the two million federal bureaucrats than there are among the 435 members of Congress" (Miller 2000, 316), but is not a universal law. Numerous illustrations from emerging and developed economies point out a more nuanced picture, one where, both illegally and legally, "bureaucrats [and not only politicians] rob the taxpayer" (*The Economist* 2012). We therefore see no reason to *a priori* think of bureaucrats as better types than politicians, nor as worse types, as sometimes suggested by the public choice literature (Niskanen 1971; Tullock 1965). We take a more pragmatic approach. We think that bureaucrats, or for that matter politicians, are good or bad depending on the organizational structure in which they operate.

In that sense, our work echoes some authors in different disciplines who, working in isolation from each other, and more implicitly than explicitly, suggest an inverted U-shaped relationship, with bad outcomes at the extremes. On one pole, where there is an almost total lack of autonomous bureaucrats because the administration is highly politicized – think of Tammany Hall party machines in late nineteenth-century America or the "democrazies" described by Paul Collier (2009) in postcolonial sub-Saharan Africa – the outcome is a highly corrupt and ineffective government. On the other extreme – when bureaucracy is extremely autonomous – we have another undesirable situation. Fukuyama (2013) uses Japan and Germany in the first decades of the twentieth century as examples of the perils of polities dominated by well-organized and powerful (mostly military) bureaucracies.

Similarly, Avner Greif (2008; with González de Lara and Jha 2008) considers that good government is based on "administrative foundations," because it is bureaucrats – and not constitutions – that can truly prevent rulers from undertaking opportunistic actions. Nevertheless, Greif (2008) notes that a polity entirely dominated by administrators could have negative effects just as much as one controlled by an unconstrained ruler. Again, Greif (2008) refers to a curvilinear relationship between bureaucratic power – vis-à-vis politicians – and quality of government. Finally, in an encompassing within-country empirical analysis, Krause, Lewis, and Douglas (2006, 785) also find that the best outcomes tend to happen where there is an "organizational balancing" between politicians and bureaucrats. In the following section, we will try to show how such a balancing act can help explain comparative differences in government performance.

The comparative literature in public administration has generated an impressive list of studies pinpointing the similarities and differences among national bureaucracies (see, e.g., Christensen and Lægreid 2001; 2007; Hood 2007; Page and Wright 1999; Peters and Pierre 2001; 2004; Pollit and Bouckaert 2011; for an overview see Page 2012), which have given us a good picture of the bureaucracies in European and other OECD countries. What's more, specifically for the US case, several sophisticated studies of political control over bureaucracy have also been carried out (see, e.g., Calvert et al. 1987; Epstein and O'Halloran 1994; Huber and Shipan 2002; Lewis 2008; McCubbins, Noll, and Weingast 1987). However, precisely the emphasis on the inherent complexities, or the particularities, of the US case have also made these studies less useful for testing general propositions on differences across the globe (Moe 1997, 455). In this book, we will therefore work with broader comparisons between a large set of countries, to which we will return in the design and methods section at the end of this chapter.

In summary, we take inspiration from the comparative political economy literature in the way the question is asked and studies are designed. In our empirical analysis later in the book, we will also take into account the variables suggested in this literature. But we notice the absence of a theory and empirical tests on the role of bureaucracy. Therefore, we depart from the public administrative literature, which fosters a deeply rooted insight about the importance of how the relations between politicians and bureaucrats are organized, and the consequences thereof. We differ in three respects from mainstream public administration. First, we note that there is no consensus about a definition of a Weberian bureaucracy, and the definition often used is too broad, according to scholars such as Olsen (2008). As we will return to soon, we use a narrow definition and mainly focus on the recruitment system and the career system created by it. Second, we do not place as much confidence in the rules and regulations of the bureaucracy as is often done. Our approach instead emphasizes incentives for corruption and effectiveness created by career prospects. Finally, we use a broader comparative design than is often used in public administration.

Our main objective in the following sections of this chapter is thus to provide testable propositions for why some governments perform better than others, and describe the mechanisms causing the effects. In doing so, we hope to take a step toward the goal for public administration, as expressed by Robert Dahl more than sixty years ago. Dahl (1947, 11) writes,

...no science of public administration is possible unless... there is a body of comparative studies from which it may be possible to discover principles and generalities that transcend national boundaries and peculiar historical experiences.

Two Symptoms of Bad Government, and How They Can Be Reduced

As just described, the organization of the relations between politicians and bureaucrats has long been debated, and there is important insight from the recent public administrative literature on the same issue, also describing the far-reaching consequences of a dysfunctional system. There are, however, limitations to what we know from this research. One important challenge concerns the definition of the problem. So far, we have discussed the problems that high quality of government institutions are supposed to solve in quite vague terms. In the next sections, we will therefore describe what we believe are the two most important symptoms of bad government, and then explain in more detail how these symptoms may be reduced by an institutional arrangement that separates the careers of politicians and bureaucrats.

Preventing Bad Activities

In a series of papers, Gary J. Miller (1992, 2000; with Hammond 1994; with Falaschetti 2001; with Knott 2008) explains the reasons for an important assumption in political economy, and thus for this book: No matter what we do, no matter how many formal constraints we impose on our rulers, they will always have the option to take opportunistic actions in their personal and constituency's interest, at the expense of social welfare. This is a pervasive idea in political constitutionalism, devised by Alexander Hamilton and James Madison, and in political science, with contributions by Mancur Olson (1965, 1982, 2000) and Fukuyama (2011). Fukuyama's *The Origins of Political Power* can indeed be interpreted as an illustration of how cohesive factions have brought down entire civilizations since the beginning of history. Put together, public governance should be seen as a realm with many opportunities for rent-seeking that, at the same time, can be easily captured by small factions highly motivated to advance their interests at the expense of social welfare.

Because of this insight, it is common to argue that the main problem any polity faces is constraining politicians' moral hazard (Miller 2000; North 1990; North and Weingast 1989). Politicians can, from their privileged position, systematically undermine social efficiency for their own good (Miller and Hammond 1994). The reason is that politicians have access to all extra goods, what is sometimes called the residual, that any policy generates and thus benefit from large residuals. Consider, for example, an infrastructure project. Apart from contributing to social welfare, it produces benefits to the specific community in which the project is located, to contractors and subcontractors, and to workers in construction and maintenance. When they decide on projects like this, politicians have the opportunity to manipulate them in order, for instance, to benefit their cronies. In democracies with a patronage bureaucracy, such as the early twentieth-century United States, these perks can be turned into votes (Folke, Hirano, and Snyder 2011). As a result, in all polities, irrespective of their political regime, there is always a potential inconsistency between the self-interest of rulers – who are tempted to use their policy-making powers to benefit some more than others – and social efficiency.

Miller (2000; Miller and Hammond 1994) pushes this argument another step by interpreting Holmstrom's (1982) impossibility theorem as logical proof that we cannot get rid of this problem. And this is true even if we are conscious of politicians' moral hazard problem, as we cannot devise an incentive system that credibly eliminates the possibility of taking advantage of the residual. Corruption is probably one of the clearest cases of creating large residuals, and we know from empirical research how destructive it is (for an overview see Holmberg, Rothstein, and Nasiritousi 2009). Consequently, we consider it to be one of the main symptoms of bad government.

Since the moral hazard is a built-in problem for all organizations, there cannot be a definite solution to it. Instead, the goal should be to minimize its consequences by organizing the decision-making process in a way that credibly constrains rulers' morally hazardous behavior. This is where the relations between politicians and bureaucrats enter the picture. In one of the most influential formulations of this idea, Miller (2000; see also Miller and Whitford 2016) suggests that the potentially most problematic decisions should be delegated to external actors, such as a group of autonomous bureaucrats. Similar to Thomas Schelling's (1960) path-breaking analysis of nuclear deterrence, Miller (2000) considers that the key to success is delegating to someone whose preferences are "known to be different from your own" (Miller 2000, 299). Miller admits that there are also possibilities that bureaucrats will exploit the residual to their personal advantage. But he still puts his hope in them because of bureaucratic characteristics such as the code of ethics signed by civil servants when joining a bureaucratic corps, deferred compensation schemes according to which civil servants feel compelled to adopt a long-term perspective, secure tenure that prevents opportunistic dismissals, and standard operating procedures that guarantee an impartial treatment of different social interests, which are in fact mechanisms to prevent power abuse by bureaucrats (as well as by politicians). Even if we agree with Miller (2000) that how these relations are organized is indeed crucial, we think he focuses too much on how bureaucrats should monitor politicians. We think it is just as important that politicians monitor bureaucrats. Therefore, the separation of careers between the two groups is more important than protecting the bureaucracy from political influence. This might seem a small difference but, as we shall see later on, it elicits quite different expectations.

Fostering Good Activities

However, good government is not only about constraining central actors from abusing their position but also about encouraging positive achievements in the administration. We see two related problems. First, the incentives for both public managers and public employees must be geared toward effectiveness and not toward some other goal. There are at least two mechanisms through which incentives originating from different career systems affect government effectiveness. We do not need to go to the extreme case of corruption to find two-way monitoring between politicians and bureaucrats useful. There is probably much wasteful spending in all polities, within the framework of the law, and, if no one dares to speak truth to power, this will be higher than it needs to be. A professional management has also been shown to positively affect production in both the private and public sectors (Chong et al. 2014; Gennaioli et al. 2013; Teodoro 2014). In a politicized system, for example, the public managers will probably not have service production as their only goal but will to at least some degree be affected by political considerations, which should hamper management. One cannot be a true professional if one is restricted by "political considerations," as has been argued by different generations of scholars studying professionalism at managerial levels (Misner 1963, 539; Teodoro 2009, 187). Politicization will also influence incentives for rank and file public employees. If they think their future careers are dependent on political considerations, rather than on how good they are at their jobs, the production of public goods will probably suffer.

Second, public employees must be willing to make investments in new reforms if the sector is to approve. This is a daunting task because, contrary to what is sometimes assumed, every detail of how superiors and subordinates in an organization should cooperate cannot be regulated in contracts (Falaschetti and Miller 2001). Therefore, convincing employees to undertake organization-specific efforts that may not be useful for them in other employment is inherently difficult (Williamson 1985). And yet, workers' contributions to the organization's goals will be greater the more they acquire "skills and routines that do nothing to increase their employability outside the firm" (Miller 2000, 300). As is easy to imagine, this problem of organization-specific skills is aggravated in the public sector, where the transferability of skills in some activities, consider national defense and security, but also welfare services that are monopolistically provided by government agencies in many countries, is fairly weak. Newly appointed bureaucrats need to make costly investments in policy expertise and in policy-making capacity that are relationship-specific and, thus, subject to hold-up problems (Gailmard and Patty 2007). That is, if the employment relationship is interrupted, the bureaucrat may not recover her investment and, rationally anticipating this, she may prefer not to invest in expertise in the first place. The ruler needs to convince employees in the public sector to invest in skills needed, which are often specific and therefore less transferable, and to work once they are in a secure position.

The underlying problem is that once employees have made these investments, workers are in a weaker bargaining position vis-à-vis managers (Klein, Crawford, and Alchian 1978). Paying for what you do, instead of for your position – which will be the subject of analysis in Chapter 6 – provides an example of this problem. On the one hand, some studies have recorded increases in productivity in firms that move from flat salaries to performance-related pay (Lazear 1996). On the other hand, in many cases, such as in the classic example of the Du Pont fibers division (Hays 1998; Miller 1992), the introduction of performance-related pay did not alter productivity because employees suspected the management would, *ex post*, manipulate the incentive system to its advantage at the expense of the workers. For instance, once a manager knows that employees can make 20 pieces a day, she might not keep the initially promised reward of $10 per piece but rather cut it down.

We are therefore again in a dilemma (see Miller 1992 for a seminal analysis of this quandary) as to which effect it is important to minimize to achieve good government; but how is that accomplished? The conventional answer, regarding public as well as private sector organizations, has generally been to give a large margin of maneuver for managerial intervention (Foss, Foss, and Vázquez 2006, 797). The explicit or implicit underlying theoretical framework of this literature is the standard principal-agent theory, according to which the main source of organizational problems tends to be the agent (e.g., employee or subordinate). Consequently, the more power the principal (e.g., manager, superior) accumulates, the better the organization will be able to curb problems created by agents who unavoidably have informational advantages over the principals.

The principal-agent mindset has permeated the literature on public organizations as well (Miller 1997). Administration scholars have underlined that public employees are ultimately agents of a political principal and, since they know more about their own true nature and their own behavior than the latter, public bureaucracies may suffer as a result of persistent problems of shirking and opportunism (Kettl 1993; Moe 1984). That is the reason why concentration of political powers in a few hands has been well received by many scholars. If political principals are fragmented, their agents (i.e. public employees) will take advantage. For example, one of the most conventional hypotheses in delegation theories is, in fact, that the more political principals, the more difficult the control of bureaucratic agents will be (Bendor, Glazer, and Hammond 2001, 245), that is, a hypothesis that goes in the opposite direction of this book's.

We depart from the principal-agent view and instead discuss why motivation takes preference over surveillance. As several researchers have noted, the obsession with control frequently backfires, leading to a "control paradox" (Miller 2005, 99; Miller and Whitford 2002; Miller and Whitford 2016) or a "paradox of trust" (Murnighan, Malhotra, and Weber 2004, 293). If you control your employees too closely, you may develop their resistance and mistrust instead of their cooperation. Psychologists have actually indicated that high degrees of surveillance may produce paranoid social cognition even among normal individuals. It is probably more fruitful to rediscover the concept of mutual gain among superiors and subordinates in a given organization (Levi 2005). There have been some theoretical developments of this idea for public bureaucracies. For instance, Brehm and Gates (1997) consider that to achieve organizational efficiency superiors must take responsibility for the actions they supervise and provide a perception of trustworthiness, treating employees as if they were trustworthy, that is, reducing overall levels of surveillance. In other words, the carrot matters more than the stick in getting public employees to make an extra effort.

We follow a line of organizational research that shows that the chances for mutual trust in an organization are much higher when the power at the top is balanced. Traditionally, organizational economics have used insight from law, economics, and organizational theory, but not often from politics. Yet, a new strand of organizational research has used insight from political science to better understand hierarchical dilemmas. Similar to the well-known case of post-1688

English monarchs (North and Weingast 1989; Root 1989), whose hands were tied by a stronger parliament, some scholars have argued that the margin of maneuver of employers should be constrained in a way that any promise they make to their employees becomes credible (Falaschetti and Miller 2001; Foss, Foss, and Vázquez 2006; Miller 1992).

The most obvious way to constrain the margin of maneuver of employers is by dividing the employers into groups. As Miller and Hammond (1994, 22) show for the provision of public goods, there is an inherent advantage in those political systems that, instead of relying on an all-powerful ruler, have plural decision-makers with known different interests. In line with this research, we think that relations at the top of the organization determine the contours of the intra-organizational psychological or relational contract, because these relations not only define the incentives at the top but throughout the state apparatus. A clear separation of careers between politicians and bureaucrats into two distinguishable chains of accountability – political officials to the ruling party and bureaucrats to their peers – represents in our view the best (or the least bad) relational contract in public institutions. This will have two important consequences; public employees will be more motivated to contribute to an effective service delivery and will also be more motivated to make new investments necessary for reforming the administration.

Why Separation of Careers of Politicians and Bureaucrats Is Good for Quality of Government

As we have already mentioned, the conventional answer in the public administration literature to how to decrease corruption, for example, and strengthen government effectiveness emphasizes the "characteristics of Weberian bureaucracy" for constraining public officials' behavior and thus limiting their possibilities for opportunism (Miller 2000, 289; but see also Evans and Rauch 1999; Rauch and Evans 2000). They put their hope in rules regulating the behavior of bureaucrats as the most important mechanism for increasing quality of government. These rules are both formal, such as legal constraints, and informal, such as professional norms.

Quite differently, we think that the key elements are not rules but incentives created by career prospects for bureaucrats and politicians.

We focus in particular on whether the incentives of politicians and bureaucrats are separated or integrated, which is a distinction already recognized as important in the administrative literature (Pierre 1995a; Pollit and Bouckaert 2011; Rouban 2012). We argue that a separation of politicians' and bureaucrats' careers generates, first, an embedded system of mutual checks and balances between officials, because they are responsive to two different chains of accountability. This reduces the first symptom discussed above, as politicians are responsible to the electorate and bureaucrats to their professional peers, and as a consequence their interests are often not the same. Quite the contrary; it is, for example, probably harmful for the career of a bureaucrat to not expose a corrupt politician and the other way round. They therefore have incentives to monitor each other and, even more important, they anticipate this monitoring function and are thus less willing to engage in corrupt exchanges, for example. Second, government effectiveness will probably be higher in separated career systems, as public employees will not depend on contacts but instead on their performance. This pushes the incentives for public employees away from opportunistic behavior and toward higher effectiveness. Third, and related to the discussion in the previous section, organizational research has shown that trust is necessary for convincing employees to make an extra effort to increase efficiency, and it depends on how the relations between owners (i.e. politicians) and managers (i.e. top bureaucrats) are organized (Miller 1992). Because employees trust managers rather than owners, the separation of careers between politicians and bureaucrats helps to solve the credibility problems that all employers face in inducing employees to undertake necessary but costly investments.

Interestingly enough, the degree of separation of careers also varies dramatically from country to country, sometimes within relatively similar contexts, such as the OECD. For instance, scholars have called attention to the remarkable divergence between "those countries where membership of the ruling party is compulsory for senior civil servants and those where such officials are forbidden to belong to political parties" (Hood 2002, 310).

We argue that this variance, which may seem innocuous at first sight, helps to both prevent bad and foster good government, precisely because it critically alters the incentives for politicians and bureaucrats. Consider first the prevention of, for example, corruption, and think of a senior bureaucrat who owes her position to the minister, and thus her career prospects to the fortunes of the ruling party. She will have very few incentives to check the residual generated by a particular policy, and, for example, report an excessive benefit to a particular geographical constituency at the expense of the overall community. And this incentive will possibly trickle down in the departmental pyramid. That is, a junior bureaucrat who aims to become a senior bureaucrat will probably try to replicate the exact same compliant behavior, and so on and so forth travelling down in the bureaucratic hierarchy. This perverse incentive certainly therefore reaches formal political appointees, but it is important to note that it also affects those who have been recruited through competitive exams and have any type of career ambition, if the rest of their career is in the hands of politicians.

We could push this fictive example a bit further and put the senior bureaucrat in a tougher situation. Imagine that she truly disagrees with a particular policy proposal launched by the minister. Again, since her career depends on the minister's career, she has very few incentives to challenge the minister's proposal. Speaking the truth to the minister, reporting behind the minister's back to another party colleague, and whistleblowing to fellow civil servants, the media, or any institution formally in charge of checking and auditing government are not wise career moves. There is a well-grounded suspicion that the bureaucrat's career prospects may be seriously damaged in the case that she challenges her superior's decision, irrespective of the outcome of the challenge. If she loses and the minister wins, her reputation will suffer. If she wins and the minister loses, the fortunes of ruling party A will suffer as a result of the conflict, and rival party B may eventually take over, which will inevitably lead to poorer career prospects for the bureaucrat. As a matter of fact, when the careers of politicians are integrated, a career strategy based almost exclusively on remaining loyal to political superiors – no matter what happens – may yield better results for any given bureaucrat than a strategy based on working as hard as possible and excelling at job tasks.

The Spanish case provides some empirical illustrations of how the integration of careers hampers the internal control exercised by public employees. For instance, civil servants testifying before court about how twenty-seven public contracts totaling €2.4 million had been rigged to favor some politically connected private contractors admitted that, despite thinking that it was "shameful and scandalous," they knew that if they did not play along their jobs would be at stake (*Cadena SER* 15-12-2014).

Similarly, many employees of the municipal government of Santa Coloma (118,000 inhabitants) "looked away" while the municipal government was making shady deals with private firms and the local debt was skyrocketing from €8 million to €85 million between 2003 and 2009. One public employee dared to blow the whistle and the Major warned her: "here we all must row in the same direction, and you are rowing against" (*La Información* 15-09-2015). A whistleblower in this highly politicized environment did not have very good career prospects. She was not only fired from the Santa Coloma municipality: She could not get any job in the public sector despite her qualifications, not even as a consultant for other administrations in the surrounding area, because, as a colleague told her: "...you have done a fantastic job, but if you send us a bill with your name in it, you ruin us" (*La Información* 15-09-2015). Finally, she had to take a job in a bookshop. Interestingly, she was rationally anticipating this outcome before she blew the whistle: "several people told me 'if you see something, do not whistleblow, [otherwise] they will destroy your life.' Yet I was stubborn and I told myself: I will end up selling baguettes, but I am not going to shut up" (*La Información* 15-09-2015).

The effects of recruitment and career paths on incentives are well known. Max Weber describes at length how loyalty to the profession, instead of to the ruler, concerns the very basis of modern government (Weber [1948] 1998). One important reason is that when the careers of politicians are integrated, the administration becomes what Victor Thompson (1965) calls a monocratic system. Thompson refers to an organization where there is only one point or source of legitimacy (Thompson 1965). The consequences of this lack of legitimate conflict are twofold and are directly connected to the other symptoms that are of interest to us. First, a bureaucrat loyal to the ruling party will generally not dare to propose an innovative policy (something inescapably risky, because novel implies by definition some uncertainty) that directly challenges the policy suggested by her superior from the same party when her future career is at risk. As noted both by Heclo (1977) and Peters (2001), policy innovation comes both from politics and bureaucracy. But, in situations where the careers of politicians and bureaucrats are integrated, they do not dare to challenge each other, and these should thus be settings that exhibit low levels of innovation (understood in a broad sense, from novel policies to addressing social problems to efficiency-enhancing organizational changes). There are, in comparison with administrations where the careers of bureaucrats are tied to the fate of their political masters, few incentives to push through new ways of looking at policy or organizational problems, even when they are suspicious about going against the minister's view.

Second, Thompson (1965) notes that in a monocratic organization, the incentive system is dominated by rewards such as career promotions initiated by the ruler. Conformity and compliance with what the superior proposes are rewarded, and thus they become the safest route to making a bureaucratic career in an integrated career system. This will make it rational for an employee to please the ruler regardless of whether that goes directly against government effectiveness. Moreover, these problems are aggravated when bureaucrats reach the top echelons of an agency or a bureau. As Thompson (1965, 6) argues, "the more success one attains, the higher he goes, the more vague and subjective become the standards by which he is judged. Eventually, the only safe posture is conformity." In other words, the closer we are to the top policymaking positions in a governmental department, or managerial ranks of civil service, the more we should expect bureaucrats to reject any course of action or any statement that could endanger their career prospects.

For instance, in the following four-layer hierarchical chain from Minister (1) to Subdirector General (4) – via Secretary of State (2) and Director General (3) – a Subdirector General unsatisfied with a given policy may find it extremely difficult to reveal her preferences, since this may hamper her aspirations to be promoted in the future to any of the three levels above her. The Subdirector General can be a trained civil servant, with years of experience and socialization in the *esprit de corps* of a particular administrative body and, yet, his career prospects make him "largely dependent upon the extrinsic rewards distributed by the hierarchy of authority [i.e. the ruling party]" (Thompson 1965, 7). In summary, we consider that allowing for an integration of politicians' and bureaucrats' careers increases, rather than decreases, the two symptoms of bad government depicted above, because it leads to weak monitoring of rent-seeking behavior and a lack of motivation to do a job well and to improve performance by innovations.

Furthermore, it is important to note that an integrated career system could both be a consequence of a "politicization" of the bureaucracy and a "bureaucratization" of politics (Aberbach, Putnam, and Rockman 1981, 16). Here is thus an organizational paradox that goes mostly unnoticed in discussions of the design of administrative systems. Countries in which civil servants do not face limitations to being active in politics, and therefore have the top positions in the state hierarchy at reach, far from benefiting from this situation may end up suffering from efficiency-detrimental risk aversion. The political ambitions available to bureaucrats are so tempting that preoccupations on the internal distribution of power and status gain preference over intrinsic motivations, such as the accomplishment of organizational goals.

By contrast, in systems in which the careers are separated, we have two parallel hierarchies of accountability. Alesina and Tabellini (2007, 169–70) describe how these two hierarchies cohabit, "...the main difference between top-level politicians and top-level bureaucrats lies in the ways in which they are held accountable. Politicians are held accountable, by voters, at election time. Top-level bureaucrats are accountable to their professional peers or to the public at large, for how they have fulfilled the goals of their organization." As a result, the careers of bureaucrats are independent of the careers of political incumbents. The future prospects of bureaucrats, inside or outside the bureaucracy, will instead depend on their professional status and not on pleasing their political masters. In a separated career system, professional bureaucrats will not have much to gain from playing along if they observe corrupt behavior among politicians. For example, when facing a dilemma in the design of a particular policy implementation (e.g., deciding that the road should go through town X or Y), they have no interest in rewarding the supporters of any particular politician, because their career is not dependent on the re-election of any political sponsor but on the judgment of their professional peers. However, they have much to lose by not exposing corrupt behavior. Their careers will be seriously damaged if they are revealed to have known about corruption and failed to expose it. Basically the same argument applies to elected officials or political appointees when they discover potentially corrupt behavior in merit-recruited civil servants. As a result, a separation of careers increases the chances for both types of actors to reveal and expose corrupt acts committed by the other type. In other words, creating different lines of accountability enables whistle-blowers on either side of the divide to take action against corruption. It is thus only when the career prospects of politicians and bureaucrats are clearly separated that we can have an efficient two-way monitoring mechanism where, essentially, politicians watch bureaucrats and bureaucrats watch politicians.

Likewise, in a system with a separation of careers, we will face the reverse situation of the organizational paradox pointed out above. Since bureaucrats have limited access to top political positions, they will be more eager to focus their energy on working hard, on fulfilling intrinsic motivations to achieve professional rewards. With their political ambitions tied to the mast, like Ulysses, the bureaucrat will be able to listen to the siren's songs. For instance, the Subdirector General we mentioned before will be more prone to push through a promising, and yet unavoidably uncertain, novel solution, even if it could challenge the minister's current preferred policy approach. In sum, a system that decidedly separates the career prospects of politicians and bureaucrats will foster the motivation for both to report government malfeasances and give priority to professional goals over power goals.

Narratives from both historical and contemporary Spain show the problems related to career integration and how hard it is to change. Indeed, with almost two centuries of difference, we find strikingly similar statements made by reform-minded politicians linking the integration of careers to the low performance in the Spanish public sector. In 1838, one MP stated before Parliament that the main problem of Spain's public sector was "the man who does his duty and, nevertheless, is not sure about his fate" (quoted in Lapuente 2007, 42). And, in 1840, another MP raised the issue of the lack of motivation of a pivotal group of public employees: "which kind of interest, for example, a provincial administrator will have? Which reforms will he take? Which works will he make when he knows that – because of any reason, intrigue, betrayal or because someone is closer to the minister – he will be dismissed?" (Lapuente 2007, 42). Consequently, one of the most reformist politicians of nineteenth-century Spain, Prime Minister Bravo Murillo, enacted a Royal Decree, which his successors immediately overturned, radically limiting the politicization of bureaucrats' careers because, in his own words, "the administration of public affairs is impossible when employees do not have any kind of stability" (quoted in Nieto 1976, 234). Almost two centuries later, Spain's "best-known economist" (*The Wall Street Journal* 11–12-2015) and one of the leaders of the centrist *Ciudadanos* party, Luis Garicano, considers that the most important reform to improve public sector efficiency is "fighting patronage politics and cronyism" (*The Wall Street Journal*

11–12-2015). In Garicano's view, if the major government parties behave "like occupying armies when they take over government" (*The Wall Street Journal* 11–12-2015), including the appointment of local hospital heads, the result is mismanagement, corruption, and white elephants.

Taken together, we would therefore expect that, with an integration of careers, the problem of political moral hazard will be aggravated, and we would thus see more opportunistic and rent-seeking behavior, less effective service delivery, and fewer efficiency-enhancing reforms. In other words, we think it would be more likely that politicians and bureaucrats join forces and form what Madison (1787) called a "faction," and Acemoglu and Robinson (2012, 95) an "extractive" elite, in states where politicians and bureaucrats are effectively responsive to a single chain of accountability (see also Miller and Whitford 2016, ch. 5). To the contrary, where the careers of politicians and bureaucrats are separated, we should observe less corruption, greater effectiveness, and more efficiency-enhancing reforms because politicians and bureaucrats have incentives both to monitor each other and to contribute to government effectiveness.

Weberian Institutions and Separation of Careers in the Real World

In the previous section, we attempted to explain why we would expect positive effects of a separation of careers between bureaucrats and politicians as well as outlining the main alternative explanation, namely the existence of a closed Weberian bureaucracy protected from political influence. The difference between our view and the closed Weberian one might seem small, and perhaps only of academic interest. However, we would argue that they often have very different institutional implications. Consequently, this section gives some empirical illustrations of our hypothesis and the closed Weberian view, and differentiates the two from each other. Using existing research in public administration, we will argue that they form a two-dimensional space in which we can place bureaucracies around the world.

On the one hand, comparative scholars have noted the stickiness of administrative structures. For instance, the most discussed topics concern the impact of administrative traditions (Christensen and Lægreid 2011; Yesilkagit 2010) and culture (Verhoest 2010) on attempts to reform bureaucracies. On the other hand, researchers have also noted the increasing global convergence toward a new type of administration (OECD 1995) or the emergence of a "European administrative state" (Olsen 2003).

As mentioned earlier, operationalizing Weberian bureaucracy is challenging, even if we focus only on staff policy. Recent years have witnessed the emergence of many comparative studies. Scholars generally distinguish between two models, although the labels differ. There are career versus position-based, closed versus open, Weberian versus post-bureaucratic, *Rechtsstaat* versus Public Interest, and Continental versus Anglo-American (Auer et al. 1996; Bekke and Van der Meer 2000; Bossaert et al. 2001; Massey 2011; OECD 2008; Peters and Pierre 2004; Raadschelders, Toonen, and Van der Meer, 2007, 2015). One key variable in understanding this difference is the legal system: While the career-based, Weberian, *Rechtsstaat*, or Continental are more prevalent in countries in the Civil or Roman Law tradition, the position-based, public interest, or Anglo-American mostly belong to the Common Law tradition (Horton 2011). However, these classifications are quite general, with within-group variation almost as significant as between-group variation (Demmke and Moilanen 2010).

This book tests another approach and builds on two underlying variables in the comparative literature. We use the separation of careers, already described in this chapter, as one distinguishing feature. We then use the closed versus open terminology to describe the second dimension. Public administration scholars have emphasized that the extent to which public employees are regulated by encompassing special employment laws that protect their careers from external competition and guarantee lifelong contracts is important for how the bureaucracy works. In the literature this is sometimes known as a career-based (OECD 2008), closed (Auer at al. 1996), organization-oriented (Silberman 1993), or "classic administrative model" (Heady 1996), since they are closer to the classic Weberian legal-bureaucratic administration. They put more emphasis on what the literature (Pierre 2011) refers to as "public law" (or *Rechtsstaat*). Its opposite is administrations where posts are "open" (OECD 2008, 27) to competition from inside and outside the public sector, and public employees are less protected by special employment laws and are subject to the more flexible "practices and processes applied in the private sector" (Demmke and Moilanen 2010, 10). Using the trade-off noted by

Table 2.1 *Two dimensions of bureaucracy*

	Open	Closed
Integration	1. Patronage For example, *Tammany Hall* party machines in the US, pre-"public-service-bargain" Britain and most of Western Europe during the nineteenth century, and currently many emerging countries	2. Corporatist For example, countries with a relatively high politicization of the administration and bureaucratization of politics, such as France, Spain, Italy, Japan
Separation	3. Managerial For example, Australia, Canada, New Zealand, Sweden where the personnel systems are private-like but still have clearly different career paths for politicians and bureaucrats.	4. Autonomous For example, closed systems with clear limits for the politicization of the administration and for the bureaucratization of politics, such as in Germany or South Korea

Comment: The horizontal axis dichotomizes open and closed systems, while the vertical axis dichotomizes whether the careers of politicians and administrators are primarily separated or integrated. Together, the table suggests four types of administrations.

Peters (2002) and Pierre (2011), this Closed Weberian model emphasizes law rather than management. Consequently, we refer to this dimension as Closed Weberian versus Open Bureaucracy.

We provide a classification of public administrations building on these two dimensions and present it in Table 2.1. The horizontal axis is a dichotomization of the open/closed dimension and the vertical axis dichotomizes whether the careers of politicians and administrators are mostly separated or integrated. This dichotomization allows us to represent four "ideal types," which of course does not capture the complexities of the real world but may still help us to illustrate that the two dimensions are indeed distinct (Barberis 2011). As Olsen (2005, 4) puts it: "...practice at best approximates the ideal-type, and public administration is never a fully developed bureaucracy." The ideal types – *Patronage, Corporatist, Managerial* and *Autonomous* bureaucracy – are thus what Weber would refer to as "pure types" and "'pure types, after all, are to be considered merely border cases which are of special and indispensable analytical value, and bracket historical reality which almost always appears in mixed forms" (Weber 1978, 1002).

The left column represents open bureaucracies – that is administrations where both the recruitment and promotion of public employees largely follow human resources practices and regulations that are usual in the private sector, such as screening CVs and job interviews of the candidates for a particular vacancy. The flexibility of open bureaucracies obviously characterizes the public administration practices in many highly politicized contexts – think of nineteenth-century prevailing spoils systems in most Western countries where political bosses hired and fired public employees at will and twenty-first-century patronage practices in many emerging countries – but also the flexible human resource procedures that are currently customary in most Nordic and Anglo-Saxon countries for a large number of posts. In open bureaucracies, management (be it for "good" or "bad" purposes) prevails over law, and incentives over rules. This is in sharp contrast to the closed bureaucracies depicted in the right column, where stringent civil service rules prevail over high-powered incentives. Law dominates over management. This is the case in the heavily regulated administrations of the "classic administrative system," where recruitment for the vast majority of positions is based on formalized exams (Heady 2001, 192).

Following the well-known distinction in economics between the "twin theories of screening and signaling," it can be argued that recruitment is in fact qualitatively different in the left and right columns (Riley 2001, 474). In the open bureaucracies to the left, most public employees are selected after a screening process (through their CVs and their performance in job interviews). In contrast, the preferred way of recruiting employees in closed bureaucracies is through signaling. Candidates signal their abilities in a competitive exam or, to be more precise, in a long series of strictly formalized competitive exams. Two examples where this procedure is used are the French *concours* and the Spanish *oposiciones*. The group of contenders who are ranked above a given threshold will join the civil service, not a particular position, but a particular ladder in an administrative body.

It is an important remark that the state apparatus in closed bureaucracies tends to be structured around administrative bodies, ranging from the top *grands corps de l'Etat* or *Grandes Cuerpos del Estado* to bodies covering street-level bureaucrats. In practical terms, this means that access and promotion to the bulk majority of positions in, for instance, core welfare state services, such as public education and health care, are subject to heavy regulations and signaling mechanisms similar to those for central administration bureaucrats. Almost irrespective of their task, in closed bureaucracies the immense majority of the public workforce has a civil service status. Consequently, public workers are less likely to be covered by the general labor laws applicable to private sector employees of the country, and more likely to be covered by special employment laws.

In contrast, open bureaucracies have either never had special employment laws for public employees or have abolished them. For instance, Sweden de-regulated the personnel policy for the public sector to make it more like policy in the private sector in a series of decisions starting during the 1970s (Sjölund 1989). Through these decisions, the bureaucrat's role changed more toward a manager-like position, and only very few positions had formal civil service status (Petersson and Söderlind 1993; Pierre 1993). New Zealand went through a similar process in the 1980s, when many of the personnel powers were decentralized and permanent civil service contracts were substituted for more performance-related contracts (Halligan 2001). However, even in open bureaucracies, not all positions have private sector–like procedures, and there are obviously competitive exams for some particular public sector jobs, such as the British Civil Service Fast Stream. Yet, these recruitment procedures are limited to particular positions, and are subject to fewer procedural regulations and formalisms than a standard *concours* or *oposición*. Instead, they are closer to other non-governmental recruitment procedures aimed at detecting young talents, such as the access tests for a PhD program in an American university.

As mentioned above, the bureaucratic differences illustrated on the horizontal axis in Table 2.1 also coincide with existing dichotomizations of civil service systems in the comparative literature. On the left side, we would encounter public sectors where most positions are open for wide competition, while those in the right column are closed for everyone except members of a given administrative body. As a result, the literature makes the distinction between open and closed civil service systems (Auer at al. 1996; Bekke and Van der Meer 2000). Likewise, Silberman (1993) differentiates two basic ways of structuring bureaucracies: on the one hand, those dominated by an "organizational orientation," where there is a "high value placed on early commitment by the individual" (Silberman 1993, 10) to the organization, which are the administrations on the right; on the left, there are administrations with a "professional orientation" (Silberman 1993, 12), where the training of the bureaucrat, for example a lawyer, an economist, or an engineer, is more important for her career than her possible membership in an administrative body. In professional bureaucracies – Silberman (1993, 74) takes the United States, Great Britain, Canada, and Switzerland as examples – there is more "flexibility" at all levels, which is reflected in structural characteristics such as "lateral entry, interdepartmental mobility, greater range of vertical mobility, and mobility across public and private organizations." These features are in sharp contrast to those of the more rigid "organization oriented" bureaucracies – Silberman (1993, 11) names Japan, France, Germany, Spain, and Italy – where the "entry level is highly uniform" and the career is "very consciously dominated by the organization."

On the vertical axis, the relevant feature is the degree to which the careers of politicians and bureaucrats are separated or integrated. We build on previous elaborations of this specific bureaucratic characteristic (Pierre 1995a; Pollit and Bouckaert 2011), and we would like to emphasize both politicization of bureaucracy and bureaucratization of politics (Aberbach, Putnam, and Rockman 1981). These two aspects tend to go hand in hand but need to be distinguished because it is often the case that reforms intended to tackle one part of the problem, for example decreasing an excessive number of political appointments in the bureaucracy, may increase the risk of the second part by overprotecting civil servants, which may help them into political careers, as in Japan or Spain. When we say separating the careers of politicians and bureaucrats, we mean both an absence (or minimum) of political appointments in the bureaucracy and an absence (or minimum) of trained bureaucrats in politics. In other words, we should not find either a significant number of political appointments in the state structure or a significant number of bureaucrats occupying political positions.

Cell 1 describes the administration traditionally classified as Patronage (for recent discussions of the concept see, e.g., Grindle 2012; Kitschelt and Wilkinson 2007; Kopecký and Mair 2012; Piattoni 2001). Following Grindle (2012, 19), we exclusively refer here to the "micro-foundation of patronage," that is, that there is a "discretionary appointment to a position in government." Patronage systems create extensive pyramids of informal contracts between the political superiors, more or less cohesively grouped around a political party or several political factions, where public sector positions are traded for personal or political loyalty. In principle, patronage should thus be understood as a structural characteristic, not as an outcome. As Grindle (2012, 23) notes, the "...association of patronage systems with incompetence... must be seen as an empirical question, not an assumption." Similarly, the distinction of patronage with corruption is "particularly important" (Kopecký and Mair 2012, 8), since it is not only seen as legitimate and non-corrupt in many contexts but is open and above board.

Although the hypotheses of this book make the opposite prediction, many scholars have claimed that there are positive effects of patronage under certain circumstances. For instance, Grindle (1977) notes how patronage was key to accomplishing some basic activities of government in Mexico and to fostering policy change. In particular, when extraordinary efforts are required of public employees, such as happens in wars, patronage could lead to good outcomes. And, according to some administrative scholars, one hidden factor that explains the good outcomes obtained by the war administrations of Lincoln in the United States and Churchill in the United Kingdom was precisely the increase of patronage appointments and the decrease of bureaucratic positions by both presidents (Fry 2000; Nelson 1982).

On the opposite side, we have scholars who note the pernicious effects of patronage in postcolonial countries. Zaire under the rule of Mobutu Sese Seko (1965–1997) is an extreme case of discretionary staff policy, where access to high rank in all state agencies depended directly upon presidential favor (Acemoglu et al. 2004; Young and Turner 1985). By regularly rotating government posts, Mobutu managed to maintain uncertainty and vulnerability (Leslie 1987). Patronage thus helped Mobutu to survive in power via mastering the loyalty of a large number of supporters and would-be supporters. Yet this came at the expense of one of the world's poorest government performances of the second half of the twentieth century. Another example of the deleterious effects of patronage is the Dominican Republic under Trujillo (1930–1961), whose principal method for controlling the state machinery was the constant shuffling and reshuffling of officeholders. In what probably represents the most extreme example of a patronage administration one can think of, Trujillo kept a file of signed but updated resignations for all government employees. Officials frequently arrived at work only to learn that Trujillo had filled in the date and that they had resigned (Acemoglu et al. 2004; Wiarda 1968). But there are many other well-known empirical illustrations of the negative effects of patronage, from the Tammany Hall party machines in the United States or the Old Corruption in Britain, to the clientelistic networks in postwar Italy and Greece.

Cell 2 depicts what could be called Corporatist bureaucracies. This cell is of particular importance, as the cases in it should perform well according to the mainstream Weberian view, while we would predict lower performance. On the one hand, these are closed civil service systems where politicians have limited discretionary powers to reshuffle the departments they run. Staff policy is in principle firmly controlled by autonomous administrative corps of civil servants (Bekke and Van der Meer 2000). On the other hand, and this is a key part of the argument we developed above, since there are no limits to the political activities of bureaucrats, and because formal rules are always possible to circumvent, we observe both an intense politicization and bureaucratization in these cases (see, e.g., Dierickx 2004; Parrado 2004; Sotiropoulos 2004). As a matter of fact, individuals interested in pursuing a political career are encouraged to become civil servants first and, once they have joined an administrative corps, they can enter a chain of promotions that will lead them from purely administrative positions first to hybrid positions later and to purely political positions at the end. The lack of career separation is so obvious that most MPs and ministers come from the ranks of different administrative bodies. France is a historical pioneer of this model of integration of careers with a political elite (including most presidents of the V Republic) trained as civil servants (generally, at the *École Nationale d'Administration*). Japan and Spain are also well-known examples of this administrative system: highly Weberian on paper, but with a high integration of careers (Dahlström and Lapuente 2011). For instance, in the first government appointed by the conservative Prime Minister Mariano Rajoy in Spain (December 2011), eleven out of the fourteen ministers (including the Prime Minister himself) were trained civil servants.

Cell 3 collects what can be called Managerial systems. It is noteworthy that the countries in this category, such as Australia, Canada,

New Zealand, and Sweden, top almost all available rankings of quality of government, whether in terms of control of corruption or in terms of government performance (see, e.g., the World Bank's Governance Indicators). The administrations of these countries are also generally seen as innovative in adopting efficiency-enhancing reforms (OECD 2004). And, quite like the cases in Cell 2, this is not what should be happening according to the closed Weberian hypothesis. This is instead where we should see problems, as these countries often have weak protection of the civil service or, such as in Sweden, no special protection at all (Pollitt and Bouckaert 2011). These cases should thus be contrasted to the cases in Cell 2. So, if we compare, for example, Spain, Italy, and Greece, which are countries closer to the closed Weberian ideal of strongly regulated bureaucracies, to, for example, Sweden and New Zealand, it should be surprising for any proponent of the closed Weberian view that the latter seem to be better functioning. This book, however, presents a reason why bureaucracy works better in the latter group of countries (Cell 3).

A key issue that we would like to emphasize here is that their flexibility, the high level of discretion they leave to officials, does not translate into high levels of opportunism, because the careers of civil servants are separated from those of politicians. This thus means that bureaucrats do not have the incentive to protect politicians if they, for example, take advantage of their position, as the bureaucrats' careers do not depend on that politician. Instead, the bureaucrat has the incentive to work hard and, when it is called for, make investments in specific skills, as her future career depends on her own performance.

In Cell 4, we find administrations that simultaneously have rather closed bureaucracy and a relatively clear separation of careers between politicians and bureaucrats. An example is Germany, which, although it has politicization at the top level of the administration, has also created two separate chains of accountability: one electoral for political appointees and one professional for the majority of bureaucrats (Fleischer 2011). As noted by administrative historians, the combination of high regulation and a relatively high level of separation of careers has long historical roots. Prussia is considered the first country in modern European history to have elaborated and applied a merit system (Fischer and Lundgreen 1975). Rules for recruitment were very strict almost from the start. In particular, it was the judiciary that was the first section of the Prussian state to establish the merit system, and by 1775 every candidate had to pass two examinations (Finer 1932). In addition, several regulations protecting functionaries from being arbitrarily fired by the executive were enacted, somewhat paradoxically, under the absolutist rule of the Hohenzollern dynasty in Prussia. An example of the high level of protection of German bureaucrats is a 1759 sentence by the *Reichskammergericht*, setting a precedent of enormous influence in the decades and centuries to come; the court decided that the removal of a civil servant could not be decided by the executive but could only be established by a well-founded judicial sentence (Nieto 1976). It is difficult to conceive a greater degree of tying the hands of the political masters of a bureaucracy than this.

Altogether, we have tried in this section to show that countries that score high on a closed scale do not necessarily have a separation of careers and *vice versa*. Using some examples, we have also pointed out that there is indeed much variation that cannot be explained by the level of regulation but can easily be explained by the integration/separation of careers. We therefore think that it is indeed valid to investigate the relationship between careers and performance more systematically.

Research Strategy

Previous sections in this chapter have tried to explain why a separation of careers between politicians and bureaucrats should have consequences that are desirable for everyone interested in well-functioning societies. More specifically, we suggest three implications of the theory sketched above that can be tested empirically. We have also identified an alternative explanation for why a certain way of organizing the bureaucracy should have effects similar to those suggested by us, namely the closed Weberian hypothesis, and this alternative therefore merits special attention.

The three empirical implications we suggest are that countries in which the careers of politicians and bureaucrats are separated should:

(1) be less corrupt;
(2) have higher government effectiveness; and
(3) have an administration where efficiency-enhancing reforms are more successfully implemented.

The main alternative explanation, which according to previous research could have the same positive effects as the ones we suggest, is the prevalence of a bureaucracy protected from political influence. Such a closed Weberian bureaucracy should be characterized by life-long career tenure, for example, and special employment laws should protect the bureaucrats.

While all alternative explanations, such as type of regime and economic development, will be discussed together with our model specifications, the closed Weberian hypothesis deserves special attention. It is vital for this book to show that a closed bureaucracy might not have the expected consequences before we move on to study the empirical implications of our theory. When this is done, we will devote one chapter to each of the empirical implications of our suggestion.

Methods

The empirical analysis in this book is based mainly on a broad comparison between, most often, more than one hundred countries. We can use this research strategy, as unique data are available to us that are designed to measure characteristics of the public administration in a broad range of countries (the data will be discussed in detail later in this section). The methods we use are fairly straightforward. In each chapter, we take three analytic steps. First, we show that there is indeed a strong and positive correlation between, on the one side, our indicators of separated careers for politicians and bureaucrats and, on the other side, indicators of corruption, effectiveness, and efficiency-enhancing reforms. Second, we move from bivariate to multivariate analyses, with a series of cross-country Ordinary Least Squares (OLS) regressions, where a large number of economic, political, and cultural control variables previously suggested in the literature on corruption, effectiveness, and public sector reforms are included. Third, we test for the robustness of the results and address potential endogeneity biases. Endogeneity is particularly important, as it could indeed be a serious objection to our results; therefore, in this third step, we try to demonstrate that the institutions separating the careers of politicians and bureaucrats precede our three dependent variables. That is, we want to show that the separation of careers is not a consequence of a less corrupt, more effective, or more flexible administration but a factor explaining the latter. We do this by two means. First, we use an instrument-variable technique, with an external regressor that captures the division between politicians and bureaucrats in a longer perspective – from Charron, Dahlström, and Lapuente's (2012) codification of Western bureaucracies in 1800. Second, we discuss historical trajectories when fighting corruption, strengthening effectiveness, and introducing administrative reforms in, for example, Denmark, Spain, Sweden, the United States, and the United Kingdom and conclude that the historical experiences in these countries are compatible with our theory.

In addition to providing the quantitative data material, we also carefully describe and analyze a number of historical and contemporary cases. Our cases are for the most part from Spain and Sweden, as these two countries in many ways exemplify different ways of organizing the relations between politicians and bureaucrats. However, we also discuss Argentina, Brazil, the Dominican Republic, France, Germany, Greece, Italy, Japan, the United Kingdom, the United States, Venezuela, and several other countries at some length.

The Quality of Government Expert Survey

In contrast with economics, broad comparisons are very rare in public administration because of a lack of data. To our knowledge, the only exception, where the structure of bureaucracy is measured in a broad set of countries, is Peter Evans and James Rauch's pioneering work (Evans and Rauch 1999; Rauch and Evans 2000). Their dataset has some limits, however, since it covers only thirty-five developing countries and focuses on the period 1970–1990. It is also restricted to the economic sector, leaving other sectors aside. While the Evans and Rauch data provide important insight into the bureaucratic structures of a particular group of countries that experienced unprecedented growth rates with the help of autonomous bureaucracies, it remains unclear whether the same results hold for other parts of the world.

The data we use are from the Quality of Government Expert Survey (referred to here as the QoG Expert Survey), which is collected by the Quality of Government Institute, Department of Political Science, University of Gothenburg (Teorell, Dahlström, and Dahlberg 2011). The general purpose of the QoG Expert Survey is to measure the structure and behavior of the public administration across countries. It includes assessments from 1053 public administration experts from a total of 135 countries. The experts are highly qualified professionals, often with an academic background in public administration

(72 percent have a PhD), who are usually residents of the country for which they answer (92 percent). The QoG Expert Survey uses the conceptual basis of Evans and Rauch's (1999; Rauch and Evans 2000) data on bureaucracies as a theoretical tool, but other perspectives such as New Public Management and administrative impartiality have also had a role in the questionnaire design (Pollitt and Bouckaert 2011; Rothstein and Teorell 2008).

The experts were asked to make an assessment on a variety of topics that are seen as relevant to the structure and functioning of public administration according to the literature, such as meritocratic recruitment, internal promotion and career stability, salaries, impartiality, NPM reforms, effectiveness/efficiency, and bureaucratic representation. For example, if it is the skills and merits of the applicants for a civil service position in country X that matter to get the job, this is measured on a 7-point scale, where 7 means "almost always" and 1 "hardly ever." A list of the questions analyzed in this book is provided in Table 2.2 (for a more detailed discussion of the QoG Expert Survey, including the entire questionnaire, see Dahlberg et al. 2013).

The data were collected in three waves, the first running from September 2008 to May 2009, the second running from March to November 2010, and the third from late 2010 through 2011. In this book, we use a pooled dataset combining all three waves. The number of respondents per country in the QoG Expert Survey varies from one to twenty-eight, with a mean of 7.8 (Table 2.3). However, to enhance the quality of the data, we include only the 107 countries for which at least three expert responses were obtained. This can be compared with Evans and Rauch's (1999) data, which ranged between two to three experts per country.

We take our indicators of the separation of careers from the QoG Expert Survey. As we have indicated, we think there are good reasons to believe that career prospects are most clearly signaled through recruitment. We would therefore like to have an indicator that captures the signal sent to employees. We will consequently primarily rely on an indicator that captures the level of meritocratic recruitment in the public sector. However, we will also use an additive index containing four indicators of professionalism among bureaucrats and the level of politicization of the public sector for robustness. The index combines four different items from the QoG Expert Survey that we, together with Jan Teorell, showed in a previous study to form a coherent

Table 2.2 *Items from the QoG Expert Survey*

Indicator of:	Question	Scale	Prof. index	Closed Weberian
Meritocratic recruitment	When recruiting public sector employees, the skills and merits of the applicants decide who gets the job	1 (hardly ever) 7 (almost always)	Yes	No
Political recruitment	When recruiting public sector employees, the political connections of the applicants decide who gets the job	1 (hardly ever) 7 (almost always)	Yes	No
Politicians' involvement in careers of senior officials	The top political leadership hires and fires senior public officials	1 (hardly ever) 7 (almost always)	Yes	No
Internal recruitment of senior officials	Senior public officials are recruited from within the ranks of the public sector	1 (hardly ever) 7 (almost always)	Yes	No
Formalization of recruitments	Public sector employees are hired via a formal examination system	1 (hardly ever) 7 (almost always)	No	No
Career tenure	Once one is recruited as a public sector employee, one stays a public sector employee for the rest of one's career	1 (hardly ever) 7 (almost always)	No	Yes
Special labor laws	The terms of employment for public sector employees are regulated by special laws that do not apply to private sector employees	1 (not at all) 7 (to a very large extent)	No	Yes
Competitive salaries	Senior officials have salaries that are comparable with the salaries of private	1 (hardly ever) 7 (almost always)	No	No

Table 2.2 (*cont.*)

Indicator of:	Question	Scale	Prof. index	Closed Weberian
	sector managers with roughly similar training and responsibilities			
Performance-related pay	The salaries of public sector employees are linked to appraisals of their performance	1 (hardly ever) 7 (almost always)	No	No

Comment: Questions are from the QoG Expert Survey. For the entire questionnaire and further detail about the survey see Dahlberg et al. (2013). For the dataset see Teorell, Dahlström, and Dahlberg (2011).

Table 2.3 *Experts per country*

Number of Experts	Countries
1–2	28
3–6	42
7–11	32
12–28	33
Total	135

Comment: The table summarizes the number of experts per country in the pooled QoG Expert Survey. Note that the twenty-eight countries with less than three experts are not included in any analyses.
Source: Dahlberg et al. (2013).

dimension (Dahlström, Lapuente, and Teorell 2012b). In the just-mentioned publication, we use a principal components factor analysis to demonstrate that the four indicators of meritocracy, politicization, political recruitment of senior officers, and internal recruitments load on the same factor. The index is additive, with equal weight for each component.

In addition, we use two separate indicators of bureaucratic closedness, also from the QoG Expert Survey. The first concerns long career tenure, the second special employment laws. They are both selected as indicators of the extent to which the bureaucracy is closed, or in other words institutionally isolated from politics. In the analyses in this volume, we use the indicators separately, combine them in an additive index with equal weight of each component, and interact them with each other, depending on the research question in the particular analysis. The aforementioned publication (Dahlström, Lapuente, and Teorell 2012b) shows that in Europe and North America formal examination systems should also be added to the closedness dimension, but this is not true for Latin America, Africa, and South-East Asia, which makes us inclined to go for the more limited index. This decision is strengthened by the results presented in Sundell (2014), where he explains that formal examination systems might work differently depending on the level of risk for patronage.

However, although the QoG Expert Survey provides probably the most extensive data available on bureaucratic structures, it relies on the honesty and knowledge of the expert included and, as in all expert surveys, its validity can therefore be questioned and there are reasons to worry about respondent perception bias. In order to investigate if there are reasons to worry, Dahlström, Lapuente, and Teorell (2012b) and Rothstein and Teorell (2012) conducted cross-source validation of three indices created from the QoG Expert Survey and demonstrated that these indicators correlate with other available measures, such as bureaucratic quality from the International Country Risk Guide (ICRG), data on human relations from the OECD, and, for the overlapping countries, with the data from Evans and Rauch (1999) in an expected way.

Furthermore, Dahlberg et al. (2013) and Dahlström, Lapuente, and Teorell (2012b) investigate whether there are systematic respondent perception biases because, if perceptions vary systematically by observable expert characteristics, the extent to which they reflect a common underlying reality could be questioned. That would imply, for example, that the estimate for a particular country is determined by the make-up of the sample of experts rather than by its bureaucratic structure. There are data on six expert characteristics (sex, education, year of birth, birthplace, where they live, and government employee). Dahlberg et al. (2013) regress all items of the survey questionnaire for these characteristics, while Dahlström, Lapuente, and Teorell (2012b) do the same for the professionalism index. They hold the object of evaluation (i.e., the bureaucracy of a specific country) constant, and thus rely on the within-country variation among experts, and show that for the most part there are no systematic respondent perception biases. There is, however, a tendency among government employees to assess their bureaucratic structures differently than non-government employees (more positive), and respondents that assess countries in which they do not live also perceive their bureaucracies differently than experts living in the country they assess (more negative). Although we must acknowledge that these systematic differences appear in the data, they are not very large in absolute terms. When it comes to relative differences in country scores, the results obtained are extremely robust to these controls for expert characteristics (average country scores with and without controls for expert characteristics correlate at .99). By and large then, whereas these sources of perception bias introduce some noise in our data, they are not serious enough for us to question the overall validity of it.

Corruption, Effectiveness, and Reforms

On the dependent side, we use indicators from several different sources. To measure corruption, we use the most recent versions of the World Bank's Governance Indicators (2013) Control of Corruption. This perception-based indicator is widely used in the literature. Control of corruption aims at "...capturing perceptions of the extent to which public power is exercised for private gain..." (Kaufmann, Kraay, and Mastruzzi 2010, 3). To create these indicators, data from about thirty different sources were combined into one aggregate measure ranging from -2.5 (low control of corruption) to +2.5 (high control of corruption) (for a discussion of the methodology see Kaufmann, Kraay, and Mastruzzi 2010). However, we also exchange the measure on corruption for the Corruption Perception Index from Transparency International (Transparency International 2013) and the corruption indicator from the International Country Risk Guide (ICRG 2013).

We use two different indicators for government effectiveness that we think come fairly close to the mechanisms discussed above. We first use an indicator of Wastefulness of Government Spending from the World Economic Forum's Global Competitiveness Report (Schwab 2012). The indicator is taken from the annual Executive Opinion Survey, which is carried out in the business community by the World Economic Forum and includes more than 14,000 executives from 140 countries (for more detail on the data collection see Browne, Geiger, and Gutknecht 2012). Our second measure is from the Bertelsmann Transformation Index (BTI), provided by the Bertelsmann Stiftung. The BTI evaluates, among other things, political management in 128 developing and transition countries, and the indicator we use is called "management performance" (Bertelsmann Transformation Index 2012). For robustness, we tested several other indicators on the dependent side, among them the government effectiveness indicator from the World Bank and indicators from Djankov et al. (2003) and Chong et al. (2014).

Regarding our third dependent variable, no readymade measure of efficiency-enhancing reforms is available for a large sample of countries. However, there has been a consensus since the late 1970s that public administrations worldwide have experienced intense reforms, many of which are in line with what is generally known as New Public Management (NPM). But these reforms have come in very different shapes, degrees, and depths (for overviews of NPM see Christensen and Lægreid 2011; Peters and Pierre 2001; Pollitt and Bouckaert 2011). Relatively similar pressures exerted by increasing globalization, stringent budget constraints, and a prevailing managerial discourse seem to have fostered all-encompassing administrative reforms in some countries – such as New Zealand, the United Kingdom, and Finland – while hardly any changes have occurred in others, such as Italy and France. The variation between countries around the world is therefore a good case for testing our third hypothesis.

NPM is in itself a broad concept, however, and this book focuses only on one NPM reform: the introduction of performance-related pay (PRP) in the public sector. We measure the degree of PRP in the public sector with the help of expert assessments from the QoG Expert Survey. Again, it is measured on a scale from 1 to 7, and the exact wording of the question asked to the country experts can be found in Table 2.2. Since this means that we have indicators on the independent and dependent sides from the same survey, we re-ran all the models with another indicator of PRP to check robustness (available for twenty-five countries from the OECD 2004).

Control Variables

Our models also include a very large number of control variables suggested in prior studies. These controls are, however, often specific to each dependent variable (corruption, effectiveness, and efficiency enhancing reforms), and we therefore discuss them together with their underlying theories in each empirical chapter.

3 | A Closed Weberian Bureaucracy

A Dubious Promise

In the foregoing chapter, we pointed out that, while indeed advancing knowledge as to what causes corruption and government effectiveness, much of the comparative literature in economics and political science has not paid enough attention to the bureaucracy (see, e.g., Acemoglu and Robinson 2012). There are important exceptions, however, including contributions from scholars such as Peter Evans and James Rauch (1999; 2000) and Gary Miller (2000), who suggest that a closed Weberian bureaucracy provides the protection from political and market influence for bureaucrats necessary to achieve well-functioning administration. We have taken much inspiration from these scholars but, as we explained in Chapter 2, our suggestion differs from theirs in an important way: Instead of focusing on the dimension that goes from administrations with an open staff policy to administrations with a more closed staff policy (the columns in Table 2.1), we focus on the dimension that goes from administrations where politicians' and bureaucrats' careers are integrated to administrations where those careers are separated (the rows in Table 2.1).

While the general purpose of this book is to bring bureaucratic factors to the forefront of the discussion of how to curb corruption and achieve high effectiveness in the bureaucracy, the goal of this chapter is specifically to test the closed Weberian hypothesis. The public administration literature has long noted that corruption can be curbed and that a better functioning administration can be created by fostering a bureaucracy that is isolated from the interference of politicians in a closed Weberian bureaucracy. Institutional characteristics normally associated with this involve guaranteeing lifelong careers and specific legal protections for public employees that differ from those covering private sector employees. The means to achieving a better functioning government are thus formal regulations. Several public administration scholars have argued that such institutions prevent governmental malfeasances (detailed reviews of this argument can be found in Olsen (2005, 2008); and Pollitt and Bouckaert (2011)). Yet, we largely lack empirical tests of the closed Weberian hypothesis. This chapter provides tests of this kind.

As it is a competing theory, we try to give it as good a chance as possible. We therefore first discuss the mechanisms implied by the closed Weberian hypothesis so that we can identify proper empirical indicators. We then turn to a cross-country comparative analysis that includes over a hundred countries, where we start by comparing the two dimensions – regulations and career incentives – that we suggested in Chapter 2. We next look at bivariate correlations between indicators of a closed Weberian bureaucracy and three dependent variables on corruption, government effectiveness, and efficiency-enhancing reforms in the public sector. After this, we bring in a minimum of controls and run simple OLS regressions. In the broad comparative analysis, we also conduct a series of model alterations and robustness checks to exclude the possibility that the closed Weberian hypothesis works only if several institutions are in place at the same time or in more or less developed parts of the world.

In a nutshell, the answer given by these analyses is negative for the closed Weberian hypothesis. Even under the favorable conditions in which we test it, this interpretation of a Weberian administration as a bureaucratic rule fails to deliver in every single aspect of quality of government that is explored. Therefore, finally, we more carefully analyze a number of the European countries belonging to the Napoleonic administrative tradition and describe why a bureaucracy organized in a closed way fails to contribute to the expected good outcomes and in fact often are counterproductive.

Two Virtues of a Closed Administrative System

In Chapter 2, we mapped public administrations around the world according to two dimensions associated with the Weberian bureaucratic ideal: the degree of bureaucratic rules and the degree of political incentives for bureaucrats. This chapter explores the ability that bureaucratic rules have to foster quality of government, and this section briefly summarizes the theoretical arguments for why one should expect bureaucratic rules to have such a positive effect. In particular, our focus is on the norms encapsulated in closed systems, such as "...rules for hiring, firing, pay and fringes, promotion, and the processing of grievances" (Moe 1984, 764).

Scholars have given numerous reasons as to why civil service rules should be essential to having a better government. The main function of these rules is that they isolate civil servants from external forces, such as market competitive forces or politicians' discretionary powers. There are two chief mechanisms in this theoretical framework. The mechanisms are interlinked, but they are conceptually and empirically distinguishable. First, it is argued that a closed Weberian bureaucracy generates an *esprit de corps* in the public workforce, achieved through socialization. The strong *sens du public service* among top civil servants who have spent, or are expecting to spend, their entire careers in an administrative body may foster impartiality and respect for the rule of law (Vandenabeele, Scheepers, and Hondeghem 2006, Horton 2011). The special status of civil servants, their sectorial closure or *Berufsbeamtentum* (Meyer and Hammerschmid 2006), fosters a public service ethos or *Beamtenethos* (Du Gay 2000), which in turn helps top career-based bureaucrats to take into account opposing preferences from different social groups (Horton 2011) and apply law in a fair way (Ziller 2003). In particular, Meyer and Hammerschmid (2006, 102) identify the following values associated with a closed civil service system: legality, correctness, neutrality, equity, objectivity, loyalty, security, secrecy, continuity, and stability.

The second mechanism would be that bureaucratic closedness gives public employees a longer (beyond the electoral cycle) time horizon through the provision of life tenure. Civil service restrictions in public personnel management are a crucial incentive for expertise creation in the civil service (Gailmard and Patty 2007). Contrary to the prevailing view of these restrictions as a source of public sector inefficiency, these stringent civil service regulations may provide incentives for public employees to acquire appropriate expertise in which they would otherwise not be eager to invest their time and effort. Effectively, civil service protection "dulls the incentives of bureaucrats" (Gailmard and Patty 2012, 11) who do not need to fear punishment in the case of poor performance; yet, since it provides a long time horizon, it offers public employees the guarantee that if they dedicate themselves to developing expertise in their policy area, this would pay off.

In the seminal articles by Peter Evans and James Rauch, the first mechanism is well argued theoretically and nicely captured empirically (Evans and Rauch 1999; Rauch and Evans 2000). Their indicator of what they refer to as Weberianness is correlated with several desirable societal outcomes, such as high economic growth and low corruption, in a set of thirty-five developing countries. A key causal explanation for these correlations is that strong norms emerge among public employees once they are protected from political interference. The socialization to shared norms reinforces civil servants' adherence to codified rules, and "...ideally, a sense of commitment to corporate goals and 'esprit de corps' develops" (Rauch and Evans 2000, 52). With the norms in place, bureaucrats would, in this view, act according to the classical mechanism pointed out by John Gaus decades ago – that is, as an "inner check" (1936, 40) that would prevent abuses. The identification of civil servants with their "confrères in office" would create "internalized intangible costs for corrupt activities" (Evans and Rauch 1999, 752).

A typical example of socialization into group norms underlined by several scholars occurred in the US Forest Service (Kaufman 1960; Miller 2000). Despite being geographically dispersed, their professional norms motivated forest rangers to pursue organizational goals and constrained them to support shortsighted policies such as aggressive clear cutting.

Similarly, a bureaucracy isolated from external influences by strong rules is viewed positively among numerous scholars and practitioners in countries with a "strong state tradition," such as France and other Napoleonic countries (Meininger 2000, 189). A bureaucracy embedded in the stringent rules of Napoleonic legalism has enjoyed a good reputation because it was historically introduced as a counterweight to political power (Kickert 2011). Issuing bureaucratic rules was largely a way authoritarian rulers in these countries could signal their commitment to the protection of very basic property rights. By writing very detailed laws, autocrats were telling potential foreign investors that their regimes were constrained by the rule of law (Prats 1984). Think of Franco's regime (1939–75) in Spain, where he delegated most policymaking to bureaucrats from the grand administrative corps who enacted a highly encompassing legal framework to offer guarantees of predictability in the day-to-day activities of the state (Lapuente 2007).

Consequently, closed bureaucratic systems, especially in countries with a relatively recent authoritarian past, are still seen as safeguards against corrupt practices because they limit the flexibility of private sector-like contracts. The strict and highly regulated administrative processes were "...originally established to protect the administration against political interference and to secure its integrity" (OECD 2012, 29). For that reason, scholars have criticized attempts to introduce elements of open bureaucratic systems into Southern European administrations, and abandoning the special labor laws protecting public employees and the guarantee of secure tenure could create uncertainty among civil servants over their future careers (Cádiz Deleito 1987).

This points toward the second mechanism, which is also discussed by Evans and Rauch (1999). Evans and Rauch (1999, 752) argue that the "...expectation of a series of promotions related to performance and conformity to organizational norms create disincentives to corrupt behavior." This mechanism relies less on socialization and more on the advantages of long-sightedness and job security. Miller (2000) provides one of the most compelling explanations of how job security is an essential underlying reason for a connection between, on the one hand, a closed Weberian bureaucratic structure and, on the other, a good and efficient government. Using Axelrod's (1984) famous expression, Miller notes that secure tenure "lengthens the shadow of the future" for bureaucrats and entrenches them against potentially illegitimate "political pressures that come laterally and informally, often with the intention of bending or undoing the original legislation" (Miller 2000, 317–18). According to Miller (2000) and Miller and Whitford (2016), closed systems isolate bureaucrats from political interests, and only when they have secure positions can civil servants therefore confidently confront politicians and senior officers, and report their possible malpractices. Bureaucratic rules are thus what give bureaucrats that courage, and that is crucial for good government.

In addition, the guarantee of a long-term career not only prevents bad behavior but also promotes good behavior, both among public employees and among economic agents, according to proponents of the closed Weberian hypothesis. To start with, public employees who enjoy secure tenure can make costly asset-specific investments in human capital that "may do nothing to enhance the bureaucrat's value in a competitive market outside the bureau but may enhance long-term productivity in the bureau" (Miller 2000, 318). Think of an employee whose job requires a constant investment in skills that have low transferability to the private sector. Without the security of lifetime employment, bureaucrats, such as state lawyers, tax officers, law enforcement agents among many others, would not make the inherently risky investments in human capital that their jobs require. At the same time, economic agents – imagine a young entrepreneur with an innovative business idea – will also feel encouraged to undertake investments that could be subject to *ex post* expropriations by opportunistic politicians. All in all, bureaucratic regulations should protect individuals in society "from the devastating effects of political rent-seeking" (Miller 2000, 319).

A Strategy for Testing the Closed Weberian Hypothesis

The next two sections discuss empirical analyses of the effects of a closed Weberian bureaucracy. Throughout, we have tried to design the empirical tests so that they are favorable for the closed Weberian hypothesis, because we think it is an important alternative interpretation to our suggestion. We will check whether the structural features traditionally linked to the closed Weberian administrative model, discussed above, exhibit significant effects on levels of corruption, government effectiveness, and the scope of administrative reforms. Are governments with Weberian rules less corrupt, more effective, and more innovative?

We have divided the analyses of the closed Weberian hypothesis into two sections. We start with a large-N analysis, and then continue to a qualitative analysis of a set of countries with highly regulated Weberian bureaucracies belonging to the so-called Napoleonic administrative tradition (Painter and Peters 2010). The broad cross-country comparison serves the purpose of testing whether the effects of closed Weberian bureaucracies are generally present from a statistical point of view. We will see that there do not seem to be any significant relationship between the closed Weberian indicators we use and our indicators of quality of government. The narratives from the Napoleonic countries show that causal mechanisms, often assumed, do not connect closed Weberian bureaucracies with good government performance, but instead sometimes have unintended consequences.

The large-N analyses that cover around one hundred countries are conducted in five steps. The first step is to map world bureaucracies according to the two-dimensioned theoretical model presented in Chapter 2. We will see how the two dimensions – rules and career incentives – give a meaningful description of the real world of public bureaucracies. Countries end up in each one of the four combinations of the two dimensions. In other words, the administrative world can at least to some extent be divided into *Patronage, Corporate, Autonomous,* and *Managerial* bureaucracies. The main purpose of this first step in the analysis is to demonstrate that the dimension we suggest is actually not the same as the one previously suggested in research.

In the second step of our analysis, we move to an explanatory level by looking at simple correlations between closed Weberian indicators and three different indicators of the quality of government: corruption, government effectiveness, and, as a proxy for administrative reforms, the prevalence of performance-related pay in the public sector. We will observe that, even in a simple bivariate model, and thus under favorable conditions for the closed Weberian hypothesis, no significant positive effect on government performance can be detected.

In a third step, we move to multivariate analyses by employing cross-section OLS regressions with control variables capturing the most prevailing cultural, political, and economic factors in the quality of government literature: Protestantism, years of democracy, and (log of) GDP per capita. All of these have been shown in earlier cross-country studies to impact differences in corruption and can be suspected to affect government effectiveness, performance, and efficiency-enhancing reforms (Treisman 2007). We focus on only a few controls in order to make it as easy as possible for the competing hypothesis. If we still do not see the suggested effects under these conditions, we feel reasonably certain that we should question the closed Weberian hypothesis.

In the fourth step, we try alternative specifications of the closed Weberian hypothesis, mainly because it could be the case that the Weberian institutions complement each other, and that the positive effects consequently occur only as a result of additive effects. We therefore combine our two indicators into an index and re-run the analyses described above. For the same reason, we also analyze whether there are interaction effects between the two indicators, again re-running the analyses.

In the fifth and final step of the analysis, we address issues of robustness, and most importantly a significant objection, namely that there might be a circular relationship between, for example, corruption and closed Weberian institutions. It could be the case that it is mainly countries with an already high risk of patronage (or some other malfunction of the bureaucracy) that need closed Weberian institutions. This selection mechanism could thus suppress an otherwise positive relationship. It is definitely not an easy challenge. Ideally, we would use an instrument variable, correlated with the closed Weberian institutions, but not with the error term of the regression, and not with the rival hypotheses suggested by this book (Sovey and Green 2011). It is, however, hard to come up with such an instrument, and we have consequently been unable to find one. Instead we follow Sundell (2014) and control for the risk of patronage in order to tease out a potential correlation. For the same reason, we divide our sample into regional sub-samples in order to see whether the effects of closed Weberianness are present in some parts of the world and not in others. Finally, as a robustness check of the results, we substitute our variables on the dependent side for alternative indicators.

For a measure of closed Weberianness, we rely chiefly on data from the QoG Expert Survey (Teorell, Dahlström, and Dahlberg 2011; see Chapter 2 for a more detailed discussion of the data). We use the two items that we think are close to the mechanisms described in the previous section. One measures how common lifelong careers are in the public sector (the esprit de corps mechanism) and the other measures whether it is common that public employees are protected by special employment laws (the protection mechanism). (See Table 2.2 in Chapter 2 for the exact questions.)

Regarding the dependent variables, we employ several indicators. For the corruption level and government effectiveness, we rely on the World Bank's Governance Indicators (World Bank 2013). For a measure of efficiency-enhancing reforms in the public administration, we use a measure from the QoG Expert Survey on the level of performance-related pay in the public sector. As just mentioned, however, we also substitute the variables on the dependent side for alternative indicators using indicators from Transparency International (2013) and the International Country Risk Guide (2013) for corruption, from the Bertelsmann Stiftung (2012) and the World Economic Forum (Schwab 2012) for government effectiveness, and from OECD (2004) for performance-related pay. The three control variables are, first, on the cultural side, the proportion of Protestants in the population in 1980, from La Porta et al. (1999). Second, on the political side,

Table 3.1 *Descriptive statistics*

Variable	Obs	Mean	Std. Dev.	Min	Max
Special law	107	5.7	.73	3.5	7
Long career	107	4.7	1.1	1.67	6.8
Web. index	107	5.2	.81	2.8	6.8
Control of Corr.	191	-.06	.99	-1.7	2.4
Gov. Effectiv.	191	-.058	.99	-2.2	2.2
PRP	107	2.96	.94	1.2	5.6
GDP/cap (log)	179	8.74	1.26	5.72	11.12
Dem. years	171	18.16	21.60	0	70
Protestant	193	13.11	21.29	0	97.8
OECD	107	.27	.45	0	1
EU27	107	.23	.43	0	1
HT region	195		2.6	1	10
Risk index	137	.54	.29	0	1

Comment: Table 3.1 summarizes all variables. All variables are available in the QoG standard dataset (Teorell et al. 2013) or the QoG Expert Survey (Teorell, Dahlström and Dahlberg 2011).

we control for the years of democracy, from Treisman (2007). Third, relating to economic development, we control for the natural logarithm of GDP per capita, from the United Nations Statistics Division (2013). Finally, we take a measure on patronage risk from Sundell (2014). He has constructed a patronage risk index from four factors, which research has shown to be correlated with higher patronage. The factors are (i) ethnical fractionalization, where more fractionalization tends to go together with more patronage (Alesina et al. 1999), (ii) education, where lower levels of education should correlate with higher patronage (Hollyer 2011), (iii) media independence, when more independence should be associated with less patronage, and (iv) an independent judiciary, which should reduce the risk of patronage. Except for the International Country Risk Guide (2013) indicator on corruption, all variables are taken from the QoG dataset (Teorell et al. 2013). The variables are summarized in Table 3.1.

After these cross-country analyses we move on to the section where we analyze the causal mechanisms – or the lack thereof – connecting closed Weberian bureaucracies and government performance. Why does the closed Weberian hypothesis fail to deliver? We analyze experiences from countries belonging to the Napoleonic tradition, France, Spain, Italy, Portugal, and Greece, which, given their strong emphasis on bureaucratic rules, offer us numerous examples of the (in)ability bureaucratic rules have to prevent abuses and to promote high levels of effort when they are not paired with a separation of politicians' and bureaucrats' careers.

Does the Closed Weberian Hypothesis Deliver?

We argued in Chapter 2 that, from a theoretical perspective, the separation of careers in the public sector and rules designed to protect bureaucrats from political influence should not correlate strongly, but instead form a two-dimensional space. This suggestion was backed with country examples and existing classifications in the public administration literature (Auer at al. 1996; Bekke and Van der Meer 2000; Heady 1996; Silberman 1993). In this section, we empirically investigate this claim, analyzing the cross-country data in order to see the extent to which this two-dimensional conceptualization of bureaucracies reflects public administrations worldwide. To do so we use an item from the QoG Expert Survey, designed to measure the level of meritocratic recruitment, as an indicator of separation of careers in the public sector. To capture the degree of bureaucratic rules, we build an additive index from two items from the same survey. We consider these items to be related to the two causal mechanisms suggested by the closed Weberian hypothesis and discussed earlier in this chapter: a measure of how common lifelong careers in the public sector are (indicative of the esprit de corps mechanism), and a measure of whether there are special employment laws for public employees (indicative of the protection of public employees mechanism).

We start by looking at a limited number of countries from rich parts of the world. The reason is that the closed Weberian concept was developed for European countries and has mainly been used to study Europe and the United States (Weber 1978[1921]; Wilson 1887). These are also the countries that public administration scholars have studied the most (see, e.g., the chapters in Peters and Pierre 2012). A sample restricted to these countries should therefore make it possible both to group the countries in a meaningful way and to compare the outcome with previous studies.

Figure 3.1 Dimensions of bureaucracy in the OECD countries

Comment: Figure 3.1 plots twenty-nine OECD countries in a two-dimensional space. On the X-axis is a seven-point closed Weberian index, while the Y-axis measures the level of meritocratic recruitment, also on a seven-point scale. Data are from the QoG Expert Survey (Teorell, Dahlström, and Dahlberg 2011). The scatterplot is divided into cells representing four types of bureaucracies: Managerial (upper left); Autonomous (upper right); Patronage (lower left); and Corporatist (lower right).

Figure 3.1 plots the twenty-nine OECD countries in our sample. The X-axis represents the seven-point closed Weberian index, while the Y-axis measures the level of meritocratic recruitment (our indicator of career incentives) in the public sector, also on a seven-point scale. The two measures have a negative correlation (-0.25), which is not statistically significant. The twenty-nine OECD countries are consequently spread out over the two-dimensional space, according to our expectations. The scatterplot is divided into cells representing the four theoretically defined categories that we discussed in Chapter 2. There are no pre-defined cut-off points where we should draw the lines, so these have to be arbitrary. For illustrative purposes, we opted for the mean value of both variables. It is important to underline that we are not claiming that bureaucracies of the world can be divided into four crisp categories. Boundaries between them are indeed blurry. What we think is interesting, though, is that the theoretical categories discussed in Chapter 2 are fairly well represented in our data, and that this fits what is known about the different cases already. But the graph also illustrates that there is significant variation in both dimensions.

Starting from the upper left corner, the first cell is the Managerial bureaucracies, covering countries with relatively few bureaucratic rules, and thus a low degree of closed Weberianness, as well as a high degree of separation of careers. Accordingly, we find countries such as New Zealand, known for extensive reforms in the public sector (Halligan 2001), the Netherlands, and several of the Nordic countries, which are consistently portrayed as forerunners in terms of administrative reforms and government performance. These countries are also seen as having a clear separation of careers for politicians and bureaucrats (Grønnegård Christensen 2004; Pollitt and Bouckaert 2011, 241, 272, and 287).

If we move to the cell on the upper right we find the countries with an Autonomous bureaucracy – that is, countries whose administrations have a clear separation between the careers of politicians and bureaucrats as well as a relatively closed bureaucracy. We can see that countries well known for the autonomy of their bureaucracies, such as South Korea (Dahlström and Lapuente 2010) and Germany (Schröter 2004), end up in this category, but it also includes countries from diverse administrative traditions, such as Norway, Ireland, or Spain.

In the lower left cell we find countries known for having bureaucracies with relatively high levels of patronage. In Mexico, the country that scores the lowest on the separation of careers, scholars have noted that thousands of public employees change jobs when there is a change of government, indicating that the careers of bureaucrats are indeed dependent on the fortunes of political parties. Patronage is a deliberate political strategy among Mexican politicians to survive in office. Merilee Grindle (2012, 172) concludes, "...perhaps nowhere were political officials more conscious that maintaining the political basis of the administrative system was essential to the functioning of the political system–the public service was a spoils system with a purpose."

Finally, the cell in the lower right corner includes countries having what we regard as Corporatist bureaucracy: a mixture between closed bureaucracy rules and a relatively high level of integration of careers. These are countries that tend to fall in the traditional category of closed

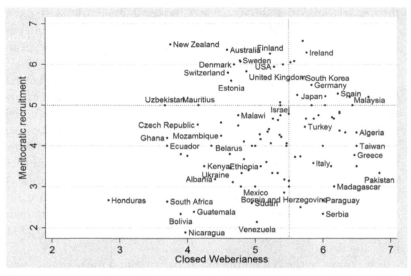

Figure 3.2 Dimensions of Bureaucracy, in 107 countries around the world

Comment: Figure 3.2 plots 107 countries on a two-dimensional space. On the X-axis there is a seven-point closed Weberianism index, while the Y-axis measures the level of meritocratic recruitment, also on a seven-point scale. Data are from the QoG Expert Survey (Teorell, Dahlström, and Dahlberg 2011). The scatterplot is divided into cells representing four types of bureaucracies: Managerial (upper left); Autonomous (upper right); Patronage (lower left); and Corporatist (lower right).

civil service systems (Auer at al. 1996; Bekke and Van der Meer 2000) but, at the same time, there is a fairly low level of separation of careers, with political appointments occupying administrative positions and, importantly, civil servants occupying political positions. Italy and Greece are probably the clearest examples of this administrative system, but other Napoleonic countries, such as France, also exhibit relatively high levels of politicization and a rather closed bureaucratic structure.

Figure 3.2 includes all 107 countries. In this full sample the correlation between meritocracy and closed Weberianism is even weaker, although on this occasion it goes in the positive direction (0.15). Again, we divide the space into four cells. We hold the cut-off points constant from Figure 3.1, however, which expands the number of countries that end up in the bottom categories, especially in the Patronage cell. Nevertheless, this is probably the best way of representing a global sample, where most Latin American (Grindle 2012, chapter 4), African (Hyden 2010), and post-communist countries (Meyer-Sahling 2010) are considered to have substantial levels of patronage. More generally, North, Wallis, and Weingast (2009, 2) note that most contemporary states would still belong to a category where "personal relationships" remain the fundamental "basis of social organization," which would also be consistent with the picture emerging in Figure 3.2, where, overall, merit seems to matter relatively little in public bureaucracies worldwide.

After these first, and very simple, analyses we think that a basic conclusion can be drawn, namely that there are at least two different dimensions, and thus, that our suggested dimension is not the same as closed Weberianism. This analysis is, however, not enough to say anything about exactly where the cut-off between different categories is, or that there are indeed any sharp boundaries at all.

Now we continue with the bivariate cross-country correlations, on the one side of our two indicators of the closed Weberian hypothesis and, on the other side, the dependent variables of the three components of quality of government. On the independent side, we use the same items from the QoG Expert Survey but start by using them separately. On the dependent side, we utilize the three indicators of corruption, government effectiveness, and performance-related pay in the public sector. The correlations between our two closed Weberian indicators and national levels of corruption are illustrated in Figures 3.3 and 3.4. The first figure shows the correlation between the control of corruption measure from the World Bank and having special employment laws protecting public employees. This variable should be understood as a proxy for the degree of institutionalized additional job security in the public sector.

The second figure shows the measure of lifelong careers on the X-axis. This indicator is a proxy for the opportunities and motivations that civil servants have for developing common norms or esprit de corps: the longer and more secure your career prospects are, the more opportunities and motivation you have to interact with your colleagues and acquire the values and norms attached to your administrative body or corps. As is evident in the figures, there are no significant correlations between these indicators of closed Weberian bureaucracy and the level of corruption (note that higher values for control of corruption are better, as this indicates more control). In other words, neither

68 — A Closed Weberian Bureaucracy

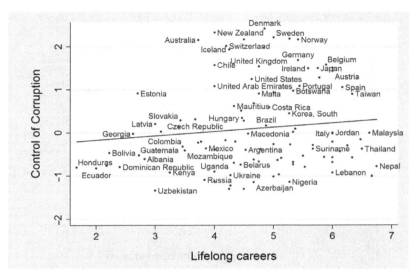

Figure 3.4 Lifelong careers in the public sector and control of corruption
Comment: The Y-axis shows the level of corruption on a scale from −2.5 (highly corrupt) to +2.5 (very clean). Data come from the Control of Corruption Index and are provided by World Bank Governance Indicators (2011). The X-axis reports how often a public employee stays for the rest of the career from 1 (hardly ever) to 7 (almost always). Data cover 105 countries and come from the QoG Expert Survey (Teorell, Dahlström, and Dahlberg 2011) and the QoG Standard Dataset (Teorell et al. 2013).

contribute to efficiency-enhancing reforms in the public sector, at least not when it is measured as performance-related pay.

However, these bivariate correlation analyses may be too simple. We therefore take another step in our analysis and apply an OLS regression including some controls from the existing research on quality of government. The regressions in Table 3.2 include three control variables from the most prevailing cultural (Protestantism), political (years of democracy), and economic (log of GDP per capita) factors noted in the literature as significant (Treisman 2007). In Table 3.2, the columns report the regression coefficients when we examine the closed Weberian hypothesis but take into account that the relationship could have been suppressed by cultural, political, or economic factors.

Columns 1 and 2 report the coefficients for control of corruption, while columns 3 and 4 report the coefficients for government effectiveness and, finally, columns 5 and 6 report the coefficients for our proxy for

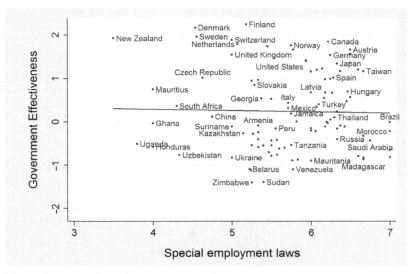

Figure 3.5 Special employment laws and government effectiveness
Comment: The Y-axis shows the level of government effectiveness on a scale from −2.5 (highly corrupt) to +2.5 (very clean). Data come from the Government Effectiveness Index and are provided by World Bank Governance Indicators (2011). The X-axis reports the extent to which public employees are protected by special employment laws measured from 1 (not at all) to 7 (a very great extent). Data cover 105 countries and come from the QoG Expert Survey (Teorell, Dahlström, and Dahlberg 2011) and the QoG Standard Dataset (Teorell et al. 2013).

administrative reforms – the prevalence of performance-related pay in the public sector complementing flat salaries. While the control variables generally have the expected effects, most striking from these analyses throughout are the lack of effects for the special employment laws and lifelong career indicators. With one exception, these features inextricably linked to the closed Weberian ideal bureaucracy do not exhibit any statistically significant effect on our different indicators of government performance. What's more, the only exception concerns the existence of special employment laws and, tellingly, the statistically significant result (with p<0.10) actually points in the opposite direction of what we could expect from the closed Weberian hypothesis: if anything, special employment laws for public employees seem to make it harder to implement efficiency-enhancing reforms, not the other way around. The narratives from the Napoleonic countries provided in the following section will help a bit to illuminate this puzzling result.

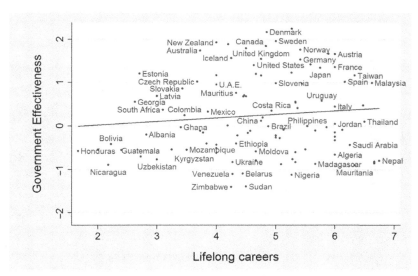

Figure 3.6 Lifelong careers in the public sector and government effectiveness

Comment: The Y-axis shows the level of government effectiveness on a scale from −2.5 (highly corrupt) to +2.5 (very clean). Data come from the Government Effectiveness Index and are provided by World Bank Governance Indicators (2011). The X-axis reports how often a public employee stays for the rest of the career from 1 (hardly ever) to 7 (almost always). Data cover 105 countries and come from the QoG Expert Survey (Teorell, Dahlström, and Dahlberg 2011) and the QoG Standard Dataset (Teorell et al. 2013).

One can, however, have at least four objections to these analyses: (i) it is possible that several institutions need to be in place at the same time for the causal effect to occur; (ii) it is possible that a positive correlation is suppressed if only countries with a high risk for patronage have introduced closed Weberian institutions; (iii) there could be different effects in different parts of the world, depending, for example, on the administrative tradition or on levels of economic development; and (iv) it is also possible that the indicators of government performance are problematic, which could bias the results.

We try to handle the first type of objections in two ways. First, we create an additive index of the indicators (special employment laws and lifelong careers) and, second, we interact the two indicators. The results are presented in Table 3.3. The closed Weberian index is the independent variable, and the dependent variables are control of corruption (column 1), government effectiveness (column

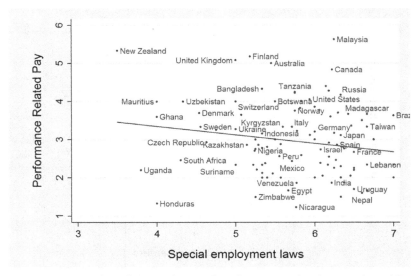

Figure 3.7 Special employment laws and performance-related pay in the public
sector
Comment: The Y-axis shows the degree of performance-related pay in the public sector.
The X-axis reports the extent to which public employees are protected by special
employment laws measured from 1 (not at all) to 7 (a very great extent). Data cover
107 countries and come from the QoG Expert Survey (Teorell, Dahlström, and Dahlberg 2011) and the QoG Standard Dataset (Teorell et al. 2013).

2), and prevalence of performance-related pay in the public sector
(column 3). All three columns report results similar to those in
Table 3.2. We then continue by interacting our indicator of special
employment laws with the indicator of lifelong careers and report
the results in columns 4 to 6. In the first two columns, where
control of corruption and government effectiveness are on the
dependent side, the results are again similar. When it comes to
performance-related pay in the public sector, the results change in
an interesting way. Although only statistically significant on the
0.10 level, lifelong career has a positive effect, while the interaction
term is negative. This indicates that lifelong careers are good for
performance-related pay in the public sector, but only when special
employment laws are not used to a great extent. This positive effect
diminishes with higher values of the special employment law indicator and is close to zero when special employment law has a value of

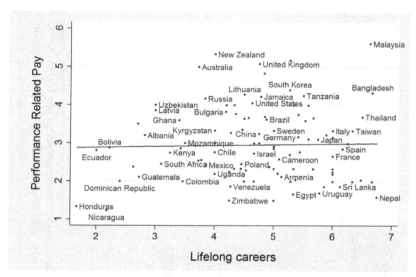

Figure 3.8 Lifelong careers in the public sector and performance-related pay in the public sector

Comment: The Y-axis shows the degree of performance-related pay in the public sector. The X-axis reports how often a public employee stays for the rest of the career from 1 (hardly ever) to 7 (almost always). Data cover 107 countries and come from the QoG Expert Survey (Teorell, Dahlström, and Dahlberg 2011) and the QoG Standard Dataset (Teorell et al. 2013).

6 on the 7-point scale; at that value the statistical significance goes below the standard threshold.

We deal with the second and third objections in new series regressions. Table 3.4 replicates the regressions from Table 3.2, but this time with the risk index included. We can see, however, that this does not alter the result in favor of the closed Weberian hypothesis. With the exception of the special employment laws and performance-related pay in the public sector, all correlations between our two indicators of closed Weberianism and indicators of corruption, effectiveness, and efficiency-enhancing reforms are statistically non-significant, while the risk index is, as expected, negatively, and in most cases statistically significantly, associated.

We also re-ran the analysis from Tables 3.2, 3.3 and 3.4, including a division of the sample into sub-samples of OECD/non-OECD and EU27/non-EU27 and controlling for other regions of the world (results not shown but available upon request). When we divide our sample

Table 3.2 *Special employment laws, lifelong careers and corruption, government effectiveness, and performance-related pay*

	(1) Control of corruption	(2) Control of corruption	(3) Gov. effect.	(4) Gov. effect.	(5) PRP	(6) PRP
Special laws	0.0067 (0.075)		-0.052 (0.065)		-0.21* (0.12)	
Long career		0.052 (0.046)		0.025 (0.040)		0.0169 (0.075)
GDP/cap (log)	0.45*** (0.061)	0.45*** (0.060)	0.50*** (0.053)	0.49*** (0.052)	0.22** (0.099)	0.18* (0.098)
Dem. years	0.012*** (0.0030)	0.012*** (0.0030)	0.0087*** (0.0026)	0.0088*** (0.0026)	0.00081 (0.0049)	0.0019 (0.0049)
Protestant.	0.014*** (0.0028)	0.014*** (0.0028)	0.0092*** (0.0024)	0.0097*** (0.0024)	0.0092** (0.0045)	0.011** (0.0045)
Constant	-4.47*** (0.60)	-4.64*** (0.54)	-4.34*** (0.52)	-4.66*** (0.47)	2.05** (0.96)	1.10 (0.88)
N	101	101	101	101	101	101
R^2	0.75	0.75	0.76	0.76	0.20	0.18
adj. R^2	0.74	0.74	0.76	0.75	0.17	0.14

Comment: Entries are OLS regression coefficients (standard errors in parentheses). The dependent variable in models 1 and 2 is the Control of Corruption Index from the World Bank Governance Indicators (2011). The dependent variable in models 3 and 4 is the Government Effectiveness Index, also from the World Bank Governance Indicators (2011). The dependent variable in models 5 and 6 is the degree of performance-related pay in the public sector from the QoG Expert Survey (2011).

* $p < 0.10$, ** $p < 0.05$, *** $p < 0.01$

Table 3.3 Weberianism and potential interaction effects on corruption, government effectiveness and performance-related pay

	(1) Control of corruption	(2) Gov. effect.	(3) PRP	(4) Control of corruption	(5) Gov. effect.	(6) PRP
Web. index	0.057	0.0059	-0.067			
	(0.067)	(0.058)	(0.11)			
Special law				-0.041	-0.030	0.51
				(0.30)	(0.26)	(0.48)
Long career				0.053	0.12	1.01*
				(0.38)	(0.33)	(0.61)
Interaction				0.0014	-0.012	-0.18*
				(0.066)	(0.057)	(0.10)
GDP/cap (log)	0.45***	0.45***	0.19*	0.46***	0.50***	0.20**
	(0.060)	(0.053)	(0.098)	(0.063)	(0.054)	(0.099)
Dem. years	0.012***	0.0089***	0.0020	0.011***	0.0083***	0.0013
	(0.0030)	(0.0026)	(0.0049)	(0.00031)	(0.0027)	(0.0049)
Protestant	0.014***	0.0095***	0.010**	0.014***	0.0092***	0.0077*
	(0.0028)	(0.0024)	(0.0046)	(0.0029)	(0.0025)	(0.0046)
Constant	-4.67***	-4.58***	1.43	-4.50***	-4.68***	-2.22
	(0.57)	(0.50)	(0.94)	(1.68)	(1.46)	(2.66)
N	101	101	101	101	101	101
R^2	0.75	0.76	0.18	0.75	0.77	0.23
adj. R^2	0.74	0.75	0.14	0.73	0.75	0.19

Comment: Entries are OLS regression coefficients (standard errors in parentheses). The dependent variable in models 1 and 4 is the Control of Corruption Index from the World Bank Governance Indicators (2011). The dependent variable in models 2 and 5 is the Government Effectiveness Index, also from the World Bank Governance Indicators (2011). The dependent variable in models 3 and 6 is the degree of performance-related pay in the public sector from the QoG Expert Survey (2011).
* $p < 0.10$, ** $p < 0.05$, *** $p < 0.01$

Table 3.4 *Special employment laws, lifelong careers and corruption, government effectiveness, and performance-related pay, controlling for patronage risk*

	(1) Control of corruption	(2) Control of corruption	(3) Gov. effect.	(4) Gov. effect.	(5) PRP	(6) PRP
Special laws	0.047 (0.074)		-0.092 (0.058)		-0.26** (0.13)	
Long career		0.063 (0.045)		0.049 (0.036)		0.034 (0.080)
GDP/cap (log)	0.33*** (0.084)	0.32*** (0.082)	0.37*** (0.066)	0.36*** (0.065)	0.12 (0.14)	0.070 (0.15)
Dem. years	0.0079** (0.0030)	0.0078*** (0.0029)	0.0045* (0.0024)	0.0049** (0.0023)	-0.0029 (0.0052)	-0.0011 (0.0052)
Protestant	0.012*** (0.0028)	0.013*** (0.0028)	0.0076*** (0.0024)	0.0087*** (0.0024)	0.0076 (0.0045)	0.0097** (0.0045)
Risk index	-1.026*** (0.311)	-1.000*** (0.308)	-1.014*** (0.244)	-0.989*** (0.245)	-0.931* (0.533)	-0.894 (0.547)
Constant	-2.391*** (0.905)	-2.878*** (0.864)	-2.298*** (0.710)	-2.916*** (0.686)	3.794** (1.551)	2.508 (1.532)
N	90	90	90	90	90	90
R2	0.79	0.79	0.83	0.83	0.26	0.22
adj. R2	0.77	0.78	0.82	0.82	0.22	0.18

Comment: Entries are OLS regression coefficients (standard errors in parentheses). The dependent variable in models 1 and 2 is the Control of Corruption Index from the World Bank Governance Indicators (2011). The dependent variable in models 3 and 4 is the Government Effectiveness Index, also from the World Bank Governance Indicators (2011). The dependent variable in models 5 and 6 is the degree of performance-related pay in the public sector from the QoG Expert Survey (2011).

* $p < 0.10$, ** $p < 0.05$, *** $p < 0.01$

into sub-samples, the results change in two intriguing ways. First, the variable of years of democracy loses statistical significance in some model specifications. Second, and more interesting, the effect of both indicators actually becomes negative and statistically significant for government effectiveness and performance-related pay in some sub-samples. We are unwilling to draw any far-reaching conclusion from these unexpected effects but, if anything, these results also speak against the expectations of the closed Weberian hypothesis.

Moreover, we have used a measure of the percentage of Protestants in 1980, originally from La Porta et al (1999). The reason is that this measure is commonly used in corruption studies. One can, of course, object that this relatively old measure is outdated. We have therefore substituted it with data from the Association of Religion Data Archives (www.thearda.com/) from 2010, and re-ran the regressions reported in Table 3.2 without observing any substantial changes.

Finally, we re-ran the analysis again, but this time substituting the indicators on the dependent side. For corruption, we instead tried indicators from Transparency International (2013) and the International Country Risk Guide (2013); for government effectiveness, we used one indicator from the Bertelsmann Stiftung (2012) and one from the World Economic Forum (Schwab 2012); and, for performance-related pay, we used an indicator from the OECD (2004). With one exception, the results are not altered in any substantial way. The exception is that when the International Country Risk Guide's (2013) corruption indicator is used the existence of lifelong careers in the public sector has for the first time an effect in the expected direction, and this is also statistically significant ($p<0.05$). This result is unstable, however: either when control variables are excluded, or when controls for regions are included, or in bivariate correlations, the lifelong career coefficient turns non-significant. We therefore consider it to be more of a statistical artifact than a stable empirical result.

Our conclusions from the analyses in this section are that the indicators have a surprisingly weak association with overall levels of perceived corruption, with indicators of government effectiveness, and with proxies for the implementation of efficiency-enhancing reforms, which speaks against the closed Weberian hypothesis.

The next section will look more closely at a group of countries that traditionally – as well as in our dataset – are seen as having a closed bureaucracy, namely the countries belonging to the Napoleonic tradition. In our perspective, these overviews of Napoleonic countries help us to understand why systems constrained by numerous bureaucratic rules fail to deliver quality of government.

The Napoleonic Tradition and the Dangers of a Closed Weberian Bureaucracy

This section provides qualitative evidence that we hope can help to explain the lack of statistical correlation between, on the one side, indicators of a closed Weberian bureaucracy and, on the other, low levels of corruption and an innovative and effective public sector. We focus on the public administrations of countries belonging to the Napoleonic tradition, namely France, Belgium, Italy, Portugal, Greece, and Spain. The name comes from the fact that its institutional characteristics were set by Napoleon and were exported to many other European countries in the early nineteenth century (Wunder 1995). These countries score high on our indicators and are also often considered to have closed institutions for public employees (OECD 2008; Ongaro 2011; Painter and Peters 2010). Although reforms in some countries, such as Portugal, have made this group of countries increasingly diverse, they still represent a relatively homogeneous group (Demmke 2010, 8). Consequently, a large literature underlines the similarities between the Napoleonic countries (Bezes and Parrado 2013; Kickert 2007; Painter and Peters 2010; Peters 2008).

Although there are differences in the tradition, especially between the original French model and the Southern European versions, scholars have noted how these countries combine a strong administration with notable politicization (Ongaro 2010; Painter and Peters 2010; Rouban 2012). On the one hand, stringent laws and regulations, such as the so-called *Etat de droit* in France, the *Stato di diritto* in Italy, and the *Estado de Derecho* in Spain, have traditionally bound their administrations. A basic feature of the Napoleonic model is the "predominance of a career civil service" (Ongaro 2010, 177), and attempts to reform the system of recruitment and promotion have largely failed (Lapuente 2007; Spanou 2008). These are countries with a marked "strong legal body of provisions ruling bureaucratic life" (Bezes and Lodge 2007, 123) and a "statute that organizes the professional life of all civil servants" (Statut General des Fonctionnaries; Estatuto de la

Función Pública). Administrative scholars have indeed observed the high degree of legal formalism, and that the law prevails over management in how the public sector is run (Painter and Peters 2010; Panozzo 2000; Pierre 2011).

On the other hand, their legalism is paired with a politicization that has historical roots and, at least to some extent, has become "structural" (Rouban 2004, 83; see also Charron, Dahlström, and Lapuente 2012). According to Ongaro (2010, 176), "in all five countries [France, Greece, Italy, Portugal and Spain] clientelistic relationships are well rooted in the system." In the case of Spain, the politicization may have increased (Bezes and Parrado 2013) as a result of the expansion of political appointments (Cejudo 2006), ministerial cabinets (Parrado 2004), and the return to a modern version of the spoils system (Alba 2001). In contrast to countries like Britain, where the potential disagreements between politicians and bureaucrats in the period of expansion of state activities in the late nineteenth century were solved via entrenching a neutral civil service, Napoleonic countries opted for a different strategy, and politicization of the administration became the prevailing norm of the relationship between politicians and bureaucrats (Rugge 2003). The result is that Napoleonic countries show a "persistence of forms of pre-Weberian style patronage (local notables)" (Ongaro 2011, 111).

Critical for the argument presented in this book, the careers of bureaucrats and politicians are thus, in comparison to other European countries, more integrated in Napoleonic administrations (Rouban 2004). As Peters (2008, 124) notes, "the Napoleonic tradition tends to have fewer barriers between the political and the administrative than most other traditions." Some authors even detect an "increased porousness" (Ongaro 2010, 179) or "interpenetration of politics and administration" (Rouban 2004, 83) in recent years. This might seem counterintuitive, given that legal boundaries are there to protect bureaucrats from political influence, but "the frontier between administration and politics has been eroded" (Rouban 2004, 99). This combination of stringent rules formally separating politicians and bureaucrats and, at the same time, a practice according to which the careers of both groups are remarkably intertwined, is possible for two reasons.

First, ministers enjoy a margin of maneuver to appoint a large number of political appointments, in the two, three, or even four

tiers below their positions, in the strategically crucial ministerial
cabinets, populated by advisors who can exert a notable influence
over the administrative apparatus, as well as in the formal departmental hierarchy, for example as Junior Ministers, General Secretaries, General Directors, and even Deputy General Directors. This
politicization has even increased during the latest decades in some
countries, and, in a survey of Belgian civil servants, for instance,
these "deplored the politicization phenomenon" and defined "the
situation as bad and going from bad to worse" (Dierickx 2004,
185). Likewise, but on a much larger scale, numerous observers of
the Greek civil service have noted the extensive penetration of the
public administration by successive governments (Lyrintzis 1984;
Sotiropoulos 1999, 2004; Spanou 1996).

Second, trained civil servants occupy a large proportion of all
appointed and political positions. In his description of France, Rouban
(2004, 83) consequently writes "...civil servants are at the heart of
political life and outnumber other actors." Likewise, in some Spanish
governments bureaucrats represent over 70 percent of the political
appointments to top administrative positions in all ministries (Parrado
2004, 252). High profile politicians, and ministers in particular, tend
also to come from the ranks of the civil service, with an average of
52 percent in France (Rouban 2004, 84). In the latest Spanish government headed by Mariano Rajoy (2011-), we find eleven civil servants –
including Rajoy himself – out of a total of fourteen ministers. In sum,
in Napoleonic countries, not only are the careers of bureaucrats and
politicians integrated, but "...a career in the civil service is a necessary
step in any political career" (Rouban 2004, 84). Judging by the Spanish case, a civil service career is almost a requirement for a successful
political career, but it also pays off if one aims to have a successful
professional career in any company within economic sectors in which
government regulation or support may be key (Molinas 2013). Generally speaking, in Napoleonic countries, "administrators often have
political careers, both as active politicians and as appointees to positions in ministerial cabinets and similar structures that are linked to
political leaders. Indeed many politicians begin their careers as civil
servants trained by the state and then move into political careers"
(Peters 2008, 124).

From a comparative perspective, scholars have observed that the
legal entrenchment of Napoleonic systems has not prevented, but has

actually facilitated, the creation of the factions we discussed in Chapter 2. The Napoleonic countries are consequently characterized by the existence of an "exclusive administrative class" (Painter and Peters 2010, 34), such as the French *grand corps* or the *Spanish Grandes Cuerpos*, that is "slipping back and forth from a civil service to a political role" (Painter and Peters 2010, 34). In France, the members of the grand corps, "selected from the Ecole Nationale d'Administration, with few opportunities for later entry into the elite positions" (Peters 2008, 125), have traditionally played a role of "brokers" (Rouban 2004, 85). To an even larger extent, in the second half of the twentieth century in Spain, elite civil servants were judged as meeting Mills' (1956) criteria of a power elite because they "could control the nomination of the political masters" (Parrado 2004, 253). And, since the democratic transition in the late 1970s, the Spanish parliament was "filled with civil servants who came from top ministerial echelons" (Parrado 2012, 121). In his sharp criticism of the Greek administrative system, Sotiropoulos (2004, 258) describes the civil service not as an "innocent bystander" or "victim" but as a group that has been truly "protagonists," who have taken advantage of their privileged position to get additional income, exclusive rights for their associations (think of generous pension plan schemes), and the like.

Franco's Spain, especially in the period 1959–75, has been defined as a government of bureaucrats (Crespo and Fernando 2003, 335; Nieto 1976, 574; Parrado 2000). Some have argued that the Weberian prophecy – or nightmare? – was fulfilled completely under the Franco regime (Villoria 1999, 103), where legislation, in turn accompanied by burdensome regulations and administrative procedures, was written by bureaucrats themselves. To the classical powers of the French administrative corps, the Spanish added a critical feature that would only be slowly removed during the subsequent democratic regime: self-financing capacities (Beltrán 2001). Once in her post, the bureaucrat achieved such a degree of stability that the legal term created in Spain to mean a permanent position was "a plaza en propiedad" (literally, "a place of your property") and the all-powerful bureaucratic corps treated the administration as a part of their own patrimony (Parrado 2000, 255). The degree of autonomy of the bureaucratic corps was so extensive that it could be argued that entire sections of the public administration almost became their private properties (Baena 1999;

Suay 1987). The Spanish public sector resembled a "feudal state society" (De la Oliva and Gutiérrez-Reñón 1968, 18) or a "confederation of corps" (De la Oliva and Gutiérrez-Reñón 1968, 146) where administrative bodies enjoyed autonomous independence from each other and from politicians. Even if to a much lesser extent, some of these characteristics have survived until today (Parrado 2000; Lapuente 2007). For example, serious attempts to weaken the grand corps was made in the 1980s but "the power of the corps was unaffected" (Bezes and Parrado 2013, 37). The highest echelons of Spanish society thus form a political-bureaucratic elite that has been labeled as the "state nobility" (Bagues and Esteve-Volart 2008), "la casta" (Montero 2009), or an "extractive elite" (Molinas 2013).

In addition, there is a marked difference between the *de jure* bureaucratic regulations and the *de facto* way of conducting business in Napoleonic administrations. Legal entrenchment can actually breed "double talk – the rules are 'observed' through elaborate procedures, but outcomes are achieved by informal arrangements, including corruption" (Painter and Peters 2010, 34). In Belgium, staff policy "officially was supposed to be governed by the bureaucratic rules of the merit system" but in practice political masters "appoint and promote as many of 'their own people' as possible" (Dierickx 2004, 184–5). The contrast between *de jure* rules and *de facto* norms is probably sharpest in Greece, where, "while officially all relevant procedures are standardized and meritocratic, unofficially it is widely admitted that politicization is quite extensive" (Sotiropoulos 2004, 260). Greek civil servants are open about this. As a 1995 survey showed, almost half the respondents acknowledged that they owed their position to either straight patronage (30 percent) or to a combination of examination and patronage (18 percent). Even more worrisome, only 16 percent of the civil servants considered that promotions mostly obeyed "objective criteria" – with an overwhelming majority understanding that the prevailing criteria of promotion included patronage considerations (Sotiropoulos 2004,).

How is it possible that highly formalized recruitment systems allow for politicized appointments? There are several ways. First, there are always alternative venues to join the civil service – one could even argue that the more stringent the procedures surrounding the regulated way of entering the civil service, the more need for *ad hoc* mechanisms to respond to unexpected peaks of job demand. For instance, in Italy and France, formal meritocratic recruitment systems have frequently been bypassed by the phenomenon known as "titularization," according to which many candidates enter with temporary contracts and, when the number of individuals with these contracts becomes high enough, a law is enacted that changes the nature of the employment contract, transforming thousands of employees from temporary into permanent civil servants. In Italy, the public employees recruited through "titularization" have, in some periods, outnumbered those hired through regular exams (Cassese 1993, 325).

Second, it is an empirical question whether legal rules are effective. For example, when there is a need to fill a vacancy in a public institution, there are guidelines that have not been devised with the aim of guaranteeing an impartial procedure, but are designed instead to tie the hands of the selection committee. A look at official administration bulletins including job advertisements reveals some strangely detailed list of the desired characteristics for a particular post – characteristics that seem to have been included to favor a very particular candidate. Obviously, it is extremely difficult to identify, let alone to prove before a court, that a special requirement for a post was deliberately inserted to favor a certain person. Nevertheless, scholars and civil society organizations have listed some bizarre conditions that have been included in job descriptions for Spanish public administrations, such as "knowing how to ride a horse" or "having been manager of a ceramics factory" (Iglesias 2007, 124) – which are hardly proxies for skills. In other words, the regulated entry procedures in closed civil service systems like Spain do not make the administration immune to nepotism and politicization; quite the contrary, they seem to create unexpected opportunities for bending meritocracy. Furthermore, the existence of a densely regulated and formalized process becomes the perfect argument for politicians interested in creating *ad hoc* agencies filled with politically appointed officials. That, for instance, seems to have been the case in the municipality of Marbella in the 1990s, where the newly elected mayor, Jesús Gil, ran on a platform to make the local government more similar to (his) private firms – with the result of extensive politicization and rampant corruption (Dahlström, Lapuente, and Teorell 2012a).

High politicization also means the threat of a constant "...turnover in higher positions" (Rouban 2004, 83). For instance, the conservative takeover of the Spanish government in 1996 implied that 89 percent of

270 top positions in the central administration changed hands, which contributed to low government effectiveness (Parrado 2004, 227). In Greece, the turnover in a context of a very polarized party system coupled with a use of politicization as a "source of generating votes rather and as an instrument of policy implementation" is much broader and difficult to quantify (Sotiropoulos 2004, 257). Although with levels of politicization way below the Greek ones, other Napoleonic countries may be heading in a similar direction, such as France, where surveys directed to civil servants detect a worrying "sense of growing politicization" (Rouban 2004, 92). It is important to note that this turnover implies an inherent instability for those directly affected by potential dismissals; they work with, relatively speaking, shorter time horizons than their counterparts in other countries with less penetration of politics in administrative positions. Yet, at the same time, since these countries also present strong politicization from below, this means that, to the X number of appointees with a short time horizon in the, let's say, two to three tiers below the minister, we need to add Y number of positions in the, let's say, four to six tiers below the occupants that may expect to be short-lived.

Thus, all in all, Napoleonic administrations show a large number of officials who either feel uncertain about their survival in office or are anxious about the possibility of getting promoted, which are hardly optimal conditions under which to undertake costly efforts and long-term investments. Let's take the city of Madrid, where municipal government battles with several huge challenges, such as having one of the highest debt figures of European capitals (\$9.2 billion), while it needs to "figure out what to do with some of its half-built or under-used sports centers" after failing to be named the Olympic host in 2013 (The New York Times, 08–09-2013). Instead of fostering an environment of hard work and creativity to see how the city can re-invent itself, observers note that many civil servants in the local government divert their efforts to "stab" each other in order to find themselves supporting the winning horse in the next local elections (*El País* 08–09-2013).

Another negative effect of Napoleonic characteristics on government performance is captured by an OECD (2012) report on governance in Greece. It underlined a core feature of the Napoleonic administrative system as the common denominator that helps to explain poor government performance in all areas covered by the review. To start with, the excessive and detailed administrative processes make Greek bureaucracy inflexible. And the legal formalism also leads civil servants to devote much more attention and effort to administrative processes than to substantial work.

When the OECD evaluated the output of Greek ministries in 2010, they found that policy implementation and coordination represented only a small proportion, while much more work was devoted to producing regulations. For instance, only 2 percent of efforts were dedicated to performance assessments, while 29 percent went to writing extremely detailed "circulars, decrees, laws and ministerial decisions" (OECD 2012, 28). What's more, according to the OECD, legal formalism also disconnects the public administration from the economy and society. Since the focus is on writing as detailed regulations as possible, without making existing evidence a basis for policy decisions, public actions seem to be the result of a "largely internal 'conversation' within the government" (OECD 2012, 28).

Last but not least, in an extreme case of the general pathology of Napoleonic countries, the Greek administration presents the paradoxical situation that administrative provisions initially enacted to prevent clientelism and corruption have, in fact, allowed "ample opportunities for rent seeking, in which resources of the public administration (human or other) are appropriated for political, economic or social advantage, without generating any added value" (OECD 2012, 31). Clientelism is systematic, and there is a widespread perception that, in general, parties have used the Greek state not as an instrument of policy implementation but for their interests (Lyrintzis 1984; Sotiropoulos 1999, 2004). This situation obviously undermines the motivation of public-spirited civil servants (OECD 2012, 31).

Although to a much lower extent, other Napoleonic countries seem also to suffer from an increasing "dichotomization" in their public workforces between highly politicized civil servants – those whose careers are inextricably linked to their political masters – and those who are not active in politics – i.e. those politically neutral civil servants who resemble more their counterparts in other OECD countries such as Britain or Sweden (Rouban 2004, 99). In France, Rouban (2004) notes that the "tension between the two groups is a major force in the recurrent sectorial social conflicts within the public service in France as this dichotomization opposes bureaucratic worlds which do not understand each other."

Given that Napoleonic administrations operate with a rigid legality and emphasize "law" more than "management," one should expect less flexibility and permeability to reforms (Bezes and Lodge 2007; Pierre 2011, 675). The evaluation by scholars of managerial reforms across Napoleonic countries is not unanimous, and generally not positive. It has been noted that administrative reforms are happening later than in other comparative countries, have low priority, and generally that Napoleonic countries are laggards with a resistance to change (Gallego 2003; Kickert 2007; Ongaro 2008; Parrado 2008; Peters 2008; Pollit and Bouckaert 2011; Rouban 2008). Although it has been claimed that one should not be "too pessimistic" (Kickert 2011, 803), there is consensus as to how difficult it is to reform Napoleonic administrations (Howard 1998; Pollit and Bouckaert 2011; Rouban 2008). And, if reforms are finally implemented, they present "missed opportunities" and "implementation gaps" that, overall, appear to be larger than those experienced in some Anglo-Saxon and Northern European countries (Ongaro 2008, 110).

Examples are Italy and Spain, where, despite the fact that some public sector organizations have undergone notable reforms, the mainstream bureaucracies have lagged behind (Parrado 2008). In France, many think there is a need for certain managerial reforms, such as moving from the seniority principle (ancienneté) and pay systems "without any relation to individual performance" in local administrations for reasons of efficiency (Kuhlmann and Bogumil 2007, 147). Nevertheless, substantial reforms have not been passed.

In addition, administrative reforms in Napoleonic countries, when implemented, have frequently resulted "in status quo or modest changes" (Bezes and Parrado 2013, 34). For instance, despite the introduction of performance-related incentives to all French directorates in 2006, "there is no evidence that performance pay has gone beyond increasing the wages for top civil servants" (Bezes and Parrado 2013, 38). A similar result has been seen in Spain, where performance-related payment has only been used very modestly in some agencies (Parrado 2008). Likewise, the attempts to adopt a budgeting process that required public works and infrastructure programs in Spain to have measurable objectives and indicators – that could have minimized the "white elephants" described in Chapter 1 – failed (Ballart and Zapico 2010). In other countries, reforms have backfired. Take for instance the case of Greece, where new public management reforms not only have not been properly implemented, but also have produced a "massive returning to extensive pre-Weberian style patronage and favoritism" (Ongaro 2008, 105).

Conclusions

This chapter has presented empirical evidence against the closed Weberian hypothesis. We have seen that a closed administration with stringent and special employment laws does not seem to lead to lower corruption, more government effectiveness, and a more innovative administration. Although we have tried using several different specifications, we cannot see evidence for the closed Weberian hypothesis in our sample of about one hundred countries.

We have seen that a closed staff policy, even if it originally served the purpose of guaranteeing an impartial public action free from political opportunism, is not an antidote to politicization. Politicians manage to circumvent regulations to colonize public administrations with fellow party members, and civil servants enjoy numerous opportunities to colonize the political layers of government, as an unintended side effect of regulations that give trained civil servants stability, privileges, and, thus, freedom to enter political activities.

As the narratives from countries belonging to the highly regulated Napoleonic administrative tradition indicate, the borders between bureaucracy and politics are blurred. In fact, given the generous leave of absence in these countries, which may include retaining part, or all, of the higher salary received in a political post when returning to the original administrative position, and other privileges enjoyed by civil servants who decide to enter active politics, it can be argued that there is hardly a more secure path to the highest political offices than becoming a civil servant to start with. Qualifying as civil servants was in fact the first step in the political careers of eleven out of the fourteen current ministers of the Spanish government. Not only is a bureaucratic career not a liability to pursuing a political career, it can become a critical advantage in these countries. Conversely, a career in a political party can be a good asset to start a successful career at top administrative positions. The consequence of having both a highly politicized bureaucracy and highly bureaucratized politics is that there is a lack of incentives for bureaucrats and politicians to act as watchdogs for each other. We do not have two separate chains of accountability but a single one: careers depend on the fortunes of the ruling party and, for those bureaucrats loyal to the main opposition party, on the fortunes of that party.

Generally speaking, the chapter sends a cautionary message to policy-makers keen on stringent regulations to achieve quality of government. This actually seems to be the conventional approach among reformers in many Napoleonic countries in the aftermath of the financial crisis, where underlying problems of governance became apparent (Fernández-Villaverde, Garicano, and Santos 2013). For instance, reform proposals enacted to fight corruption tend to be accompanied by encompassing and very detailed laws and regulations. Yet, as we have seen here, more laws regulating the civil service do not seem to have a significant effect on curbing corruption, nor do they seem to strengthen government effectiveness. They also create "solid veto points" (Bezes and Parrado 2013, 45) that impede administrative reforms and consequently hinder reform trends that we see in countries where the careers of politicians and bureaucrats are effectively separated.

This problem was actually noted two millennia ago by the Roman statesman Tacitus, who famously noted "the more corrupt the state, the more numerous the laws" (quoted in Lewis and Catron 1996, 702). Although we have not presented any evidence for this reverse relationship, and we are indeed skeptical of the existence of such causality, it is clear that more laws regulating the civil service are not conducive to better government. Thus, our policy implications for how the civil service should be regulated would be similar to what Don Quixote recommended to his servant Sancho Panza when he appointed him governor of Barataria Island: "...do not issue many regulations; and if you have to, try to make them good" (de Cervantes, 1615, chapter 51).

4 | Corruption

The Inventions of Prudence

One of the main implications of the theory presented in Chapter 2 is that a separation of interests between politicians and bureaucrats in general, and of their careers in particular, decreases the risks of misbehavior in both groups. It is therefore crucial that the careers of bureaucrats do not depend on politicians, so that they cannot, for example, use bureaucrats to draw on public resources in order to enrich themselves or their party. Bureaucrats should have incentives to protest if they are used in such ways, without this being harmful to their careers. And it is equally important that politicians, who should have other loyalties than those of bureaucrats, oversee their behavior and take action if they see examples of corruption. It is only under these circumstances that an efficient two-way monitoring mechanism emerges, which will in turn diminish corruption and other types of misbehavior.

Chapter 3 demonstrated that a closed Weberian organization of the bureaucracy, contrary to what earlier research in this field has led us to believe, does not have the desired consequences. Countries with a closed bureaucracy have no less corruption, are not more effective, and implement fewer efficiency-enhancing reforms. Our suggestion is instead that positive outcomes are more likely achieved through institutional mechanisms that guarantee an effective separation of politicians' and bureaucrats' careers. Consequently, a recruitment process for bureaucrats that relies on professional merits is especially important because it prevents the emergence of relationships of loyalty and subordination of public officials toward their political masters. When officials are recruited (and promoted) according to merit criteria, we thus have two chains of accountability – one based on political criteria and the other on professional peer review criteria – cohabiting in the state apparatus and checking each other.

Our argument echoes James Madison's (1788) famous solution to avoiding political abuses by the legislature deployed in Federalist 51, if we simply replace the term legislature for state apparatus. According to Madison (1788), the goal should be "to divide the legislature [in our case the state apparatus], into different branches [in our case, a political and a bureaucratic branch], and to render them by different modes of election [in our case, political procedures, such as elections and merit-based procedures, respectively], and different principles of action [in our case, reelection and professional ambitions, respectively], as the nature of their common functions, and their common dependence on the society, will admit." Rendering politicians and bureaucrats by different "modes of election" – for instance, democratic elections for political officials and meritocratic recruitment for bureaucrats – will create incentives for mutual monitoring. As Madison reasoned, "the constant aim is to divide and arrange the several offices in such a manner as that each may be a check on the other; that the private interest of every individual, may be a centinel over the public rights" (Madison 1788). By creating different modes of election, we give the different parts of government the ability to "resist encroachments of the others" (Madison 1788).

We argue that, in governments where the professional fates of politicians and bureaucrats are intertwined, bureaucrats cannot resist the encroachments of their political superiors because, ultimately, their career prospects depend on their active or passive support. If separating the interests of the different branches of government were, for Madison, the key "inventions of prudence" to prevent a gradual concentration of powers, we claim that a similar invention of prudence is necessary in the state bureaucracy. To prevent widespread corruption, accountability mechanisms of politicians and bureaucrats should be divided so that incentives of the latter do not depend on the former.

The goal of this chapter is to empirically test the suggestion that a separation of careers between politicians and bureaucrats has a negative effect on corruption. We try to give our theory as tough a test as possible. We bring a large set of alternative explanations, which are described in the next section of this chapter, into our models. However, the current literature on deterrents of corruption focuses mainly on the political side of the state, for example, the effect of democracy, electoral systems, or veto players, and our controls therefore come primarily from this literature. In the next section, however, we also specify different causal mechanisms through which a bureaucracy can affect corruption and investigate the extent to which our suggestion is supported by the empirical evidence as compared to other mechanisms that have been suggested.

In our research strategy, we rely primarily on broad cross-country comparisons between about one hundred countries (this differs between model specifications). Our main independent variables come from the QoG Expert Survey (Teorell, Dahlström, and Dahlberg 2011). The original data have already been discussed in Chapter 2, but the indicators used in this chapter are explained in the section on research strategy.

We show in the following section that there is indeed a strong bivariate correlation between our indicators of the separation of careers and corruption, and proceed by noting that it also holds when a large set of controls is included. We then pay special attention to specific bureaucratic characteristics and see that the features closest to our causal mechanism are also the strongest predictors. Finally, we address a potential objection, which is the possibility of endogeneity bias, using instrumented variable and lagged dependent variable techniques. In the subsequent section, we describe historical experiences from the process of fighting corruption in countries such as Denmark, Sweden, the United Kingdom, and the United States. The two purposes of this section are, first, to illustrate our causal mechanism by showing how civil service reforms aimed at separating the careers of politicians and bureaucrats led to a curbing of the relatively high levels of corruption these countries suffered during the nineteenth century and, second, to note that the sequencing between the separation of careers and decrease in corruption levels that we suggest is compatible with the historical experiences in these countries.

Deterrents to Corruption

Since a series of pioneering studies at the end of the twentieth century, in particular Ades and Di Tella (1997), La Porta et al. (1999), and Treisman (2000), there has been an explosion of comparative research on cross-national differences in corruption. Encompassing reviews of the first decade of research on this issue are found in Holmberg, Rothstein, and Nasiritousi (2009), Svensson (2005), and Treisman (2007). This theoretical section has two aims. We will start by discussing the theory behind the previously suggested explanations. For the sake of clarity, we have divided the different explanations under a number of subheadings. After discussing the main political, economic, and cultural alternative explanations, we will turn to the group of factors most in focus in this book, namely those related to the bureaucratic structure of the state. We will discuss the different bureaucratic approaches to curb corruption, together with our own suggestion, before going into the empirical strategy.

Virtuous Institutions vs. Virtuous Societies

The most consistent finding in the existing literature is that high economic development is strongly correlated with low perceived corruption (Ades and Di Tella 1999; La Porta et al. 1999; Treisman 2000, 2007). There are two conflicting interpretations of the strong correlation between economic development and levels of perceived corruption or, for that matter, almost any other indicator of quality of government, since they are all highly correlated to income levels. Some scholars suggest that institutions come first and others that they are the result of economic growth. According to the latter interpretation, economic development explains why some countries managed to build up good institutions (Boix and Stokes 2003). The basic idea is that, in one way or another, economic development creates a demand for good government and institutions develop in response (Charron and Lapuente 2010; Demsetz 1967; Lipset 1960; Svensson 2005, 27; Welzel and Inglehart 2008. The fact that current levels of perceived corruption correlate robustly with indicators of economic development from as far back as 1820 lends further support to this interpretation (Treisman 2007).

Nevertheless, other important studies tell another causal story and show positive effects that certain institutions have historically had over long-term economic development (Acemoglu et al. 2001; North 1990; Acemoglu and Robinson 2012). The debate between those who think that "institutions rule" (Rodrik et al. 2004) and those who say that "institutions don't rule" (Sachs 2003) is far from over. Therefore, we will control for levels of economic development in our analysis, as is usual in the literature on corruption.

We will also control for levels of education, following human capital theory, according to which both economic development and high quality institutions were caused by the accumulation of human capital (Glaeser et al. 2004). Yet, since the spread of education was slower in Catholic and Muslim countries than in Protestant ones (Landes 1998), we will also control for another characteristic traditionally associated with a virtuous society, namely the proportion of Protestants in the population. Again, there are several alternative mechanisms apart from the fastest spread of education that may explain why Protestant countries have been found in many studies (e.g., La Porta et al. 1999; Treisman 2000) to have low levels of corruption. For instance, Protestant churches may have played a more active role as watchdogs of state officials, perhaps reporting their misbehavior. The reason would be that these churches were born out of opposition to a state-sponsored Catholic religion (Svensson 2005).

As regards other social characteristics, we will also control for two further important variables in our empirical analysis. First, we include a measure of ethno-linguistic fractionalization, given that ethnic divisions have been found to be significant in explaining several related variables such as political stability, civil conflicts, and the delivery of private goods instead of public goods (Alesina et al. 1999; Easterly and Levine 1997). Second, we control for a standard proxy for trade openness. We follow here a large literature that has found that a country's openness to international trade is significantly associated with lower corruption (Ades and Di Tella 1999; Gerring and Thacker 2005; Sandholtz and Gray 2003; Sandholtz and Koetzle 2000; Svensson 2005; Treisman 2000, 2007). *Ceteris paribus*, an open economy should reduce the opportunities that bureaucrats have to extract bribes, either from import tariffs or from the local monopolistic producers who frequently enjoy favorable treatment by government officials.

Democracy vs. Autocracy

An important part of the literature focuses on the impact on corruption of the most basic political regime distinction, namely between democracy and autocracy. Theoretically, democracies should be associated with less extractive governments (Olson 1993). Yet, empirically, studies have found a curve-linear and contradictory relationship between a country's type of political regime and its level of corruption (Harris-White and White 1996; Sung 2004). Democratic transitions can actually increase corruption in the short run and, only after several years, when democracy has truly taken root in a country, can corruption effectively be reduced (Keefer 2007; Treisman 2000).

Several mechanisms have been proposed to explain this U-shaped relationship (Montinola and Jackman 2002). Bäck and Hadenius (2008) suggest that transitional states lack the top-down instruments to repress the corruption among public officials that is characteristic of autocracies, and they have not yet been able to consolidate the bottom-up mechanisms to curb corruption that operate in fully fledged democracies. Keefer (2007; with Vlaicu 2008) says that politicians in younger democracies find it relatively costly to build reputations as impartial providers of public goods and, consequently, in order to put together successful electoral platforms, they need to rely on patrons who bring in votes in exchange for targeted, clientelistic, or outright corrupt goods. As a result, our analysis will include proxies for both the current level of democracy and the consecutive years of democracy they have enjoyed.

As relates to democracy, there is another factor that is highlighted as key in monitoring public sector misbehavior: the existence of a free press (Besley and Burgess 2001; Brunetti and Weder 2003; Treisman 2007). To get an intuitive idea of how important free media is in curbing corruption, it is probably best to look at how relevant the opposite, a government controlled media, is for those interested in fostering corrupt deals. McMillan and Zoido (2004) use a revealed preference argument to do so. They found that the former secret police chief of Peru's President Fujimori – Vladimiro Montesinos – had paid owners of TV channels up to one hundred times more in bribes than he paid, for example, judges and politicians. These authors reached the conclusion that a free media is probably one of the best ways to monitor government misbehavior. In addition, scholars have also noted that measures of newspaper circulation have a significant effect on curbing corruption (Treisman 2007).

Men vs. Women

Not only type of political regime, but also type of politicians or, more precisely, gender, seem to matter in explaining cross-country differences in corruption. In fact, the share of legislators or government ministers who are female is one of the most robust political factors in comparative studies (Dollar et al. 2001; Swamy et al. 2001; Treisman 2007). Some authors, such as Sung (2003), argue that the correlation is spurious, produced by other characteristics of a liberal democracy that tend to go hand in hand with gender equality policies. Nevertheless, the relationship between women in politics and low corruption holds, controlling for the most common proxies for other characteristics of a liberal democracy, such as free elections, years of democracy, or freedom of the press. Treisman (2007) subjects women in politics to a stringent set of robustness tests, controlling for the government party's margin of victory or the degree of fractionalization of parties, and ruling out that the effect was driven by some outliers, such as the Scandinavian countries, and shows that the effect largely holds.

Therefore, and although the mechanisms through which women in high political office lead to overall lower levels of corruption are still not clear, the significant effect shown in the research is a reason to take this relationship seriously (Wängnerud 2008). We consequently take the share of women in parliament into account in our analyses.

Decisiveness vs. Veto Players

There is also a growing political economy literature that shows the comparative advantages of those political systems that enjoy more political checks and balances (Henisz 2000) or, using Tsebelis' (1995) terminology, more veto players. Applying this argument to the fight against corruption, Andrews and Montinola (2004) find a strong correlation between the number of veto players that a country has (the number of parties in the government coalition) and the country's ability to curb corruption. The micro foundation would be the following: the more partners a government coalition has, the more coordination problems they face in engaging in corrupt exchanges. Because of their own selfish electoral interest, the different members of a governing coalition may thus find it more rewarding to reject a bribe – or whistle-blow about it – than to accept it. Consequently, we will control for the number of veto players.

Presidentialism vs. Parliamentarism

A similar mechanism has been put forth regarding the constitutional form of government. Persson, Roland, and Tabellini (2000) consider that, as elected officials in presidential systems cannot make credible commitments to each other, rent-seeking and corruption should be lower than in parliamentary regimes. Yet, quite the opposite, many authors have found a negative correlation between presidential regimes and corruption (Gerring and Thacker 2004; Lederman et al. 2005; Panizza 2001), especially when presidentialism is combined with a closed-list proportional system in legislative elections (Kunicova and Rose-Ackerman 2005). Treisman (2007) effectively finds that presidentialism is associated with higher corruption in most model specifications but, intriguingly, this becomes insignificant when there is a control for Catholicism. In other words, presidentialism could be conditional to other societal factors – giving, for instance, bad results in terms of corruption in Latin America but better results for the United States.

Majoritarian vs. Proportional

Another interesting debate deals with the characteristics of the electoral system. Research indicates that the different components of the classic distinction between majoritarian and proportional systems, such as the size of the district and the existence of plurality rule, should be analyzed separately. On the one hand, a better accountability of legislators to their constituents should be expected in plurality systems, while candidates who are elected from party lists have less individual accountability and are thus more prone to engage in corrupt activities. Empirical studies seem to confirm this expectation since a higher share of MPs elected in single member districts have been found to be correlated with lower levels of corruption (Chang and Golden 2007; cf. Kunikova and Rose-Ackerman 2005; Persson, Tabellini, and Trebbi 2003). On the other hand, one characteristic associated with proportional systems – the existence of large voting districts – has been found to have positive effects on controlling corruption. The reason would be that larger voting districts reduce the barriers to entry for new parties or candidates (Persson, Tabellini, and Trebbi 2003).

Political vs. Bureaucratic Institutions

Taking a more general perspective, we can distinguish between two major types of institutional explanations of corruption. On the one hand, most of the comparative literature focuses on political institutions, such as in the studies reviewed above. This literature has primarily explored mechanisms devised to address the problems of politicians' adverse selection (e.g., a certain electoral system that enhances accountability) and moral hazard (e.g., constraints on the executive that limit opportunistic behaviors). On the other hand, and this is the research we will summarize here, there is a minor strand in the comparative literature that has tried to open the overlooked black box of the administrative apparatus of the state.

One reason why bureaucratic institutions have been sidelined by mainstream comparative research on corruption is probably that they are less visible than ones that are political. In addition, the abundance of large datasets of comparative political institutions contrasts sharply with the scarcity of cross-country datasets on bureaucratic structures. Nevertheless, the analyses of the few that have been developed have found that bureaucratic factors seem to be key to understanding how clean of corruption a state is (Dahlström, Lapuente, and Teorell 2012a; Evans and Rauch 1999; Rauch and Evans 2000). An extensive practice of patronage appointments has been argued to be a necessary condition for the establishment of particularistic exchanges such as corruption (Kopecký and Scherlis 2008). At-will political appointments could be exchanged for bribes and they can help to cover up corrupt practices (Kopecký and Mair 2012).

Our goal here is to study which of the bureaucratic elements pointed out by the few studies of the relationship between administrative structure and corruption matter for curbing corruption. Is it a question of bureaucratic norms? That is, autonomous civil servants internalize informal rules of good conduct and are less corrupt than at-will public employees who are more mobile and, thus, less identified with the core values of a particular bureaucratic body. Or is it a question of salary? In other words, merit-based bureaucrats get better salaries than patronage-based employees and, for that reason, the former are less tempted to accept bribes. Or is it a question of career incentives?

The latter is indeed what we argue: having public employees whose professional careers are fundamentally independent from their political superiors' careers leads to the establishment of a credible system of mutual monitoring of (potentially) corrupt activities. By virtue of their professional independence, merit bureaucrats can, in Madison's (1788) words, "resist encroachments of the others," such as pressures from political superiors to acquiesce to, support, or even take part in corrupt endeavors.

According to the norm mechanism, the advantages of a bureaucratic autonomy are that it allows bureaucrats to develop a set of strong norms. The argument is that isolated bureaucracies create *better types* of public employees through intense socialization in a cohesive social group. That something like this can happen is indicated by the terms for the bureaucratic body, in French the *corps* and in Spanish the *cuerpo*, words that still carry high social prestige and evoke high moral grounds in many societies. In particular, it has been argued that bureaucrats recruited through formal examinations who expect a life-long career in a given government department would develop an *esprit de corps* with beneficial effects for curbing corruption (Rauch and Evans 2000). A set of common norms for fostering impartial and non-corrupt behavior would therefore emerge in an isolated bureaucracy by encompassing civil service protections from the interference of politicians. Those norms of conduct would be the effect of the characteristics of what the literature defines as a "closed" civil service system (Bekke, Perry, and Toonen 1996, 5; Lægreid and Wise 2007, 171), such as the existence of career stability and lifelong tenure, the prevalence of internal promotions over lateral entries to the civil service, and the development of special laws covering the terms of employment for public sector employees instead of the general labor laws prevailing in the country. These characteristics are supposed to increase the expected number of interactions among civil servants in the same bureau and would help to create a sense of common norms, which, in turn, would discourage corrupt behavior among its members. This would be the most decisive mechanism, according to Rauch and Evans (2000), in terms of why a Weberian bureaucracy (in our terminology a closed Weberian bureaucracy) would be less corrupt than one filled by discretionary appointments.

A second bureaucratic mechanism for curbing corruption has to do with the salaries paid in the public sector. In this line of work, the extent to which salaries are competitive with what is paid in the private sector is particularly interesting. There is an ongoing debate on the importance of public sector salaries between those who say that higher pay for bureaucrats should diminish corruption (Becker and Stigler 1974; Besley and McLaren 1993; Di Tella and Schargrodsky 2003; Van Rijckeghem and Weder 2001) and those who have not found robust evidence for that in cross-country studies (Dahlström, Lapuente, and Teorell 2012a; Rauch and Evans 2000; Treisman 2000).

Rauch and Evans (2000) test proxies for these two mechanisms – norms and salaries – in their pioneering comparative study of the public administrations of developing countries. It is important to note that there could be some problems of size and bias in their sample, which is restricted to thirty countries that were considered to be "semi-industrialized" in the 1980s, plus five poorer countries randomly selected to increase the representation of other world regions. This is to say that Rauch and Evans (2000) focus on countries undergoing a critical stage of economic development when data were gathered, and it is at that stage that bureaucratic characteristics should be expected to be more necessary according to the developmental state literature. This, for instance, could be the case in the archetypes of the model of the developmental state, such as Korea or Taiwan, that were explored in detail by Evans (1995) and that one might suspect to be overrepresented in a sample limited to countries in economic transition. Still, Rauch and Evans' (2000) findings are insightful. The only variable that seems to exhibit a systematic effect on the control of corruption is meritocratic recruitment. Their proxies for internal promotion and career stability, despite being linked to their main theoretical mechanism – the development of an *esprit de corps* or a "closed" bureaucracy as we refer to it here – do not show a clear effect in reducing corruption. Also, when it comes to the effect of competitive wages, Rauch and Evans (2000) do not find empirical support. Neither bureaucratic norms nor salaries seem to matter very much.

We argue that this is because there is a distinct mechanism – the separation of politicians' and bureaucrats' career incentives – that may be the relevant link between a merit-based bureaucracy and a country with minimal corruption. Our mechanism requires neither the long-term development of norms nor the payment of high salaries, which has notable policy implications. The costs of rigid civil service protection and expensive payrolls are not justified in terms of curbing corruption. At the same time, our mechanism can also be compatible with the findings of Rauch and Evans (2000): a meritocratic and non-politicized recruitment is what seems to make the difference. Unlike Rauch and Evans, however, we do not identify meritocratic recruitment with formal examinations, since, as we argued in previous chapters, we can have both: a highly meritocratic civil service without formal examinations (managerial administration) and a highly politicized civil service with formal examinations (corporate bureaucracy).

We consider that the existence of a clear separation of career incentives between politicians and bureaucrats helps both the prevention of corruption and the fight against corruption. It prevents corruption because exchanges are, *ceteris paribus*, less likely to happen when careers are separated than when they are integrated in terms of the careers of politicians and bureaucrats. Further, the fight against corruption will be easier because auditors or law and enforcement officials are, *ceteris paribus*, more likely to investigate and prosecute corruption wherever they regard their professional fates to be free of political considerations. Most important, however, as we explained in Chapter 2, is that, where there are different interests, politicians and bureaucrats will monitor each other.

It is relevant to note that the existence of a non-politicized meritocratic public workforce reduces corruption, not necessarily by virtue of selecting more competent agents but by introducing agents with interests known to be different from those of politicians. In other words, we do not contend that merit-recruited bureaucrats are better types than politically appointed ones, but that they are simply different types. Let's consider some illustrations of how the presence of (absence of) separation of political and bureaucratic careers (increases) reduces the probability of corruption.

We can take a look at how corruption increases following a rise in the integration of politicians' and bureaucrats' careers. This is what has been extensively documented in several coastal towns of Spain. Take Estepona, a popular tourist resort that enjoys 325 days of sunshine per year. After years of investigation, the police and judicial prosecutors uncovered in 2009 the details of a large corruption network formed by no less than 103 individuals who had extensively benefitted from a highly politicized public workforce. The money from the private firms interested in getting favorable treatment – for example, to approve development plans ignoring zoning rules – had been flowing to public officials at such a pace that the township did not have "double bookkeeping" – that is, an official one and a second one to illegally finance the ruling party – which is standard in highly corrupt governments. Instead, Estepona had "triple bookkeeping," with a third account registering the money directly diverted to politicians' pockets (Montero 2009, 102). All sorts of businesses fed the local officials' hunger for money – for example, a local councilor allegedly asked €42,000 from the owners of a brothel (Montero 2009, 122). Yet, despite the huge number of people, amount of money, and the many public decisions and actions that were literally bought, there were no leakages from local civil servants and, when the case came to light, it was because of an internal quarrel, an "internal war" (*El País* 27-06-2009), among the leading politicians.

Thanks to the detailed police reports, we know how such a strong pact of silence in the Estepona local administration was sustained: a systematic replacement of politically neutral public employees by an army of political appointments. The coalition parties "agreed, after the elections, the number of at-will positions for each party" (*El Periodista Digital* 02-10-2009). And, as a result, "at least 120 out of the 315 party members [of the ruling socialist party in Estepona] are or have been working for the local government. Equally, at least 42 close relatives of those party members have also been hired" (*El Periodista Digital* 02-10-2009). The political control over the administrative machinery implied that even the most honest public employees found it difficult to blow the whistle. For instance, when a civil servant denounced the local government in 2012, he was removed from his post under allegations of "neglecting his duties" (*El País* 17-02-2013).

In neighboring Marbella, under the rule of Mayor Jesús Gil (1991–2003), we encounter similar mechanisms. Mr. Gil transformed a relatively meritocratic local government into an administration mostly filled with at-will appointments. To this end, he replaced the existing bureaus in the municipal government – where he had to deal with autonomous civil servants – with a series of departments that should be run as flexibly as possible. In short, almost all local officials became accountable in a direct fashion to the mayor, even those belonging to the national bureaucratic *corps* and who are responsible for the internal auditing of local governments. Two of those key figures, the *Interventor* – that is, the officer in charge of the internal control of the economic and financial activities of the municipality – and the *Secretario* – who offers legal advice and legally backs all local government decisions – got generous housing allowances (1000€/month) and productivity bonuses (2000€/month) from the Mr. Gil-controlled local government (*El País* 10-10-2006). Not only their salaries but also their careers depended on Mr. Gil's evaluation of their loyalty. Indeed, when Mr. Gil considered that the *Interventor*, after a major corruption scandal had been unveiled, had become a "traitor" and "whistleblower," "who invents news to favor the opposition" (*El País* 12-12-2000), he opened an internal procedure to dismiss him. This micro-management of human resources in the Marbella local government allowed the development of what judges would refer to, one decade afterwards, as a "system of generalized corruption" (*El País* 4-10-2013). In the 5,774 page-long sentence of the corruption cases in Marbella, a large number of individuals – fifty-two – were found guilty.

The extensive judicial investigation of the nature of the corrupt exchanges in Marbella allows us to see how a large corruption network could have operated for many years without being stopped or even detected by regional, national, or judicial institutions. In particular, the centerpiece of the corruption network was located precisely in one of the most discretionarily run departments: the local agency for urban planning. This was headed by a close friend of the mayor, Juan Antonio Roca, whose "grip on the town hall (...) earned him the nickname JR - from his own initials and those of one of television's most infamous villains, JR Ewing of Dallas" (The Guardian, 8-04-2006). It is this "grip" on great sections of the municipal administration – where he had created a system to charge bribes up to three different times when pushing through planning applications or public contracts – that allowed him to accumulate a personal fortune estimated to be about €2.4 billion, invested in "art, vintage cars, palaces in Madrid, thoroughbred horses, fighting bulls and stuffed wild animals - including a polar bear and the heads of an elephant and rhinoceros" (*The Guardian,* 8-04-2006). Despite the sumptuary deployments of wealth by local government officials like Mr. Roca raising the eyebrows of most of the citizens of Marbella, the accusations of corruption did not make media headlines until many years afterwards because of the cohesive structure of a network of officials whose professional fates were largely dependent on the survival of Mr. Gil's party in office. There were no "whistle-blowers" that reported either to the media or to the police in a patronage-ridden local administration. No one had an incentive to reveal the nature of the game that they were playing.

The 30,000 Marbella homes currently in legal limbo as a result of years of corrupt exchanges between developers and local officials contrast sharply with the single building planned – yet not even built – by the seashore in Gotland, Sweden. In 2009, county governor Marianne Samuelsson had to resign after a professional official leaked to the media Samuelsson's intentions to grant permission to an important businessman to build by the seashore (Dahlström, Lapuente, and Teorell 2012a).

As a matter of fact, it is difficult to even find cases of corruption allegations, like the one above, or corruption convictions where politicians are involved in Sweden. The Swedish Anti-Corruption Institute has gathered all court cases on corruption from the year 2000 onward. Of a total of 193 cases, only six, or 3 percent, involve politicians. It is thus fairly probable that Swedish politicians do not have the prerequisites for creating the corrupt networks needed for cases such as the Marbella one, and therefore never try.

Returning to Spain, a politicized public workforce is more unlikely to, *ex post*, investigate corrupt deals. This is what, according to the spokesman of the largest union of police officers in Spain, *Sindicato Unificado de Policía*, explains why certain cases of corruption are not uncovered in Spain (Público 30-12-2013): the government uses personnel policy to "politicize" and "manage" the anti-corruption units in the police force. In his own words, "the fact that in two years there have been four heads of the Judiciary Police tells you everything" (*Público* 30-12-2013). By a selective use of political appointments in key positions, the minister would be able to "remote control" the corruption investigations that affect his party (El Confidencial 18-10-2013).

A similar case is found in Turkey where, in January 2014, the government, using its extensive prerogatives in appointments, removed 350 police officers – including 80 senior officers in units such as the financial crimes unit, the intelligence unit, and the organized crime unit (The New York Times 07-01-2014) – from their posts in a clear response to the corruption inquiries among high profile politicians (BBC News 7-01-2014). It is important to note that this strategy to protect politicians from corrupt investigations relies heavily on the sectors of the Turkish government where the integration of politicians' and bureaucrats' careers is highest. As an observer remarks, "by law, the government has no jurisdiction to remove judges or prosecutors, so it is cracking down on the police force, which falls under its authority" (The New York Times 07-01-2014).

A Strategy for Investigating the Effect of Separated Careers

As mentioned, the main purpose of the empirical analysis in this chapter is to investigate whether our hypothesis, that a separation of careers between politicians and bureaucrats creates less corruption, is reflected in available data. To a large extent we follow Dahlström,

Lapuente, and Teorell (2012a), but we take some additional steps regarding the causal mechanisms, the historical cases, and when addressing potential endogeneity problems. In our analysis we consider a rather large number of economic, political, and cultural variables that have previously been suggested to reduce corruption and are discussed above. In addition, we take into account a number of alternative explanations concerning the bureaucratic structure, such as the relative level of salaries in the public sector and the secure positions that public employees have in different countries. As far as possible, we finally try to pin down the causal mechanism and demonstrate that it most probably relates to the separation of careers, and that it is the monitoring mechanism we suggest.

We take four analytic steps to achieve the goals just mentioned. We rely mainly on broad cross-country comparisons between about one hundred countries, but we also discuss several historical examples in detail. First, we establish that there is indeed a strong and positive correlation between our indicator of a separation of interests and low corruption. Second, we conduct a series of cross-country OLS regression analyses using a corruption indicator as the dependent variable and a large set of control variables. We pay special attention here to the administrative explanations discussed at length in Chapter 3. We also interact our indicator of a separated career with democracy because, if we are right, the effect should be stronger at higher levels of democratization when whistle-blowing is easier. Third, we test for the robustness of the results and make a special effort to address a potential objection to our results concerning endogeneity bias. Fourth and finally, we discuss in detail the historical experiences of the reduction of systemic corruption in some established Western democracies, including the United States, the United Kingdom, and Sweden. This final step serves the purpose of demonstrating that institutions that separated careers of bureaucrats and politicians indeed preceded, or were a part of, the fight against corruption, which makes our causal story more credible.

To measure the level of corruption in different countries, we use the version of the control of corruption indicator from the World Bank's Governance Indicators from 2011. The World Bank has combined data from thirty different sources into one aggregate measure ranging from -2.5 (low control of corruption) to +2.5 (high control of corruption) (for a discussion of the methodology, see Kaufmann, Kraay, and

Mastruzzi 2010). However, we also use alternative measures on the dependent side to check the robustness of the results. These include the Corruption Perception Index from Transparency International (Transparency International 2013) and the corruption indicator from the International Country Risk Guide 2013 (ICRG 2013).

On the independent side, we use data from the QoG Expert Survey for the administrative characteristics (Teorell, Dahlström, and Dahlberg 2011) (see Chapter 2 for a more extensive discussion of the data collection). To capture the theoretical concept of greatest interest to us – the separation of interest between bureaucrats and politicians – we use an indicator of the extent to which recruitment to the public sector is made by merit. In a previous paper, together with Jan Teorell, we showed that the merit indicator is best suited, but we also test with a professionalization index containing four indicators for robustness (Dahlström, Lapuente, and Teorell 2012a).

We further take a number of other administrative characteristics measured by the QoG Expert Survey into account in the analysis. First, we control for some arrangements that were introduced in order to isolate the bureaucracy from political involvement, such as formal examinations, lifelong careers, and special employment laws for public employees, which we discussed at length in Chapter 3. Second, we include an indicator of how competitive salaries are in the public sector, which has been claimed to reduce corruption (Becker and Stigler 1974; Besley and McLaren 1993; Van Rijckeghem and Weder 2001).

As mentioned, we include a set of indicators of political, economic, social, and cultural factors suggested in previous research to reduce corruption. On the economic side, we take GDP per capita (logged), the total trade volume from the World Development Indicators provided by the World Bank, and the years of openness to trade from Sachs and Warner (1995). On the cultural and social side, we include a standard measure of ethno-linguistic fractionalization in 1985 (Roeder 2001), the proportion of Protestants in the population in 1980 (La Porta et al. 1999), and the enrollment of male secondary education in 2009 (UNESCO 2010). Finally, on the political side, we include a measure of the level of democracy from Freedom House and Polity and freedom of the press from Freedom House (from 2002 to 2006, varying for different countries), the Political Constraints Index (Henisz 2000), the percentage of women in parliament from the OECD Gender,

Institutions and Development Database (2009), the proportionality of the electoral system from the Database of Political Institutions (Keefer 2009), the years of democracy, the number of newspapers per 1000 inhabitants, and the number of television sets per 1000 inhabitants from Treisman (2007).

The dependent variable and the control variables are available from the QoG dataset (Teorell et al. 2013) and are summarized in Table 4.1.

Results of Cross-Country Comparisons

We start the empirical analysis by looking at simple correlations between our two measures of separation of interest between bureaucrats and politicians on the one side, and the World Bank's control of corruption measure on the other side.

In Figure 4.1, we graph the bivariate relationship between the level of meritocratic recruitment in the public sector and the indicator of control of corruption. The basic idea is that a meritocratically recruited bureaucracy owes its loyalty to its professional peers, rather than to politicians or to some particular agency or *corps*. The reason for paying special attention to this indicator is that the recruitment process is probably of key importance, as it is in this process that the employee in a very concrete way learns who earns her loyalty. The level of meritocracy in recruitment is reported on the X-axis and the control of corruption measure on the Y-axis. In line with our theory, the correlation is positive, strong, and statistically significant (R=0.70, $p < 0.00$).

Italy and Mexico are two countries that appear in the figure as both lacking a meritocratic administration and having high levels of corruption, which might be surprising taking into account that they are both OECD members. These are countries that the literature uses as paradigmatic examples of both a non-meritocratic administration (see for instance Cassesse 1993 for Italy and Grindle 2012 for Mexico) as well as states that have high levels of corruption (see for instance Golden 2003 for Italy and Morris 2009 for Mexico). It has been argued that the extensive patronage recruitment in Italy, for example in the period 1973–1990, when about 350,000 public employees received their positions through discretionary appointments while about 250,000 were recruited through regular entrance exams (Cassese 1993), and the "partisan political loyalty of civil

Table 4.1 *Descriptive statistics*

Variable	Obs	Mean	Std. Dev.	Min	Max
Bureaucracy 18th century	30	.47	.51	0	1
Competitive salaries	107	3.2	1.0	1.3	6
Control of corruption (2011)	191	-.06	.99	-1.7	2.4
Control of corruption (1996)	175	-.03	1.0	-2.1	2.4
Education	171	78.5	26.1	10.7	132
Ethnic fractionalization	166	.46	.27	0	.98
Formal examination	107	4.5	1.4	1.6	6.8
Freedom of the press	193	47.2	24.4	10	99
GDP/cap (log)	179	8.7	1.3	5.7	11.1
Level of democracy	193	6.7	3.1	0	10
Long career	107	4.7	1.1	1.67	6.8
Meritocratic recruitment (QoG Expert Survey)	107	4.3	1.1	1.9	6.6
Meritocratic recruitment (QoG Expert Survey II)					
Newspaper per 1000	134	100	125	0	588
OECD	107	.27	.45	0	1
Political constraints	171	.42	.31	0	.89
Protestantism	193	13.1	21.3	0	97.8
Share of legislators elected by plurality vote	162	.51	.50	0	1
Special law	107	5.7	.73	3.5	7
Trade volume	174	86.1	45.8	22.1	422
TV sets per 1000	140	233	207	0	847
Weberian index	107	5.2	.81	2.8	6.8
Women in parliament	116	16.3	10.1	0	56.3
Year open to trade	133	85.7	16.7	50	100
Years of democracy	171	18.2	21.6	0	70

Comment: Table 4.1 summarizes all variables. All variables except literacy rate 1880 are available in the QoG standard dataset (Teorell et al. 2013), and the QoG Expert Survey (Teorell, Dahlström, and Dahlberg 2011).

108   *Corruption*

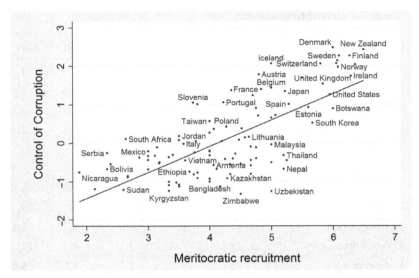

Figure 4.1 Correlation between control of corruption and meritocratic recruitment

Comment: The Y-axis shows the level of corruption on a scale from −2.5 (highly corrupt) to +2.5 (very clean). Data come from the Control of Corruption Index and are provided by World Bank Governance Indicators (2011). The X-axis reports whether public sector employees are recruited by their skills and merit, measured from 1 (not at all) to 7 (a very large extent). Data cover 104 countries and come from the QoG survey (Teorell, Dahlström, and Dahlberg 2011).

servants" leave too "extensive opportunities to engage in bureaucratic corruption" (Golden 2003, 189). In the case of Mexico, the existence of a politicized civil service, which has hindered horizontal accountability in government officials (Morris 2009, 9), is considered a major factor behind the famous dictums that "corruption is not a characteristic of the system in Mexico . . . it is the system" or that corruption is "Mexico's national sport" (Morris 2009, 1).

However, the correlations in Figure 4.1 do not include any control variables, and there is thus an obvious risk for omitted variable bias. We therefore conduct a series of cross-country regression analyses, again with the control of corruption indicator as the dependent variable, but this time including a large number of control variables. As we discussed previously in this chapter, there is no standard set of determinants of corruption, and we therefore test several alternative specifications, following the strategy of Dahlström, Lapuente, and Teorell (2012a). These specifications are reported in Table 4.2.

Table 4.2 *Meritocratic recruitment and Control of Corruption (OLS estimates)*

	(1)	(2)	(3)	(4)	(5)
Meritocratic recruitment	0.45*** (0.06)	0.28*** (0.05)	0.16*** (0.06)	0.26*** (0.06)	0.23*** (0.05)
GDP/cap (log)	0.61*** (0.11)	0.34*** (0.09)	0.067 (0.094)	0.22** (0.10)	0.23*** (0.065)
Education	-0.005 (0.005)	-0.002 (0.004)		-0.0001 (0.004)	
Ethnic fractionalization	0.19 (0.25)			0.072 (0.22)	
Level of democracy		0.064*** (0.024)	-0.009 (0.040)	0.11*** (0.024)	
Political constraints		0.23 (0.23)			
Protestantism		0.009*** (0.002)		0.009*** (0.002)	0.006** (0.003)
Years of democracy		0.006** (0.003)	0.004 (0.004)	0.006** (0.003)	0.007*** (0.003)
Freedom of the press			-0.020*** (0.006)		-0.016*** (0.003)
Newspaper per 1000			0.002* (0.001)		0.0003 (0.0005)
TV sets per 1000			-0.0003 (0.0004)		
Women in parliament			-0.006 (0.005)		
Year open to trade			-0.006 (0.004)		
Share of legislators elected by plurality vote				0.051 (0.11)	
Trade volume				0.003** (0.002)	0.002 (0.001)
OECD				0.206 (0.157)	
Constant	-7.00*** (0.720)	-4.83*** (0.551)	0.101 (1.10)	-4.37*** (0.714)	-2.64*** (0.610)

Table 4.2 (*cont.*)

	(1)	(2)	(3)	(4)	(5)
Number of countries	96	99	52	91	94
R^2	0.733	0.830	0.687	0.856	0.860
Adjusted R^2	0.722	0.816	0.620	0.838	0.849

Comment: Entries are OLS regression coefficients (standard errors in parentheses). The dependent variable is the World Bank Control of Corruption indicator from 2011. OECD=Organization of Economic Co-operation and Development. All variables are available in the QoG standard dataset (Teorell et al. 2013) or the QoG Expert Survey (Teorell, Dahlström, and Dahlberg 2011).
* $p < 0.10$, ** $p < 0.05$, *** $p < 0.01$

As Evans and Rauch (2000) is without doubt the most influential scholarly work studying bureaucratic structures and corruption, we start by replicating their model including GDP per capita (logged), level of education, and degree of ethno-linguistic fractionalization. Moving on, the second model presented in Table 4.2 follows Lapuente and Nistotskaya (2009) and takes the extent to which political power is currently fragmented or is fragmented over time. The reason is that political competition and varying time horizons create very different incentives for rulers to introduce meritocracy in the bureaucracy. This model also includes a cultural control, namely the proportion of Protestants in the country, which has previously been shown to correlate with corruption, although the causal reason is debated (La Porta et al. 1999). The third and fourth models take the departure in the two most influential reviews of the causes of corruption of which we are aware. Daniel Treisman's (2007) analysis suggests that economic development, a longstanding democracy, the freedom of and widely read press, together with a large proportion of women in parliament and a history of trade openness, correlate with low corruption. Our third model therefore includes measures for all these correlates of corruption. In the fourth, we use Persson, Tabellini, and Trebbi's (2003) study on electoral rules and corruption as a reference. This model includes Rauch and Evans' (2000) variables together with the proportion of legislative candidates elected by plurality votes for individuals, the level and number of years of democracy, Protestantism, trade volume, and a dummy for OECD members. [It should be noted that, although we prefer the measure of the percentage of

Protestants in 1980, originally from La Porta et al (1999), we have also tried to substitute it with data from the Association of Religion Data Archives without observing any substantial changes.]

In the fifth model, we keep the determinant that has been statistically significant in any of the other models. (The one exception is the Freedom House measure of level of democracy, which we omit due to collinearity with the Press Freedom Index.)

For the purpose of this book, we are most interested in seeing that the indicator of meritocratic recruitment works as a statistically significant deterrent of corruption across all these specifications. These results are also robust to the inclusion of regional controls and are substantively the same when we substitute the measure on corruption with indicators from Transparency International (2013) and the International Country Risk Guide (2013). Moreover, due to the imprecise point estimates of the World Bank Control of Corruption indicator we re-ran the all models presented in Table 4.2, taking the inverse size of the standard errors into account, which did not make any substantial differences for the results (see Kaufmann, Kraay, and Mastruzzi 2010).

However, the models presented in Table 4.2 do not include any alternative explanations from the bureaucratic structure literature. We therefore use the final model, column 5 in Table 4.2, which also includes indicators of a closed Weberian system and the one of relative pay in the public sector. As discussed at length in Chapter 3, institutional protection of the bureaucracy is probably the most important alternative explanation (Miller 2000; Rauch and Evans 2000). The results are given in Table 4.3. The first model includes an additive index combining the career tenure of bureaucrats and the extent to which special employment laws protect them. The results of the analysis show a counterintuitive, although not statistically significant, negative relationship between competitive salaries and control of corruption, and a non-significant positive relationship between the closed Weberian index and control of corruption. However, the merit indicator is positively and statistically significantly related to control of corruption.

Now we have established a stable correlation between our preferred indicator and control of corruption. Also under a control for several demanding determinants from the literature, we make some additional efforts to try to analyze whether the mechanism we suggest is reflected in the data curve. As a first step, our indicator of meritocracy is included in model 2 together with the separate components of the closed Weberian index used in model 1. The career tenure indicator

Table 4.3 *Components and mechanism (OLS estimates)*

	(1)	(2)	(3)	(4)
Meritocratic recruitment	0.22***	0.21***	0.26***	-0.20
	(0.055)	(0.057)	(0.062)	(0.19)
GDP/cap (log)	0.25***	0.23***	0.22***	0.24***
	(0.068)	(0.067)	(0.065)	(0.068)
Freedom of the press	-0.015***	-0.016***	-0.016***	
	(0.0029)	(0.0030)	(0.0029)	
Protestantism	0.0057**	0.0062**	0.0046	0.0054*
	(0.0028)	(0.0028)	(0.0029)	(0.0031)
Years of democracy	0.0073***	0.0069**	0.0066**	0.0052*
	(0.0026)	(0.0027)	(0.0027)	(0.0029)
Newspaper per 1000	0.00031	0.00030	0.00034	0.00018
	(0.00054)	(0.00055)	(0.00055)	(0.00058)
Trade volume	0.0023*	0.0019	0.0018	0.0026*
	(0.0014)	(0.0014)	(0.0014)	(0.0014)
Competitive salaries	-0.077			
	(0.051)			
Weberian index	0.0073			
	(0.058)			
Long career		0.036		
		(0.044)		
Special law		-0.013		
		(0.069)		
Formal examination			-0.038	-0.024
			(0.038)	(0.041)
Level of democracy				-0.18**
				(0.091)
Merit re. * Level of dem.				0.067***
				(0.023)
Constant	-2.69***	-2.66***	-2.52***	-2.34***
	(0.63)	(0.66)	(0.62)	(0.88)
Number of countries	94	94	94	94
R^2	0.87	0.86	0.86	0.85
Adjusted R^2	0.85	0.85	0.85	0.84

Comment: Entries are OLS regression coefficients (standard errors in parentheses). The dependent variable is the World Bank Control of Corruption indicator from 2011. All variables are available in the QoG standard dataset (Teorell et al. 2013) or the QoG Expert Survey (Teorell, Dahlström, and Dahlberg 2011).
* $p < 0.10$, ** $p < 0.05$, *** $p < 0.01$

now shows the expected positive sign, while the special employment laws are still negatively correlated to control of corruption. No component of closed Weberianism is statistically significant in this specification, however. Thus, neither the guarantee of lifelong careers nor special regulations that differ from the country's general labor laws seems to matter in terms of deterring corruption when controlling for meritocratic recruitment.

Next, we try to exclude the possibility that it is not the type of loyalty and monitoring that we suggest here, but instead isolation of the bureaucracy, which leads to low corruption. Therefore, in model 3, we take two different indicators of merit in the public sector into account. One of them is our preferred indicator of meritocratic recruitment and the other is closer to the ideas presented by Evans and Rauch (1999) and measures the use of a formal examination system for recruitment in the public sector. In the analysis, the former indicator clearly gets the upper hand. In other words, it is inconsequential whether civil servants need to pass a formal exam to join the civil service or undergo the standard recruitment procedure in the private sector through CV screening and job interviews. Comparing European countries, it is fairly easy to see that this make sense, where, for example, the Scandinavian countries have used a more private sector-like screening process, while continental countries, such as Italy and Spain, have instead tried to protect the civil service with formal exams. Our analysis indicated that whether civil servants are employed on the basis of their skills, not depending on their political connections, is what really matters and that it seems to be possible to achieve this in countries such as Denmark, without formal examinations, while it seems possible to circumvent the formal examinations of Spain, for example.

However, Sundell (2014) makes an interesting analysis that takes us one step back in the causal chain by asking what leads to meritocracy in recruitment. His results show that constraints to the recruitment process, such as formal tests, are much more strongly associated with meritocracy in countries that face a high risk of patronage compared to countries with a low risk. Formal examination systems might therefore be called for at earlier stages of development, for example (see Dahlström, Lapuente, and Teorell 2012b for similar reasoning).

Taken together, the analyses presented in the first three models of Table 4.3 support our suggested mechanism – the separation of interest, through merit recruitment – while it is not compatible with the two other main hypotheses in the bureaucratic structure literature, namely closed Weberian institutions and higher salaries. So far, we thus think that the incentives mechanism suggested here received the strongest support of the three hypotheses, but that is still a conclusion with several reservations related to the cross-sectional data and aggregate level of analysis.

However, if our theoretical mechanism, which relies on bureaucrats and politicians acting as watchdogs for each other, is correct, the effect should be stronger when accountability is more straightforward, and we should be able to find indications of this in the empirical material. As we have described elsewhere, it is reasonable to assume that accountability is more direct in democracies in which leaks and news about malfeasances can more easily reach the general public than in less democratic or autocratic regimes (Dahlström and Lapuente 2015). In model 4, we therefore analyze the interaction between meritocratic recruitment and the level of democracy and expect the marginal effect of meritocratic recruitment to be higher in more democratic countries. This interaction term is included in the fourth column in Table 4.3 together with the constitutional terms, and it shows a statistically significant slope of the interaction term, in line with our expectations. Although one of the constitutional terms (the level of democracy) is also statistically significant, this is less interesting as it reports the coefficient when meritocratic recruitment is zero, which is not represented in our sample. The solid line in Figure 4.2 indicates how the marginal effect of meritocratic recruitment changes with the level of democracy, and the plotted lines show the 95 percent confidence interval. When both plotted lines are above (or below) the zero line, the effect is statistically significant. This occurs when the level of democracy is higher than 5.4 on the 11-point scale from 0 to 10, and 68 percent of the countries in our sample are above this value (see the histogram included in the graph, and the percentage of cases reported on the secondary X-axis). Even though this is not conclusive evidence in favor of our mechanism of mutual control between politicians and bureaucrats, it points in the suggested direction.

However, the analyses presented here are all cross-sectional, and, even though they come from different sources, we should not forget that both the independent and the dependent variables are perception-based measures. Because of the cross-sectional structure of the analysis, there is a risk that the results presented above suffer from endogeneity bias. As far as possible, given that we have only cross-sectional data available, we

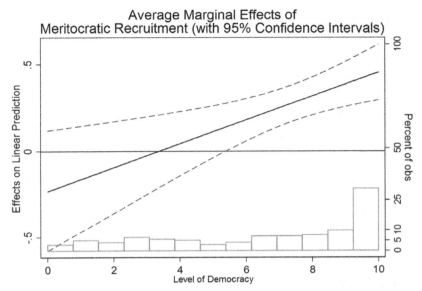

Figure 4.2 Interacting meritocratic recruitment and level of democracy

Comment: The Y-axis shows the effect of meritocratic recruitment on control of corruption and the X-axis shows different levels of democracy. The solid line reports the marginal effect and the plotted lines the 95 percent confidence interval. The histogram at the bottom of the graph shows the percentage of observations at each level of democracy, and the secondary X-axis reports the percentage scale. The variables reported in Table 4.3, model 4, are included. All variables are available in the QoG standard dataset (Teorell et al. 2013) or the QoG Expert Survey (Teorell, Dahlström, and Dahlberg 2011).

would like to minimize the risk that experts either simply perceive the bureaucracy as more meritocratic in less corrupt countries or that the causality runs in the direction opposite to the one suggested here.

We use two different strategies to get rid of potential endogeneity bias in the estimates as far as possible. First, the lagged dependent variable is included, which implies that we draw on temporal variability in the corruption perceptions. This does not solve the problem but should at least make it smaller. In column 1 of Table 4.4, we control for the earliest available measure of control of corruption, which is from 1996. As might be expected, this decreases coefficients, but the merit indicator continues to be statistically significant even when this control is included.

Corruption

Table 4.4 *Correcting for endogeneity (OLS and 2SLS estimates)*

	(1)	(2)
Meritocratic recruitment	0.11**	0.45*
	(0.045)	(0.22)
GDP/cap (log)	0.18***	-0.50
	(0.052)	(0.43)
Freedom of the press	-0.008***	-0.033**
	(0.002)	(0.013)
Protestantism	0.005**	0.0003
	(0.002)	(0.004)
Years of democracy	-0.001	0.010*
	(0.002)	(0.005)
Newspaper	0.0001	0.0002
	(0.0004)	(0.0007)
Trade volume	0.0005	-0.001
	(0.001)	(0.002)
Control of corruption (1996)	0.505***	
	(0.073)	
Constant	-1.75***	4.21
	(0.507)	(4.45)
Number of countries	94	28
R^2	0.911	0.872
adj. R^2	0.903	0.827

Comment: Entries in model 1 are OLS regression coefficients, while in model 2 they are two-stage OLS estimates (standard errors in parentheses). Model 2 uses a measure of the bureaucracy in the eighteenth century according to Ertman (1997) and coded by Charron, Dahlström, and Lapuente (2012). The dependent variable is the World Bank control of corruption indicator from 2011.
* $p < 0.10$, ** $p < 0.05$, *** $p < 0.01$

Second, we try another strategy: to instrument for the meritocratic recruitment indicator by using an exogenous regressor. More specifically, we employ a measure of whether the state administration in a country was bureaucratic or patrimonial in the eighteenth century, according to Ertman (1997), as an instrumental variable. The measure is used in Dahlström, Lapuente, and Teorell (2012a). It is originally taken from Charron, Dahlström, and Lapuente (2012), who create a dummy variable for countries based on Ertman's (1997) division of modern European countries into two major categories. On the one hand are polities such as the German states, Sweden, or Britain, in which an autonomous, merit-based bureaucracy was the result of the war-driven process of state building in the modern era. On the other hand are the countries in which the state building process led to the consolidation of a patrimonial administration; examples are France, Spain, and Portugal. If our theory is correct, this historical experience should primarily affect corruption today through the use of a non-politicized bureaucracy. On the downside, however, it only covers thirty-one OECD countries and therefore substantially limits our sample. Moreover, the F-statistics, obtained from the first stage of the 2SLS, is below 10 (not reported here), which might indicate that the instrument is too weak (Stock, Wright, and Yogo 2002). However, when calculating Anderson-Rubin confidence intervals, which are robust to instrument weakness, the coefficients retain significance. The second column reports the results with the bureaucracy in the eighteenth century as an instrument for merit in the bureaucracy today. As reported, both the merit indicators continue to be statistically significant, and the coefficient actually increases quite dramatically to .45.

All in all, the empirical analyses presented in this section show a statistically significant association between meritocratic recruitment and control of corruption. This result is robust to the inclusion of several demanding controls and to different model specifications. We can also change the dependent variable and use other indicators of corruption without any great changes. In this section, we have moreover tried to pin down the monitoring career incentive mechanism and compare it to alternative mechanisms. Finally, we addressed a potential endogeneity problem. Although we think all these analyses speak in favor of our interpretation, we will now proceed to a discussion of a few countries that have succeeded fairly well in fighting corrupt behavior in order to further explore the empirical support for our suggestion.

Historical Experiences of Fighting Corruption in the United States and North Western Europe

As a final analytic step in this chapter, we address potential endogeneity bias by adding empirical illustrations of the reduction of systemic corruption in some established Western democracies. We present historical narratives showing that, chronologically, meritocratic recruitment did not occur after administrative corruption was curbed, nor as a consequence thereof. Quite the opposite, merit reforms were enacted before systemic corruption was tamed. In many countries, merit recruitment processes were adopted at historical peaks of corruption, precisely because reformers saw this as a mechanism to fight corruption. These cases will thus also provide narratives where one can see the theoretical mechanisms of this book at work: merit adoption was devised as a way of breaking the integration of interests between politicians and (their often politically appointed) bureaucrats. Using Knott's (2011) interpretation of the Madisonian concept of factions, the idea reformers had in mind at the turn of the twentieth century was to eliminate the influence of political factions in public administration.

However, before we discuss the cases, we would like to emphasize that corruption and absence of merit (i.e., patronage) are not the same phenomenon. The literature conceptually distinguishes between patronage and corruption; as Golden puts it, the two concepts "should be analyzed as different games" (2000, 3). The relationship between them is most probably causal, and the World Bank identified as early as 1997 (World Bank 1997) a non-patronaged bureaucracy as one of the four factors correlated to low corruption. Some within-country studies have been able to pin down the circumstances under which patronage increases corruption levels in a country, such as that incumbents do not fear exposure by a credible political rival in the case of engaging in corrupt exchanges (Golden 2000, 3). So far, the first important message in this literature is that research should separate both phenomena: merit (vs. patronage) and corruption. We now proceed to offer some historical examples of the timing of the adoption of merit vis-à-vis the fight against corruption.

Nordic Countries

We will start with brief accounts from some of the earliest reformers of patronage administrations, namely the Nordic countries. These countries currently show the lowest levels of corruption in the world (Uslaner 2008). In particular, we focus on Denmark and Sweden, for which quite substantial empirical evidence has been gathered on both the adoption of merit in their administrations and corruption. Overall, their historical experience is consistent with our argument, since meritocratic recruitment reforms preceded their historical break with corruption and governmental inefficiencies. Before we look more closely at this process, however, we should remind ourselves that, up to the mid-nineteenth century, elites in countries such as Denmark were able to extract private rents, from straight embezzlement to the pervasive predominance of personal contacts over impersonal laws (Frisk-Jensen 2008). Using North, Wallis, and Weingast's (2009) ter-minology, the Nordic countries could thus be defined as particularistic limited access societies and, using Acemoglu and Robinson's (2012) concept, an extractive elite able to rent-seek from social welfare.

Scholars note for example that "...corruption was an ingrained part of public administration in Denmark at the time of the constitutional revolution" (Frisk-Jensen and Mungiu-Pippidi 2011, 65). The level of corruption in the years prior to and immediately after the 1849 liberal constitution was not necessarily higher than that of more advanced European states. Still, especially during the 1810–1830 period, it was high enough to be regarded an "epidemic of speculation" (Frisk-Jensen 2008, 192). In the subsequent thirty years, there was a decrease in the corruption recorded and, around 1860, corruption became marginal.

As in other Nordic countries, the sequence of events in Denmark indicates that merit reforms took place before corruption was curbed. Meritocracy was a cause – and not the result – of a less corrupt state. Historians explicitly mention that an early adoption of merit in Den-mark, especially after the country's traumatic military defeat in the Napoleonic wars, is one of the "chief assets of the Danish path to good governance" (Frisk-Jensen and Mungiu-Pippidi 2011, 70).

The process of adoption of merit recruitment in the Danish public administration had already started in 1736, when the University of Copenhagen launched a law exam; in subsequent decades, it sent its graduates to the nascent Danish civil service (Frisk-Jensen and Mungiu-Pippidi 2011, 70). Consequently, by the beginning of the nineteenth century, Denmark enjoyed *de facto* merit recruitment to its public administration, where only around 10 percent of its civil servants were nobles (Feldbaek 2000; Knudsen 2006). The culmination of the process of merit adoption would be 1821, when a law degree from a university was made mandatory for all would-be civil servants. In other words, Denmark achieved a merit-based bureaucracy in a process that started many years before and that ended in the middle of its worst peak of corruption, from 1810 to 1830, several decades before corruption was effectively curbed in the country (1860). We thus feel relatively confident in claiming that the adoption of merit was not the result, but, quite the opposite, a cause of Denmark's ability to become... Denmark.

As concerns Sweden, Teorell and Rothstein (2015) summarize the main impediments in the Swedish bureaucracy in the late eighteenth century and identify four types of problems: first, recruitments to the bureaucracy were to a large extent not meritocratic; second, a system of purchase and sale of office – the so-called "accord" system – was widespread; third, officials usually did not have regulated salaries on which they could sustain themselves, but got most of their income through an informal payment system - so-called *spotler*; and fourth, malfeasance, bribery, and other types of misconduct were either vaguely regulated or completely unregulated for large parts of the bureaucracy.

Although lack of cross-country data makes it almost impossible to evaluate the extent of Swedish problems compared to other countries at the time, such as France and the United Kingdom, it is clear that the Swedish bureaucracy did not meet Weberian standards when entering the nineteenth century (Bågenholm 2015). What is also undisputed is that meritocracy in recruitments increased (Sundell 2015), while purchase and sale of office, informal payments (Sundell 2014), and malfeasance (Teorell and Rothstein 2015) declined dramatically during the nineteenth century.

Partly because there is no single reform package in Sweden, such as the Pendleton Act in the United States, or the Northcote-Trevelyan Report in the United Kingdom, it is hard to be sure of both what triggered and what reinforced these changes. Rothstein (1998, 2011) links the turnaround of the patronage system to a reform period that he places between 1860 and 1875. In his view, during these years, the Swedish administration acquired most of the elements associated with a modern bureaucracy. For instance, in 1863, higher standards for degrees were established in the new rules for university education. Discriminatory regulations were also eliminated and, for example, from 1870 onward, Jews could become civil servants – as well as representatives in the Swedish Parliament. As Rothstein (2011, 114) states, despite there still being episodic cases of corruption in the aftermath of the meritocratic reforms, "they were no longer seen as 'standard operating procedure'" as they had been until the 1860–1875 meritocratic reforms.

Recent research pushes back the meritocratic reforms, noting that important improvements of the Swedish bureaucracy had already begun in the first half of the nineteenth century (Rothstein and Teorell 2015; Teorell and Rothstein 2015). Using sophisticated measures including an analysis of the surnames of all Swedish bureaucrats working for central agencies for over 200 years, Sundell (2014; 2015) explores the decline of informal payments and nepotism in the Swedish bureaucracy. His conclusion is that that these processes were incremental and difficult to link to a single reform period.

For the purpose of this book, though, what is most important is that a separation of politics and bureaucracy was introduced in Sweden before other inefficiencies were fought, and not as a consequence thereof. In Sweden, this seems to have been the case, since two cornerstone features for separating the careers of politicians and bureaucrats had already been established in the late eighteenth century, that is, before corrupt practices were curbed. First, by that time Sweden had acquired the often referred to characteristic "dualism" of the Swedish governance – that is, far-reaching independence of the agencies from the central ministries – which took shape at the beginning of the eighteenth century (Andersson 2004). Second, the principle of seniority in promotions for bureaucrats, which prevented ad hoc political interference in bureaucratic careers, was already in place at the end of the eighteenth century (Nilsson 2000).

United Kingdom

The introduction of merit in a series of reforms in Britain starting with the 1854 Northcote-Trevelyan Report should also be seen as a way of creating a less corrupt administration. There was increasing awareness in British society that at-will patronage appointments to civil service positions were one of the causes – or even the main cause – of corruption. Merit adoption was therefore seen as a solution to that underlying problem, which was particularly acute during the period between 1780 and 1860, traditionally known as the *Old Corruption* (Rubinstein 1983).

Again, despite being the world's most powerful empire, Britain was dominated in the early nineteenth century by a political elite that had some resemblances to what Acemoglu and Robinson (2012) would define as an extractive elite. Britain was a "classic case of state 'corruption'" (O'Gorman 2001, 54). Rubinstein (1983) provided some interesting examples. For instance, public officials formed a relatively high fraction of those who amassed large fortunes in the first decades of the nineteenth century. In particular, 10 percent of the half-millionaires and 23 percent of those who accumulated between £150,000 and a half million owed their riches to being engaged in public activities. The range of private abuses of public office in the patronage-based British administration went from the highest echelons of government – such as the Tory Lord Eldon, Lord Chancellor for twenty-seven years, and, who, despite his modest origins, amassed a fortune of £707,000 – to the lower ones – such as the Honorary Patrick Plunkett, who had an annual stipendium of £500 as "purse-bearer" to the Chancellor of Ireland, who, by the way, was his brother (Rubinstein 1983).

Rubinstein (1983) underlined the connection between these indications of systemic corruption and the prevailing type of access to public office in Britain at the time, which was based on nepotism and political patronage, with the Tory party being particularly rewarded. Several scholars have noted the encompassing nature of patronage in Britain, given that it started at the Crown cabinet level and penetrated all civil and military positions, all administrative levels up to local government, and up to the Church and even some professions such as law (Harling 1996; O'Gorman 2001). This association between the type of access to public service and corruption was also well known by contemporaries. Rubinstein (1983, 59) summarizes "one has only to open a radical journal or newspaper dating from the period between 1810 to 1835 to find, with almost unvarying regularity, an exposé of the extent of patronage and perquisite and an attack upon their existence."

As a result, British reformers reached the conclusion that a meritocratic administration could help to curb these excesses caused by a patronage-ridden administration where political (and personal) connections trumped merit. The reformers, following the philosophy of Jeremy Bentham, started to win some battles. For instance, they were able to convince the Poor Law Commissioners to appoint their officials only according to merit criteria (O'Gorman 2001, 63–4). The 1854 Northcote-Trevelyan Report, which stated that appointments to the civil service should be made through a process of open and competitive examinations (and not by virtue or personal or political connections), is generally seen as the turning point in the consolidation of a merit-based bureaucracy in Britain. Authors agree that the spirit of the report was indeed to eradicate corruption (Chapman and Greenaway 1980; Greenaway 2004; Harling 1996). Charles Trevelyan, head of the Civil Service (1840–59), explicitly stated the report's anti-corruption goal: "diverting ... that stream of corruption what makes the H. of Commons - what ought to be our help & support in everything that relates to the good govt. of the country, or as I should rather say the effective administration of the affairs of the country - the greatest obstacle with what We have to contend." Similarly, William Gladstone considered the report to be an essential element of the fight for good government, or, in his own words, "my contribution to the picnic of Parliamentary reform" (both quoted in Greenaway 2004).

Scholars agree that it took several years, and in some departments such as the Foreign Office and the Colonial Office even decades, until the principles of open and competitive examinations were fully implemented (O'Gorman 2001, 64). As Dunleavy and Hood (1994, 9) observe, the merit principle remained in an 'incubated' mode; as a matter of fact, it was initially charged by many as an implausible 'Chinese scheme' at odds with the particularities of the British Empire. Yet, some years after, it became conventional wisdom among practitioners and academics that there was no other way to effectively tackle corruption and bad government than a merit-based civil service that tied the hands of politicians in their appointing, promoting, and firing employees.

United States

There is probably no country with more studies on the adoption of the merit system than the United States. The great variation in the timing and geographical scope of civil service reforms at the local and state levels has been subject to intense quantitative scrutiny in past decades (e.g. Frant 1993; Hollyer 2011; Johnson and Libecap 1994; Lapuente 2010; Ruhil 2003; Ruhil and Camões 2003; Tolbert and Zucker 1983). These studies point at very different factors that can explain why some cities, states, or agencies in the federal government adopted civil service systems at a given historical moment while others delayed the adoption for years or decades.

Not all of the factors that are explored in this literature are related to corruption. For instance, some authors find that the type of local government explains the existence and strength of civil service commissions in US cities (Frant 1993; Lapuente 2010). In others, the adoption of merit freed politicians from rising patronage demands, increasingly difficult to fulfill (Ruhil 2003), and from party machines increasingly difficult to control (Johnson and Libecap 1994). The adoption of merit in some American cities has also been associated with the expansion of secondary and tertiary education (Hollyer 2011). These authors explicitly note the shortcomings of explanations of merit as the "victory of good government forces" (Ruhil 2003, 159) because of "empirical difficulties" (Frant 1993, 992), given that, despite obvious success in many senses, "the civil service reform movement was remarkably short lived, peaking in 1884 and subsequently languishing" (Ruhil 2003, 159). This literature thus indicates, first, that the adoption of merit is conceptually and empirically distinguishable from corruption and that we should study them as different variables, as we do in this chapter, and second, that the replacement of patronage appointments, or *spoils*, with merit-recruited bureaucrats obeyed to multiple demographic, social, economic, political, and cultural causes.

It is important for us, however, that the goal of the progressive era reformers who pushed for the adoption of merit was still to curb corruption. Along the lines of the theory presented in this book, the reformers carefully thought of the causal connection between separating the interests of politicians and bureaucrats, on the one side, and minimizing corruption and misuse of public funds on the other. Still, this view of government met strong opposition from party machines and political appointees who owed so much to the spoils system. Let's, for instance, keep in mind the words of the early twentieth century Tammany Hall boss George W. Plunkett melancholically remembering the good old times in which "when a party won, its workers got everything in sight" (Schultz and Maranto 1998, 56). It took a combination of political factors, explored in the quantitative literature reviewed in previous sections in this chapter, triggered by a shocking incident – the death of President Garfield at the hands of a disappointed office seeker in 1881 – to put the meritocratic reforms in motion.

By the 1880s, a coalition of religious moralists, business people, and progressive reformers started advocating a separation of politics from administration (Knott 2011, 30). They aimed at a "moral purification of government" (Arnold 2003, 205; see also Teaford 1983). Numerous contemporary observers saw the very same theoretical mechanism that we discuss in this book. For instance, William Clarke emphasized in 1897 that "as official patronage, either direct or indirect, is a great if not perhaps the chief cause of corrupt elections, it logically follows that the less patronage there is, the less corruption there will be" (quoted in Frant 1993, 994). The link between an administration with patronage positions and a corrupt administration had also been claimed by the highly influential members of the Great Triumvirate – Henry Clay of Kentucky, Daniel Webster of Massachusetts, and John C. Calhoun of South Carolina – who criticized President Jackson's patronage appointments in the US Congress in the 1830s-40s on these grounds (van Riper 1958, 63; Schultz and Maranto 1998, 17).

The opportunities for different factions of patronage appointees, often called party machines, to take both personal and party advantage out of a partial, and sometimes corrupt, policy implementation were huge and well known at the time. For instance, the collector of the highly politicized New York City Customs, noted by several scholars as a prime example of patronage (Rosenbloom 1971, 63; Schultz and Maranto 1998, 36), embezzled $1.25 million (5 percent of the federal budget!) before sailing off to Europe (Nelson 1982, 25; Schultz and Maranto 1998, 41). Together with these high profile cases, there were numerous lower profile ones that also show links between the monopoly of bureaus by patronage appointments and corruption. For instance, it was not uncommon that Jacksonian postal officials delivered party journals free of charge while they lost publications considered to be anti-Jackson (Schultz and Maranto 1998).

The increasing social awareness of corruption problems was noted by early political entrepreneurs of the civil service reform movement, such as Congressman Thomas Jenckes who, right after the Civil War, launched a bill aimed at establishing a merit-based civil service (Schultz and Maranto 1998, 51). Jenckes got the support of many businessmen distressed by the corruption resulting from the spoils system (Hoogenboom 1961), especially in the customs system (Schultz and Maranto 1998, 52). Many representatives of liberal professions, intellectuals, and religious groups joined this pro-merit movement, emphasizing the corruption problems derived from political appointments. As a matter of fact, the association between at-will appointments in the administration and corruption was seen as being so strong in the years immediately after the Civil War that some authors have argued that the spoilsman "replaced the slave owner as the jinni of evil" (Schultz and Maranto 1998, 55; van Riper 1958, 81).

In addition, scholars note the eye-opening role played by three particularly notorious corruption scandals in the 1870s, in all of which public opinion could connect political appointments to misuse of public funds for private gain (Schultz and Maranto 1998, 61). These cases helped to explain the success of the National Civil Service Reform League, created in 1881, which would become one of the most structured advocates of merit adoption throughout different administrative levels during the following two decades.

In sum, the US historical experience shows that merit adoption was seen as a key factor for curbing the high levels of corruption during the nineteenth century that in many bureaus – precisely in those with a higher rate of politicized appointments like the New York Customhouse or the postal service in certain territories – seemed to have a systemic more than an episodic nature. Reformers who pushed for a stricter separation of politics and bureaucracy triumphed in some administrations, for example those that established neutral bipartisan Civil Service Commissions, yet not in all, given the obvious opposition of many entrenched interests from party machines. As shown above, this seems to be more the rule than the exception worldwide: a clear awareness among academics, intellectuals, business, and other reformers that at-will appointments in the public administration lead to corruption. And, in front of them, a strong opposition to change by political elites and the vested interests created by large legions of political appointees.

Conclusions

In the growing literature on corruption, scholars have tended to focus most on political, economic, and cultural explanations. This chapter has, in line with the theory presented in Chapter 2, suggested that the bureaucracy should also be taken into account and that special attention should be given to the relations between bureaucrats and politicians. While there are indications that both politics and bureaucracy substantially affect corruption, they have hardly been tested together at all. The literature emphasizing political factors has had a tendency to ignore the potential influence of the bureaucracy – focusing almost exclusively on the selection mechanisms (e.g., electoral system) and incentives (e.g., incentives of presidents vis-à-vis prime ministers). The bureaucracy literature in turn has not incorporated insight on political factors and instead focused its attention on how to address public employees' adverse selection and moral hazard problems.

This chapter has tried to bridge this gap, and we have empirically tested both types of factors. The empirical results indicate that, even when controlling for a very broad range of political and institutional factors, meritocratic recruitment to the public sector is a statistically significant deterrent of corruption. This result is stable in our different model specifications, and we interpret it as supportive of the theoretical suggestions made in this book, and thus as a product of politicians and bureaucrats having different incentives and therefore monitoring each other. We tried to pin down this mechanism in the empirical analysis as far as possible, and demonstrated, for instance, that the marginal effect of the merit indicator is strongest when accountability is most straightforward.

The chapter has also addressed what we consider to be a major problem for the empirical analyses on corruption, namely a potential endogeneity bias, by including a lagged dependent variable and using an instrumental variable technique. We have also complemented these quantitative results with narratives from the historical experiences of countries that had historically experienced moderate to high levels of corruption and nevertheless were able to curb it partly thanks to the adoption of bureaucratic mechanisms devised to separate the interests of politicians and bureaucrats.

5 | *Effectiveness*

Introduction

We have just seen that the separation of politicians' and bureaucrats' careers helps to control corruption, mainly because it creates incentives for both groups to protest if they see misbehavior without fearing that their future careers will suffer. Even though low corruption is of major importance for the prosperity of a country, it is not the only factor that is important for a well-functioning society. We will thus now move to another important implication of the theory presented in Chapter 2 and try to explain why some governments are more effective than others. In short, we suggest that the career incentives given to politicians and bureaucrats largely affect how effectively governments produce service for their citizens.

We are, of course, not the first to ask why some governments are more effective than others. Scholars from different social science disciplines have divided governments into groups according to whether they make an overall positive or negative contribution to the welfare of their societies. Important observations have been made about the structure of the society and whether the access to economic entry is "open," in contrast to "limited" (North, Wallis, and Weingast 2009, 2), and whether the elites are "inclusive" instead of "extractive" (Acemoglu and Robinson 2012, 79). As discussed earlier, these categories are appealing and have taught us a great deal about long-term development. But they are difficult to operationalize and are often measured as government outcomes, and not as institutional features, which poses some problems. For example, outcomes change over time, and the categories are sometimes almost tautological; an open or inclusive government becomes, in empirical terms, almost synonymous with a productive government.

In attempts to escape these problems, scholars have tried to identify institutional features that precede and are clearly distinct from outcomes, and at the same time are measurable across countries. Laws and regulations fulfill these criteria and have therefore gained the attention of researchers interested in effective governments. As a result, we have seen an "explosion of research on the consequences of legal rules and regulations" (La Porta, Lopez-de-Silanes and Shleifer 2008, 300) during recent years.

We consider this so-called Legal Origins Theory to be the main competitor to our suggestion, for two reasons. First, it reflects the longlasting distinction in the public administration literature between the Anglo-American or 'public service' tradition – that coincides with the Common Law countries in the Legal Origins Theory – and the *Rechtsstaat* tradition of continental Europe and Scandinavia (Pollit and Bouckaert 2011). The legacy of these historical traditions has been argued to affect administrative reforms to this day (Pierre 2011; Yesilkagit 2010). Second, the legal traditions have the advantage in relation to alternative factors, such as democratization and education levels, that they can be seen as "largely exogenous" (La Porta, Lopez-deSilanes, and Shleifer 2008, 285), since they "were typically introduced into various countries through conquest and colonization" (La Porta, Lopez-deSilanes, and Shleifer 2008, 285).

We therefore review the Legal Origins Theory literature and, in line with the theory presented in Chapter 2, argue that the integration/separation of politicians' and bureaucrats' careers affects government effectiveness, even when the Legal Origins Theory is taken into consideration. In addition, like laws and regulations, career incentives are distinct from outcomes, while being measurable and transferable across countries.

We think there are at least two mechanisms by which incentives in different career systems affect government effectiveness. First, a process very similar to the one described in Chapter 4 is at play. We do not need to go to the extreme case of corruption to find a two-way monitoring between politicians and bureaucrats useful. There is probably much wasteful spending in all polities, within the frames of the law, and if no one dares to speak truth to power, this will be higher than it needs to be. Second, a professional management has been shown to positively affect production in both the private and public sectors (Chong et al. 2014; Gennaioli et al. 2013). In a politicized system, for example, public managers will probably not have service production as their only goal but will to at least some degree be

affected by political considerations, which should hamper management. This will also influence incentives for rank and file public
employees. If they think their future careers depend on political
considerations, rather than on how good they are at their jobs, the
production of public goods will suffer.

The following three sections will first describe the alternative explanation, the Legal Origins Theory, and discuss both the similarities and
differences to our theory. After that we turn to the mechanisms just
mentioned, elaborate them, and give some examples. However, the
main purpose of the chapter is to provide a systematic empirical test
of our suggestion, and we describe the strategy for this test in the
following section. We then move on to report the results of a series
of cross-country comparisons. The results show that wasteful government spending is lower and management performance is higher in the
public sector in countries with separated careers for politicians and
bureaucrats.

Two Styles of Societal Control

The literature on economic effects of laws and regulations notes that a
"heavier hand of government" tends to be correlated – sometimes as a
cause, sometimes as a consequence, many times as both – with poor
economic outcomes (La Porta, Lopez-de-Silanes and Shleifer 2008,
300; see also Aghion et al. 2010; Blanchard and Giavazzi 2003;
Djankov et al. 2002; Pinotti 2012; Shleifer 2010). Generally speaking,
many authors have relied on the classic public choice argument that
government regulations mostly benefit insiders at the expense of outsiders (Peltzman 1976; Stigler 1971; Tullock 1967). In particular, entry
regulations have been found to distort industry structure (Fisman and
Sarria-Allende 2004), delay the entry of crucial firms (Ciccone and
Papaionnou 2006c), act as a barrier to entrepreneurs (Klapper, Laeven,
and Rajan 2006), and reduce international trade (Helpman, Melitz,
and Rubinstein 2008). Similarly, excessive labor regulations misallo-
cate labor (Lafontaine and Sivadasan 2007) and reduce necessary
labor turnover (Micco and Pagés 2006).

Moreover, not only excessive regulations have perverse effects.
Several authors have noted that the regulatory levels in different sectors
tend to correlate with each other. From a theoretical point of view,
Blanchard and Giavazzi (2003) show how strict labor market regulations

go hand in hand with strict product market regulations. One way or another, insiders in the product market (i.e., incumbent firms) establish a strategic alliance with insiders in the labor market (i.e., unionized workers with permanent job contracts) at the cost of outsiders in both markets (i.e., start-ups, unemployed or workers with temporary job contracts).

Hopkin and Blyth (2012) detect an interesting empirical pattern across the OECD. Countries with stringent labor regulation also tend to overregulate product and financial markets. On one extreme are Greece and Italy, which tend to overregulate economic activities; on the other extreme are well-known liberal market economies, such as the Anglo-Saxon countries, but also, more surprisingly, countries with strong welfare states, such as Denmark. Excessive regulations have deleterious effects on economic innovation, controlling for standard factors (Hopkin, Lapuente, and Möller 2013). The explanation suggested is that governments that regulate a great deal may not interfere in market exchanges in order to level the playing field, as it is usually portrayed, but, as a matter of fact, to protect those who need protection the least, the country's strongest economic agents. Incumbent firms and incumbent employees seem to benefit from high levels of regulation more than outsider firms and employees.

All in all, several studies point out that there are countries with, relatively speaking, much regulation of economic life that benefits particularistic interests at the expense of general welfare, and countries with, relatively speaking, less government regulation that promotes general welfare. According to an argument by Hayek (1960), influential among political economists, this distinction between countries follows "profound differences in philosophies of freedom" (La Porta, Lopez-de-Silanes, and Shleifer 2008, 303). In some countries, the government unilaterally imposes the "solely valid pattern" while in others the government allows "spontaneity and absence of coercion" (Hayek 1960, 56). A central question in this research is: Why do some countries end up on the positive side of this philosophical divide and others on the negative side?

In a series of influential articles, Rafael La Porta, Florencio Lopez-de-Silanes, Andrei Shleifer, and Robert Vishny (1997, 1998, 1999) present evidence supporting the view that a country's type of legal tradition affects a large number of desirable institutions, such as judicial independence and high quality laws, which then in turn positively affect social outcomes such as a low degree of corruption and high rates of economic growth. In a paper from 2008, La Porta, Lopez-de-Silanes, and Shleifer transformed their previous evidence, together with the work of many other scholars noting the empirical association between the legal tradition historically adopted by one country and its current economic performance, into what they call the Legal Origins Theory. The Legal Origins Theory considers that there is a "sharp distinction" (Levine 2005, 65) between "two most distinct approaches to law and regulation" (La Porta, Lopez-de-Silanes, and Shleifer 2008, 290): on the one hand, the common law tradition, emanating historically from English law and currently covering Britain and all its former colonies, and on the other the civil law tradition, heir of Roman law that was crucially shaped by Napoleon, who exported it to most continental European countries, and their colonies worldwide, through direct conquest or indirect influence.

Following Hayek's (1960) claim about the inherent advantage of English legal institutions over their French counterparts, the Legal Origins Theory argues that the common law and civil law countries have distinct "styles of social control of the economic life" (La Porta, Lopez-de-Silanes and Shleifer 2008, 286). Common law is associated with a lighter hand of government and civil law with a heavier hand and, consequently, "common law is associated with better economic outcomes than French civil law" (La Porta, Lopez-deSilanes, and Shleifer 2008, 302). Indeed, the level of formalism in both the judicial sector and the administration has been found to be significantly higher in civil law countries than in common law ones (Djankov et al. 2003). Because of lower levels of regulation and, in turn, more credible protection of property and private contracts, common law "sets the stage for investment and growth" (Mahoney 2001, 27). The result is that, using a large number of outcome variables and controlling for numerous alternative factors, common law countries seem to systematically achieve higher levels of economic and social development (La Porta, Lopez-de-Silanes, and Shleifer 2008).

An explanation like the Legal Origins Theory based on the type of legal system a country adopted decades or even centuries ago presents numerous advantages from an empirical point of view. It has high analytic power, for example, and is easy to test and falsify. Consequently, a notable body of empirical evidence that shows a significant correlation between the legal origin of a country and a wide array of contemporary outcomes has emerged during recent years. In addition, if we assume that legal origins, as La Porta, Lopez-de-Silanes, and Shleifer (2008) claim, were mostly imposed upon rulers via conquest and colonization and were not voluntarily adopted, then they should be considered as largely exogenous. The Legal Origins Theory would thus avoid the almost inescapable endogeneity trap of institutional explanations.

The Close Relationship between Laws and Bureaucracies

Nevertheless, as we have argued elsewhere, the exogenous character of legal origins is not so evident (Charron, Dahlström, and Lapuente 2012). Levine (2005, 63) observes that the Napoleonic Code had a political goal, more than a judicial one, namely to "strengthen the state." And according to another author, Napoleon "wished to use the state power to alter property rights and attempted to insure that judges did not interfere" (Mahoney 2001, 505). Judges, as famously stated by Napoleon, should be transformed from independent professionals into "automata" who would implement rulers' codified sense of justice (La Porta, Lopez-de-Silanes, and Shleifer 2008, 303). High prestige judges should be turned into "largely administrative, low-prestige occupations" (La Porta, Lopez-deSilanes, and Shleifer 2008, 304). The creation of the civil law tradition should thus be seen as part of a larger interventionist enterprise, which also included the creation of a vast and invasive bureaucracy (Woloch 1994).

Russian, Spanish, Portuguese, Turkish, Latin American, and other rulers who opted for the French versions of civil law after Napoleon probably shared that interventionist goal. In fact, this is a common purpose of all kinds of rulers, regardless of the country or the culture they live in, as the numerous failed attempts to impose absolutist regimes in modern England show. The key difference, following the insight of Greif (2008, with González de Lara and Jha 2008) and mentioned in Chapter 2, is that the English kings simply could not implement their interventionist plans because they lacked a body of directly accountable administrators with strong incentives to implement their rulers' wishes.

In other words, we argue that the distinction between legal traditions to some degree captures mechanisms similar to the one presented in this book: the ability rulers have to control the state apparatus. It reveals that, according to the Legal Origins Theory scholars, "the Magna Carta established the foundations of the English legal order" given that it legally constrained monarchs in undertaking violations of civil rights and private property (La Porta, Lopez-de-Silanes, and Shleifer 2008, 306). Yet, as Greif (2008, 29–30) observes, the Magna Carta did not stop King John from abusing his powers and, ultimately, invalidating the Magna Carta itself. If King John's descendants on the English throne could not repeat his opportunistic behavior, it was not because of a legal restriction but because they had to bargain with relatively independent administrators in order to implement their policies. England, unlike France, was not a monocratic state apparatus with servants directly accountable to the executive.

The posterior progressive development of law systems reinforced these trends. To start with, judges remained largely autonomous professionals in England while in France they were supposed to mechanically implement rulers' wishes written in laws and regulations. In this sense, this book complements the Legal Origins Theory argument by stating that not only judges, but the vast majority of civil servants, were directly dependent on the ruler in Napoleonic countries while civil servants in common law countries would retain a more professional autonomy. Similarly, what may explain the surprisingly good performance of some civil law countries, particularly the Scandinavian countries, which literally represent a "problem" for Legal Origins Theory scholars, is that judges and public employees are generally, like their British counterparts, autonomous professionals (Mahoney 2001, 17).

Automata versus Autonomous

Our proposition is thus that where public employees are directly dependent on their political masters' wishes for their own careers, there will be poorer government effectiveness than in countries where public employees' professional careers do not directly depend on their political masters. In our opinion, this is a key difference among polities. The existence of a unified chain of accountability in public institutions that runs from the top executive throughout the administrative machine leads to a lower provision of welfare than a context where two chains of accountability separate the careers of political and bureaucratic officials. This separation of careers induces, from our point of view, welfare-enhancing policies more than legal constraints on the executive.

In particular, we think there are at least two mechanisms through which separation of careers leads to superior outcomes.

First, separated careers allow bureaucrats to speak truth to power and thereby act as counterweights to policies that are not illegal but may be inefficient or even wasteful (Heclo 1977). Take the "white elephants that dragged Spain in the red" we described in the introduction in Chapter 1 as an example of what can happen when politicians hear no voice of reason. The expensive Santiago de Compostela's City of Culture was a project promoted by the charismatic regional president, Mr. Manuel Fraga, and, despite that experts considered it an ill-devised project, the many political appointees ended up approving it, according to one whistle-blower, because of "fear of" Mr. Fraga (*El País* 08-01-2011). And this fear was probably rational, as the politician, this time Mr. Fraga, held the fortune of the appointees' future careers in his hand. With another system in which careers are not as closely tied together, it is reasonable to assume that there would have been greater opportunities for advice against the project.

When planning the International Airport of the Murcia Region in Spain, public employees also seemed more interested in pleasing their political masters than in properly assessing the technical viability of the project. The regional government of Murcia was not satisfied with a large airport – Alicante – located only 75 kilometers away, or with a minor reform of the half military-half civilian airport of San Javier – as close as 35 kilometers to Murcia, and promoted the construction of a completely new airport costing €200 million (*El País* 13-02-2013). As Xavier Fageda notes, although it was obvious that an airport in that location would hardly attract airlines, the project was accompanied by a strangely optimistic study contemplating the viability of the airport under three different scenarios (*Salvados* 2013a; *El Periodico* 08–12-2013). The worst scenario predicted 500,000 passengers/year; the neutral, 1 million passengers; and, under the best scenario, the authorities expected around 1.5 million passengers/year. Now, with 0 passengers a few years afterwards, it seems clear that, although the construction of the airport followed all legal requirements, individuals involved in the process shared the same optimistic bias as the initial political promoters. No one wanted to disappoint them.

And there are numerous similar examples of this bias. Journalist Alvaro Romero describes one of Spain's "ghost highways" where studies predicted daily traffic of 35,000–40,000 vehicles, but where in fact hardly 4,500 vehicles use the highway (*Financial Times* 15-05-2013; *Salvados* 2013b). Bel (2010) documents several infrastructure decisions in Spain that, after lengthy and highly regulated processes, were still based on too optimistic forecasts. Take the enlargement of the airport of León that allowed it to manage up to ten times its current number of passengers, which seems unrealistic under normal circumstances, but even more so when, at the same time, a high speed train connecting Leon and Madrid would start operation. Or take the high speed train between Madrid and Valencia that, according to a study provided by the Ministry of Infrastructure based on fantasist calculations, would generate no less than 136,000 jobs between 2010 and 2016. Similar studies have backed the expansion of a high speed railway network in Spain where over €40,000 million was invested to serve a mere 1 percent of all transportation in the country (Fageda 2013).

Why did highly qualified civil servants – recruited through formalized exams – write or authorize all these studies that gave unrealistic forecasts on the future use of infrastructure projects? It definitely seems that loyalty to their political masters, who controlled their careers and were obsessed with projects to satisfy key territorial constituencies, has played an important role (*El País* 13-02-2013; Fageda 2013).

A second mechanism through which the existence of integration (separation) of politicians' and bureaucrats' careers hampers (fosters) government effectiveness has to do with public management. Recent economic scholarship has shown that management is indeed an important factor for production in the private sector, and Chong, La Porta, Lopez-de-Silanes, and Shleifer (2013) extend this argument to the public sector. Very similarly to this book, they suggest that professional management increases government productivity. Without a credible management function, the risk of not using material and human resources effectively rises. Developing the argument from Chong et al. (2013), we think that the existence of a single hierarchy headed by political masters may break what organizational scholars refer to as "psychological contracts" or "relational contracts" (Argyris, 1960; Foss, Foss, and Vázquez 2006; Levi 2005; Tepper and Taylor 2003; Williamson 1975). These contracts are built upon trust between superiors and subordinates developed over years and are essential for organizational efficiency (Baker, Gibbons, and Murphy 2002, 39). With an integrated career system, the suspicion that the future relationships between, for instance, a public manager and a public employee can be arbitrarily interrupted by some political consideration may critically alter the relational contracts between them, notably affecting management.

Let's take the example of Spain's Tax Agency to show how this can look. It is important to bear in mind that the Spanish Tax Agency had long been regarded as a highly effective public organization and as a champion of managerial reforms (Parrado 2008). Yet during 2012 and 2013 – under the Conservative government appointed after the November 2011 general elections in Spain – the Tax Agency witnessed around 300 dismissals in the middle and top managerial layers (Saura 2013). In the Conservative minister's own words, the underlying reason for these removals from managerial positions was they were "full of socialists" (*El País* 06–12-2013).

The president of the association of Tax Inspectors, Ramsés Pérez Boga (2013), describes the effect that these changes have had on the morale of the civil servants working at the Tax Agency. He uses the metaphor of Goya's famous painting *Fight with Cudgels*, where two men with their legs buried in mud seem condemned to strike one another, to depict what the work environment at the Tax Agency may wind up to become. It is common knowledge in the agency that changes in the top positions will trigger a "cascade of changes in second-layer positions, since roughly half of the tax inspectors [trained civil servants recruited through highly competitive formal exams] occupy at-will posts" (Ramsés Pérez Boga 2013, 1). This has created a great deal of uncertainty in the Tax Agency's workforce. Thompson's (1965, 6) prediction of what happens in organizations with a single chain of hierarchy – where "the normal psychological state is one of more or less anxiety" – seems to reflect what has happened in the Tax Agency, where "every movement by Menéndez [its general director] is interpreted as a witch hunt or a political purge" (*El País* 06–12-2013).

But we would not only expect bad management from a single chain command structure. We should also consider the incentives for the public employee on the ground to work hard. In an integrated system, the employee knows that her future career does not depend on her professional success but on the fortunes of her sponsor. Thus making extra effort does not pay off. A rational employee would therefore spend more time in pleasing politicians, or other patrons, than in producing good service to citizens. It is important to say that it is not necessary that an actual "witch hunt," as described above, takes place to damage morale among public employees. As a matter of fact, both the Secretary of State of Public Finances (*El País* 10–12-2013) and many tax officials (*El País* 22-11-2013) deny that such a political purge is taking place. It is only necessary that there are "doubts" (Pérez Boga 2013), that there is a vague perception that – as the union of tax officials, *Gestha*, noted – "there is something more" behind a particular dismissal, in order to generate a "great upheaval" in the Tax Agency (*El País* 22-11-2013) and to enter the realm of monocratic pathologies described by Thompson (1965), where employees become more concerned about the uncertainty of their positions than motivated to accomplish organizational goals.

All in all, we would expect service production to be less effective in integrated career systems because of two interrelated factors: (i) the lack of checks and balances; (ii) relatively bad management, and thus employees are less motivated to do a good job. In the next two sections we will first describe a strategy for testing these suggestions and then discuss the results of our empirical analysis.

Two Components of an Effective Government and Its Determinants

In the section above, we tried to be as specific as possible about the causal mechanisms through which we expect this separation of careers to affect government effectiveness. The main purpose of the next section is to put our proposition to a systematic empirical test, but we would first like to give a more detailed description of our empirical strategy.

We will again rely primarily on broad cross-country comparisons, with about one hundred countries in most specifications. We mainly use cross-section OLS regression techniques and take three analytic steps. First, we analyze the bivariate correlations between an indicator of separation of careers and two different effectiveness measures. Each of the indicators on the dependent side is representative of the different causal mechanisms. Second, we regress our indicator of integration/ separation of careers on the same two indicators of government effectiveness, but this time include a number of fairly demanding control variables. Third, we address potential endogeneity bias and test the robustness of the results. Throughout, we discuss some cases, mainly in Latin America and Europe, in order to help us make a correct interpretation of the cross-national comparison.

On the independent side, we use the indicators from Chapter 4, namely the meritocratic recruitment item from the QoG Expert Survey (Teorell, Dahlström, and Dahlberg 2011). We also tried all analyses with the professionalism index, however, and the results are substantively the same. For a discussion about the data collection and for the full questionnaire, see Chapter 2 (see also Dahlberg et al. 2013; Dahlström, Lapuente, and Teorell 2012b).

In the main analysis we use two indicators on the dependent side, but we also used other indicators in order to assess robustness. There are several reasons why we do not trust a single indicator. To start with, measuring government effectiveness is extremely difficult, and there is no established consensus about what measure should be used, which in itself speaks for using several different indicators. What's more, we have suggested that effectiveness should be affected by a reduction of wasteful spending, better management, and more productive public employees. We therefore tried to find indicators that are fairly close to these paths to effectiveness.

The first indicator on the dependent side is an indicator of Wastefulness of Government Spending from the World Economic Forum's Global Competitiveness Report (Schwab 2012). The indicator is taken from the annual Executive Opinion Survey carried out in the business community by the World Economic Forum. The Executive Opinion Survey 2012 includes more than 14,000 executives from 140 countries, who answered the following question: "How would you rate the composition of public spending in your country?" on a scale from 1 to 7 where 1 is "extremely wasteful" and 7 is "highly efficient in providing necessary goods and services" (Schwab 2012, 395; for more detail on the data collection, see Browne, Geiger, and Gutknecht 2012).

Our second measure is from the Bertelsmann Transformation Index (BTI), provided by the *Bertelsmann Stiftung*. Among other things, the BTI evaluates political management in 128 developing and transition countries. It is based on expert assessments, and the indicator we use is called "management performance." This index captures an important implication of the second mechanism. It aims to measure whether the government has a high steering capability, uses human and material resources efficiently, and is successful in basic consensus building and international cooperation. We use the index in the main analysis but also tested only using the steering capability and human and material resource efficiency sub-components, with very similar results.

What's more, we include a number of control variables in our models. As described in the previous section, we consider the Legal Origins Theory (Djankov et al. 2002, 2003; La Porta et al. 1999, 2008) to be the strongest competing explanation. We therefore take several controls from this line of research, such as a dummy for legal origin in the country, latitude, ethnic heterogeneity, and GDP per capita (log). Djankov et al. (2010) also showed that the disclosure of financial and business among politicians is correlated to the quality of government, which makes us include a dummy of whether the economic interests of the country's parliamentarians are publically available. Further, following the work of Evans and Rauch (1999) and Rauch and Evans (2000), we add an indicator of closed Weberianism. This measure is from the QoG Expert Survey and is an additive index calculated from the two items of how common lifelong careers are in the public sector and the extent to which special labor laws protect public employees (see Chapter 2 for the exact wording of the questions).

Finally, we take two steps to handle potential problems with our analysis. It could be claimed that the causality runs in the other direction, and that our analyses are biased by endogeneity. We therefore run a two-stage regression with the same instrument variable as we used in the previous chapter, which captures whether the administration was mainly bureaucratic or patrimonial at the turn of the eighteenth and nineteenth centuries (Charron, Dahlström, and Lapuente 2012; Ertman 1997). We also run a series of robustness checks, where we take in additional controls and exchange our dependent variables. We try using the World Bank's government effectiveness indicator, which strengthens the results, and employ measures on the dependent side from Chong et al. (2014). Chong et al. (2014) have collected data on how effective the postal service is around the globe. In a very innovative effort to provide objective data, they mailed ten non-existent business addresses in 159 countries, included a return address, and noted whether the letter was returned, and in the case a response was received, how long it took for the letter to be returned. Chong et al. (2014, 10) then used data on the proportion of letters returned and the time it took to get them back, together with data on the size of the labor force in the sector, the capital invested, and the actual number of letters sent in the country to calculate a "production function" that captures government effectiveness in the sector. With this production function on the dependent side, they show how technology, capital, labor, and management affect postal effectiveness, which is in

Table 5.1 *Descriptive statistics*

Variable	Obs	Mean	Std. Dev.	Min	Max
Meritocratic recruitment	107	4.3	1.1	1.9	6.6
Wasteful spending	142	3.3	.90	1.8	6.0
Management performance	126	5.5	1.8	1.4	9.4
Bureaucracy 18th century	30	.47	.51	0	1
Ln(GDP/cap)	179	8.7	1.3	5.7	11.1
Common law	193	.33	.47	0	1
Latitude	193	.28	.19	0	.72
Education	143	7.8	2.9	1.2	13.3
Ethnic fractionalization	166	.46	.27	0	.98
Closed Weberianism	107	5.2	.81	2.8	6.8
Disclosure publicly available	172	.29	.45	0	1
Productivity in the postal sector	156	8.4	3.3	0	12.6
World region	195	4.5	2.6	1	10

Comment: Table 5.1 summarizes all variables. With the exceptions of the data on productivity in the postal sector (Chong et al. 2014) and the disclosure data (Djankov et al. 2010), the variables are available in the QoG standard dataset (Teorell et al. 2013) or the QoG Expert Survey (Teorell, Dahlström, and Dahlberg 2011).

line with our argument. For robustness, we tested whether we could replicate their results, and we can.

All variables are summarized in Table 5.1. With the exception of the letter data (Chong et al. 2014) and the disclosure data (Djankov et al. 2010), the variables are available in the QoG standard dataset (Teorell et al. 2013) or the QoG Expert Survey (Teorell, Dahlström, and Dahlberg 2011).

Separated Careers, and an Effective State

We argue that recruitment and career paths affect incentives for both politicians and bureaucrats. When the careers of politicians and bureaucrats are integrated and their incentives thus coincide, the risk increases not only for corruption but also for legal wasteful spending, indicated by the examples of "airports to nowhere" and so-called white elephants discussed earlier. What's more, management in an integrated career system will probably be less geared toward an efficient use of human and economic resources because it will be biased by

partisan considerations. Finally, in an integrated career system, public
employees will probably not have as strong incentives to effectively
deliver services as in a separated system, because their future carrier
will be determined to a large extent by political circumstances. Simplified, making the right friends is therefore as important as working
hard. We therefore expect the separation/integration of careers to
correlate with indicators of an effective use of public funds and human
resources, as well as with indicators of good public management and
an effective public sector.

As mentioned in the previous section, there are no agreed upon
measures of government effectiveness. We think that the separation
of politicians' and bureaucrats' careers will result in less careless
(although legal) government spending, because politicians and bureaucrats monitor each other, very similar to what we argue happens with
corruption. The management of the public sector will also be better,
because it will not be biased by partisan considerations to such a large
extent, and public employees will work harder to effectively deliver
service, as this is more important for their future careers. For these
reasons, we chose to work with two different indicators on the dependent side. We consequently chose one indicator reasonably close to each
of these mechanisms on the dependent side: (i) less wasteful government spending; (ii) better public sector management. On the independent side, we use the indicator on meritocratic recruitment from the
QoG Expert Survey described earlier.

We start the analysis by looking at simple bivariate correlations
between our indicator of the separation of careers between politicians and bureaucrats and a measure of wastefulness of government
spending from the World Economic Forum's Global Competitiveness
Report. Figure 5.1 below graphically illustrates the correlation
between the indicators, where 102 countries around the world are
included. Figure 5.1 has the merit indicator on the X-axis and the
measure of wasteful spending on the Y-axis. Note that the World
Economic Forum's measure of the wastefulness of government
spending ranges from 1 to 7, where higher values indicate less wasteful spending. We therefore expect the correlation between them to be
positive, and it is, and also fairly strong and statistically significant
($R=0.47$, $p < 0.00$).

In the graph, we can see the difference between OECD countries,
such as Spain, where a good deal of wasteful spending seems to take

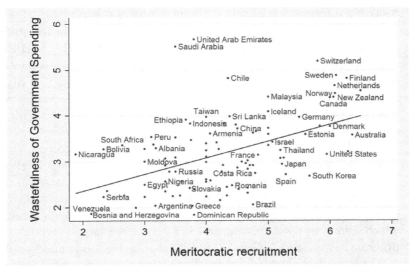

Figure 5.1 Correlation between wastefulness of government spending and meritocratic recruitment in the public sector

Comment: The Y-axis shows the level of wastefulness of government spending, on a scale from 1 to 7, where 1 is "extremely wasteful" and 7 is "highly efficient in providing necessary goods and services." Data come from the World Economic Forum's Global Competitiveness Report (Schwab 2012). The X-axis reports whether public sector employees are recruited by their skills and merit, measured from 1 (not at all) to 7 (a very large extent). Data are from the QoG survey (Teorell, Dahlström, and Dahlberg 2011) and the QoG Standard Dataset (Teorell et al 2013). 102 countries have data on both variables and are thus plotted above.

place, and Sweden, where wasteful spending seems to be minimal. According to the position of Spain, the examples we gave in Chapters 1 and 2 and the ones we give in this chapter do not seem to be exceptions but rather particular illustrations of a more disturbing pattern of wasteful spending in Spain. Sweden, on the other hand, is in the top five, both when it comes to meritocratic recruitment and low level of wasteful spending.

The observation about Sweden is in accordance with previous evaluations of both the high degree of separation of careers between politicians and bureaucrats (Dahlström and Pierre 2011; Pierre 1995b; Pollitt and Bouckaert 2011) and its use of public resources to deliver welfare-enhancing policies, such as investments in human capital (Hopkin and Blyth 2012; Lindert 2006) or a level of public capital "very close to its optimal value" (Demetriades and Mamuneas 2000, 702). Given that the embryo of a separation of careers in the state apparatus can be traced back to the development of the Swedish administration in modern Europe, when a dualistic structure separating policymakers from agency employees was consolidated, it also seems difficult to claim that a reverse causation between government effectiveness and the type of administration can help explain their high correlation (Andersson 2004; Pierre 2004; Premfors 1991).

Outside the OECD, we find Venezuela in the lower left corner, with an extremely non-meritocratic administration and a very high level of wasteful spending. Several additional sources support the position of Venezuela. To start with, scholars have long considered Venezuela an example of misuse of public funds: "an outstanding case is Venezuela, which simply stopped growing in 1979 despite the largest investment program in its history" (Gelb 1988, 122; see also Robinson and Torvik 2005). It would probably be misleading to interpret Venezuela's wasteful spending as a mere consequence of its oil resources. As Robinson, Torvik, and Verdier (2006, 451) accurately note, "for every Venezuela and Nigeria, there is a Norway or a Botswana" thus "a satisfactory model should explain why resources seem to induce prosperity in some countries but not others." In line with these economists, we argue that the underperformance of some oil-rich countries is not because they are cursed by resources, but by poor institutions (Mehlum, Moene, and Torvik 2006). Instead of the "producer-friendly" institutions of resource-rich countries like Norway, Venezuela's institutions would fall in the category of "grabber-friendly" (Mehlum, Moene, and Torvik 2006, 1121–2).

Again, the 64,000 dollar question is what makes Norwegian institutions producer-friendly and Venezuelan institutions grabber-friendly, especially if we take into account that – quite shockingly if we think about it today – both countries had similar levels of development not too long ago (Santiso 2011). We think that, following the relationship plotted in Figure 5.1 and the theoretical argument given in this book, the type of administration prevailing in each country may have played a significant role in understanding why the notable influx of income from oil has been used for political rent-seeking, as seems to have happened in Venezuela according to most accounts, or for providing efficient public goods, as has been the case in Norway (Havro and Santiso 2008; Karl 1997).

The sequencing in Norway and Venezuela is very different, as the system of separated careers precedes the detection of oil resources in Norway. This is not only seen in the data on comparative bureaucracies presented here; there is also a consensus among public administration scholars that Norway has a long history of separation of careers between politicians and bureaucrats (Lægreid 2001; Lægreid and Pedersen 1996). In contrast, there is ample evidence that Venezuela developed a particularly pervasive spoils system after its transition to democracy in 1958, a system that was reinforced in subsequent decades (Coppedge 1994; Karl 1986).

We would like to note that there are also two quite obvious outliers in Figure 5.1, however, namely the United Arab Emirates and Saudi Arabia, although the explanation for their position is probably related to their high level of GDP and their being small states, and because of natural resources. Both these oil-rich countries have much less wasteful spending than their level of meritocracy in the public sector indicates, and this speaks against our proposition. Still, while we cannot be sure why they are outside the general pattern, it is consistent with the resource curse literature discussed above, which in essence claims that countries with easily available natural resources do not need to make investments in a well-functioning administration (Mehlum, Moene, and Torvik 2006; Sachs and Warner 2001).

Another country with an enormous amount of wasteful spending that we see in Figure 5.1 is the Dominican Republic. Policymaking has traditionally been unchecked by autonomous bureaucrats and has been concentrated in a very small number of politicians. Joaquin Balaguer, who controlled Dominican politics in the second half of the twentieth century, serving several terms as president, reproduced the highly monocratic style of government of his predecessor *El Jefe* Trujillo, who tyrannically ruled the country from 1930 to 1961. Balaguer, without any bureaucratic check, came to control more than half of the government budget, misallocating expenditures on a grandiose scale (Keefer and Vlaicu 2008). Yet the opposition to Balaguer reproduced the same particularistic bias: a focus on targeting spending and neglecting public good provisions, which explains the extremely low ratio of money for education to public investment in that country, where it is as much as 50 percentage points lower than in comparable countries (Keefer 2002).

In-depth studies of policymaking in the Dominican Republic, such as the one conducted by Keefer (2002), reveal the connection between a

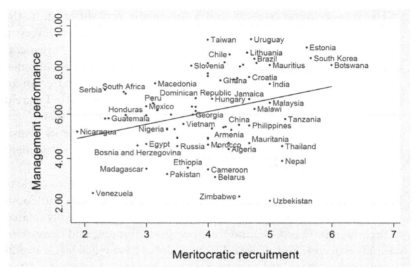

Figure 5.2 Correlation between government management performance and meritocratic recruitment in the public sector

Comment: The Y-axis shows the level of management performance on a scale from 1 to 10. Data come from the Bertelsmann Stiftung's Transformation index (Bertelsmann Transformation index 2012). The X-axis reports whether public sector employees are recruited by their skills and merit, measured from 1 (not at all) to 7 (a very large extent). Data are from the QoG survey (Teorell, Dahlström, and Dahlberg 2011) and the QoG Standard Dataset (Teorell et al 2013). Seventy-nine countries have data on both variables and are thus plotted above.

politicized administration and low government effectiveness captured in Figure 5.1. Keefer (2002, 2) summarizes his findings as follows:

as many respondents of all political tendencies insisted in interviews in February 2002, there is a strong under-current of clientelism in the Dominican Republic. One consequence of clientelism is that public spending is biased towards public and private goods that are easy to target to specific voters or groups of voters, such as jobs, buildings and highways, and away from publicly-provided goods and services that are more difficult to target, such as higher teacher salaries, improved school curricula, or regulatory predictability.

In Figure 5.2, we substitute the indicator of wasteful use of resources for an indicator from the *Bertelsmann Stiftung* that aims to capture the management performance of the government. We can include only seventy-nine countries with this indicator, but a rather similar picture as the one above emerges, although with a weaker correlation ($R=0.28$, $p < 0.05$). It should be noted that, compared to the 102 countries graphed in Figure 5.1, twenty-three of the more developed countries are missing. We still have considerable variation in the sample, but we have lost the top performers in this analysis, which probably biases the correlation downward.

Again we find Venezuela in the lower left corner, very much in line with expectations. The peak of integration of careers in the Venezuelan state was probably reached during the rule of President Hugo Chavez, who micro-managed appointments and dismissals throughout the state apparatus (Hawkins, Rosas, and Johnson 2011). In an extreme case of bad management, many employees of the state-owned oil company were not in tune with his political agenda after a strike; overnight, Chavez removed 18,000 employees – including top managers – and replaced them with tens of thousands of party loyalists who were expected to dedicate part of their working time to political goals, such as showing off in the celebration of the anniversary of his 1992 failed coup. It was clear that, if managers and employees had not gotten the message before, connections, not efficiency, was what was counted. As The Economist (18-02-2012) reported, this is also directly related to the remarkable deterioration of its efficiency indicators during the latest decade.

Mexico ends up in the middle of the distribution in management performance among the developing countries plotted in Figure 5.2, substantially better than Venezuela but not as good as the Baltic states, for example. Mexico is relatively rich but suffers from an adminis-tration structured by the decades-long political domination of the *Partido de la Revolución Institucional* (PRI). The presidential office controls the political allegiances of public employees "down to the most remote village in the country" (Grindle 2012, 169), which is represented here by its position on the X-axis (meritocratic recruit-ment). According to previous research, however, Mexican politicians were able to attract highly qualified professionals through so-called smart patronage and, in turn, achieve some important policy results, which probably explains its middle position in management perform-ance (Domínguez 1997; Grindle 1977). Still, it is without doubt that the inherent uncertainty of large-scale discretionary appointments has affected management in the public sector – especially around election time. As Grindle (2012, 170–1) notes, while the last year of an administration is overwhelmingly employed to establish "contacts for future job possibilities," the first year of a new administration resembles a "game of musical chairs, as those who were in public positions found other appointments." It thus seems that there are large periods of time where managers are more concerned about politics than about how to perform their current duties diligently.

In addition, and critically for management, the constant fluidity of the different personalistic currents in the PRI may lead public employees to find alternative loyalties to rely on in order to secure a job in the public sector. These loyalties may obviously deter managers from the pursuit of the public good in their daily activities. As Schneider (2004) describes, economic elites themselves admit that influence in appointments in the public sector is one of the most prevailing forms they have to gain favors from the Mexican institutions. Schneider (2004) also notes that entrenched business interests believe that "ambitious officials will, as they contemplate future promotions (emphasis ours), court business support and be more attentive to their views on policy."

Our interpretation of the association is also in line with results from Chong et al. (2014). They show how the quality of public management is positively correlated with higher production in the postal service sector. However, without any controls, these graphs are essentially of illustrative value, as we run an obvious risk of having omitted important variables. We therefore run a series of regressions, including several demanding controls, presented in Table 5.2. For the purpose of this chapter, most notable is that our indicator on meritocratic recruitment is statistically significant throughout. Table 5.2 includes four different specifications. Models 1 and 2 only control for GDP per capita (logged) for each of our dependent variables. But including this very powerful control does not alter the results dramatically. The coefficient of our indicator of the separation of careers continues to have the expected sign and is still highly statistically significant.

In models 3 and 4, we include a number of controls mainly from the legal origins tradition. Djankov et al. (2002) analyzed how easy, costly, and rapid it is to start a business in a country. La Porta et al. (1999) and Djankov et al. (2010) analyzed the quality of government more broadly. In the more inclusive models, we take most of the control variables from this line of research, as we think that their Legal Origins Theory is the most important alternative explanation. We include the legal origin of the country, latitude, ethnic heterogeneity, natural logarithm of GDP per capita, and a dummy capturing whether

Table 5.2 *Meritocratic recruitment, wastefulness of government spending, management performance, and postal effectiveness*

	(1)	(2)	(3)	(4)
Meritocratic recruitment	0.31***	0.51***	0.20**	0.98***
	(0.078)	(0.19)	(0.098)	(0.19)
Ln(GDP/cap)	0.11	0.80***	0.29**	0.50**
	(0.077)	(0.17)	(0.13)	(0.24)
Common law			0.52**	-0.28
			(0.21)	(0.41)
Latitude			0.70	0.056
			(0.69)	(1.24)
Education			-0.042	0.034
			(0.056)	(0.10)
Ethnic fractionalization			0.42	-0.24
			(0.39)	(0.73)
Closed Weberianism			-0.11	-0.63***
			(0.106)	(0.20)
Disclosure publicly available			-0.13	0.34
			(0.21)	(0.37)
Constant	0.84	-2.82*	0.10	1.13
	(0.62)	(1.60)	(1.10)	(2.10)
Number of countries	99	76	84	63
R^2	0.24	0.30	0.33	0.51
Adjusted R^2	0.23	0.28	0.26	0.44

Comment: Entries are OLS regression coefficients (standard errors in parentheses). The dependent variable in models 1 and 3 is the level wastefulness of government spending from the World Economic Forum's Global Competitiveness Report 2012, measured on a scale from 1 to 7, where 1 is "extremely wasteful" and 7 is "highly efficient in providing necessary goods and services." The dependent variable in models 2 and 4 is the level of management performance on a scale from 1 to 10, from the Bertelsmann Transformation Index 2012.
* $p < 0.10$, ** $p < 0.05$, *** $p < 0.01$

disclosures of financial and business interests for parliamentarians are publically available in the country (Djankov et al. 2002, 2003, 2010; La Porta 1999). We also add another control, namely one indicator of closed Weberianism (based on two indicators from the QoG Expert Survey, namely lifelong careers and whether public employees are protected by special labor laws). In total, this adds up to no less than six controls more in models 3 and 4. As we do not have data on all the controls for the entire sample, adding them also affects the size of the sample, which gives a reduction of between 15 and 17 percentage points.

Most noteworthy among the controls is probably that the log of GDP per capita is highly statistically significant in the predicted direction in all models. Surprisingly, the dummy for common law is statistically significant and points in the predicted positive direction only in model 3 (wasteful spending), while the coefficient is actually negative in model 4 (however, it is much above the standard threshold for statistical significance). It should also be noted that the closed Weberianism variable has a negative sign in all the models and is statistically significant in model 4 (management performance). This result stands in sharp contrast to the conventional view of how an effective government should be organized (Evans and Rauch 1999; Rauch and Evans 2000). However, in previous studies (Dahlström and Lapuente 2012; Dahlström, Lapuente, and Teorell 2012a), we have shown that there is very weak empirical support for this claim. The negative association of closed Weberianism and government effectiveness can actually be interpreted along the lines of our theoretical mechanism: special employment laws and lifelong careers in the public sector may protect public employees from proper scrutiny and thus help to create a group of relatively unaccountable officials, where the incentives for effective management are low.

We now turn to a discussion of what happens to the merit indicator when all controls are included. It has a reduced b-coefficient in model 3, compared to the more limited model 1, which is expected when including several controls and losing a considerable number of cases. It is now only about two thirds of what it was previously in model 1, but it is still statistically significant ($p < 0.05$). More unexpected is that including the common law dummy, the average years of school in the population over twenty-five, and the latitude of the capital actually increases the effect of merit on management performance in model 4, compared to model 2. All in all, we think it speaks for our interpretation of a causal relationship between the integration/ separation of careers and government effectiveness that our merit indicator and the three depended variables are consistently statistically significant in all the specifications.

So far, the empirical patterns found are compatible with the theory we suggested. Meritocratic recruitment is associated with low levels of wasteful government spending, high levels of management performance, and an effective delivery of postal service. A potential objection to these findings, however, concerns endogeneity bias. We therefore instrument for meritocracy by using an external regressor. Institutions separating the interests of politicians and bureaucrats have been suggested to have deep historical roots, which in itself speaks against causality running in the other direction (Painter and Peters 2010; Pierre 1995a; Pollit and Bouckaert 2011). It also means that it might be possible to find an instrumental variable that picks up this historical experience and thus primarily affects our dependent variables through the mechanism of separation of careers. We use the same measure as in Chapter 4, which captures whether the administration was mainly bureaucratic or patrimonial at the turn of the eighteenth and nineteenth centuries, according to Ertman (1997) and coded by Charron, Dahlström, and Lapuente (2012). On the downside, this variable is available for only thirty-one OECD countries and thus substantially limits the sample. It also makes it impossible to use the management performance indicator from Bertelsmann Stiftung, as only eight countries overlap the two datasets. We will thus only use wasteful spending on the dependent side in the analysis below.

Table 5.3 reports the results of using the external regressor in a two-stage regression. No controls are included in model 1, while model 2 includes all the controls from the analysis in Table 5.2. In model 2, the first stage F-statistics is, however, below the standard threshold (10), indicating potential weak instrument problems (Stock, Wright, and Yogo 2002). But using Anderson-Rubin confidence intervals instead, the merit recruitment coefficient is still significant. The effect of the merit indicator is statistically significant in both the models, even though the sample is now very restricted (twenty-nine and twenty-seven countries, respectively). We can also note that the size of the coefficient of the merit indicator increases rather dramatically compared to the analysis reported in Table 5.2, which might be indicative of a larger true effect of merit than we were previously able to capture, but it could also just be an effect of the sample being smaller. In addition, we also controlled for the earliest available measure of wasteful government spending, which is from 2004 and obtainable for only thirty-two countries. Including this control would be an alternative way of handling a potential endogeneity

Table 5.3 *Correcting for endogeneity (2SLS regressions)*

	(1)	(2)
Meritocratic recruitment	0.89***	1.93**
	(0.172)	(0.74)
Ln(GDP/cap)		-1.38
		(1.29)
Common law		-1.41*
		(0.75)
Latitude		0.72
		(2.12)
Education		-0.11
		(0.15)
Ethnic fractionalization		0.87
		(1.10)
Closed Weberianism		-0.24
		(0.37)
Disclosure publicly		-1.55
available		(0.96)
Constant	-1.14	11.00
	(0.89)	(9.23)
Number of countries	29	27
R^2	0.40	0.30
Adjusted R^2	0.37	-0.02

Comment: Entries are 2SLS estimates (standard errors in parentheses), using a measure of the state administration in the eighteenth century as an instrument variable. The
dependent variable is the level of wastefulness of government spending from the
World Economic Forum's Global Competitiveness Report 2012, measured on a scale
from 1 to 7, where 1 is "extremely wasteful" and 7 is "highly efficient in providing
necessary goods and services."
* $p < 0.10$, ** $p < 0.05$, *** $p < 0.01$

bias. The merit indicator stays statistically significant when this control
is also included (results not shown).

In order to check the robustness of the results reported in Tables 5.2 and
5.3, we re-ran all the models substituting the measure on the dependent
side for the World Bank's government effectiveness indicator, which only
strengthens our interpretation. We also used the indicator from Chong

et al. (2014), and we are able to reproduce their results, which strengthens our confidence in our interpretation of our findings. What's more, we re-ran the models including regional controls, which changes the results in three ways. First, the log of GDP per capita becomes statistically non-significant in the wasteful spending and management performance models. Second, the negative effect of the indicator of closed Weberianism becomes statistically significant and, third, the latitude variable is positively and statistically significant in the same models. Neither of these alterations, however, influences our main conclusion from the empirical analysis: a system of separated careers for politicians and bureaucrats is positively associated with higher government effectiveness.

Conclusion

This chapter has explored how separated careers in the state apparatus, proxied by the level of meritocratic recruitment in the bureaucracy, affect effectiveness. It engages in a discussion with the booming literature exploring the effects of institutions, particularly with the literature that underlines the role of legal origins. We hope to contribute to this literature by noting an overlooked institutional factor that may help explain government effectiveness: the extent to which there is an integration of careers between political and bureaucratic officials, or a "monocracy," using Thompson's term (1965). More specifically, we highlight two mechanisms through which "monocratic" governments – that is, those where the career incentives of politicians and bureaucrats respond to the same chain of authority – make less effective governments, and we provide both quantitative and qualitative empirical indications that support our suggestion.

First, we argue that legal but inefficient policy decisions, for example involving wasteful spending to satisfy a given territorial constituency that unavoidably crowds out investments in public goods, are less likely when those assisting the decision-making process – the bureaucrats – are free to speak truth to power. Second, we consider that the tasks of public managers may be hampered by introducing political considerations instead of professional. The inherent instability of politically appointed managers, since it notably shortens their time horizons, may seriously damage the psychological contract public managers have with their subordinates. The motivation of rank and file public employees may also be affected if they have doubts about the extent to which a dutiful execution of their functions or, to the contrary, a more partial policy implementation that favors incumbents' constituencies, promotes their future careers.

The empirical analyses have shown that, controlling for several alternative explanations, mainly from the legal origins literature, the existence of merit-based bureaucratic career systems contributes to higher government effectiveness. In addition, we have illustrated these mechanisms with a variety of narratives from diverse countries – such as Spain, Sweden, Norway, Argentina, Mexico, and the Dominican Republic – that seem to point in the same direction as our quantitative evidence: Integrating the career prospects of politicians with those of bureaucrats is conducive to government malfunctions.

6 | Reforms

Introduction

Chapter 5 demonstrated that career incentives for politicians and bureaucrats influence how effective the state is. When their careers are integrated, the risk of wasteful spending and bad management is high and the motivation for good job performance is low. This chapter will take the analysis one step further and explore the extent to which the same factor also affects probabilities of administrative reforms. External factors occasionally create opportunities to reform the public sector in order to increase productivity. If we look at responses to major economic crises, for example, we can see great cross-country variations. Some governments take the opportunity to make, sometimes painful, reforms in the public administration, while other governments postpone reforms even in the most critical circumstances. Following Lodge and Hood (2012, 82), it can be argued that economic crises represent a common "drama," but we find "several subplots" with very different outcomes in particular countries. What explains these subplots? Why are some governments more capable of reforming themselves than others?

For instance, compare the reforms of the public administration in Sweden after its deep financial crisis in the early 1990s, described by the *Swedish Agency for Public Management* as "dramatic," with the lack of reinvention of government in the Southern European countries heavily hit by the 2008 financial crisis (Statskontoret 1997, 127). Administrative business continues as usual. There is obviously much less business, since countries such as Greece and Spain have witnessed some of the harshest budgetary cuts in their history. Yet fundamental changes have not been made in administrative business.

More generally, a large literature observes that since the mid-1970s administrative reform has been on the agenda of almost all Western governments (Cassese 2003; De Francesco 2012; Lynn 2001; March and Olson 1983;). The underlying reason for the emergence and expansion of public management reforms aimed at adopting private sector management practices is that governments have been subject to increasing demands to perform, deliver results and do so in an efficient, customer-friendly, and flexible way (Marsden 1997; Willems, Janvier and Henderickx 2006). Rhetoric does not always go hand in hand with actual reform practice, however, and the literature refers to this situation as double-talk, or even hypocrisy (Christensen and Laegred 2001; 2010). On the one hand, governments are pressured both from international organizations, such as the OECD, the EU, the IMF, and the World Bank, and national actors to send a signal that they also adhere to the prevailing norm of what a well-functioning administration should look like (Christensen and Laegred 2010; De Francesco 2012; Finnemore 1996). On the other hand, governments can be reluctant to adopt reforms that may create, in the short term, concentrated losers, especially among politically well-located pressure groups, such as civil service associations or unions, even if the reforms would be beneficial for society at large.

Intriguingly, the positions that governments take in this dilemma depend more on the institutional setting of the country than on the political color of the incumbent (Dahlström and Lapuente 2010). For instance, both Social Democratic and center-right governments in Sweden have shown quite intense reforming zeal, while, at the same time, neither left nor right governments in France have extensively reformed their public administration. The differences are more on the country level, relatively stable across time, and related to institutional factors. We suggested in a previous paper that reforms that introduce monetary incentives in the public sector, performance-related pay being the prime example, are much more likely to be implemented in settings with "...a relative separation between those who benefit from the incentives (e.g., politicians) and those who manage the incentive system (e.g., senior civil servants)," compared to when the careers of the two groups are intertwined (Dahlström and Lapuente 2010, 577).

Consequently, cross-national differences in public management reform are remarkable. Year after year, and reform opportunity after reform opportunity, some countries exhibit a relentless ability to reform, for example in Denmark and New Zealand, while others, such as Italy or Greece, miss the same opportunities for reforms. As comparative public administration scholars have noticed, the puzzle is that "although the New Public Management (NPM) approach is often analyzed through the convergence doctrine, administrative reform policies in Western countries have differed in content, orientation and timing since the early 1980s" (Bezes and Parrado 2013, 22).

The goal of this chapter is to understand this puzzle in the light of the general theory presented in Chapters 1 and 2. Following Drori, Jang, and Meyer's (2006) pioneering comparative study of government reforms, we hope to contribute to the discussion grounded in the writings of Karl Marx and Max Weber on the extent to which modernization of government is explained by economic, cultural, or, as we suggest, institutional prerequisites. We will thus test both the most prevalent economic explanations for understanding why some governments are more willing to reform themselves than others (economic pressures from globalization and economic development) as well as the most dominant ideological (influence of the political right) and cultural accounts (Anglo-Saxon administrative tradition). In addition, this chapter aims to make a theoretical contribution by providing an explanation, rooted in the theoretical framework presented in this book as well as in our previous empirical work on public management reforms (Dahlström and Lapuente 2010), which instead of economic and cultural causes, highlights a specific institutional factor, namely the tension between politicians' incentives and those of bureaucrats.

The chapter is structured as follows. First, we describe our general dependent variable, cross-national differences in New Public Management (NPM) reforms, and justify our particular operationalization, which is whether countries have implemented performance-related pay (PRP) systems in the public sector. This is a good indicator for our purpose here, as PRP systems are a relatively new entity in the public sector. We should already at this point say that we make no effort to evaluate whether PRP is effective, or generally a good idea for the public sector. Our purpose is only to evaluate whether new characteristics – reforms – are implemented at all.

After a brief review of the existing explanations, we develop our explanation, largely based on what was argued in Chapter 2. In brief, our argument goes as follows: several organizational economists have underlined the need for a system of separation of interests in firms in order to make promises on incentives credible (Miller 1992). Similarly, we argue that reforms require a high level of trust between public managers and public employees. Reforms are therefore more likely to be implemented when there is a relative separation between those who benefit from the reforms (politicians) and those who manage the public sector (bureaucrats). Where the interests of politicians and bureaucrats overlap, reform initiatives will be less credible in the eyes of public employees, and thus less likely. We then discuss the research strategy for this chapter, and proceed to test whether a system with separated careers between politicians and bureaucrats is correlated with high levels of PRP in the public sector and, finally, discuss PRP reforms in Sweden and Spain.

New Public Management and Performance-Related Pay

Since the mid-1970s, public administration reforms have often been described as parts of a "global trend," known as New Public Management (Sahlin-Andersson 2001, 43; see also Hood 1991). The speed and scale of NPM reforms are such that the terms "striking," "sweeping," and "revolutionary" are frequently used in reference to them (Lynn 2001, 2).

Although NPM includes quite different reforms, it is probably legitimate to treat it as an analytical category worth exploring as such, given the notable common motivations behind NPM reforms and the similarities of the administrative reforms in different countries (Caldwell 2000; Lynn 2001). In one of the most influential books outlining the philosophy behind NPM, Osborne and Gaebler (1992) write that the key feature of NPM is to move away from rules and processes traditionally dominant in the administration and focus more on results. In their review of the "middle aging of New Public Management," Hood and Peters (2004, 271) summarize the NPM's core idea as one of replacing the traditional emphasis on *ex ante* controls of public bureaucracies' activities for a new emphasis on *ex post* evaluation of the results administrations actually deliver. Put simply, NPM aims to introduce managerial changes in public administrations to increase productivity by learning from the private sector (Hood 1991; Ongaro 2008). Authors remark that, in practice, NPM implies the introduction of the "market logic into public organizations" (De Francesco 2012, 1280) and the change of "rule-based authority-driven processes with market-based, competition-driven tactics" (Kettl 2000, 3). The adoption of private sector tools can be seen in several NPM reforms, ranging from contracting out and agencification to the partial replacement of flat salaries for performance-related pay. To a certain extent, it can thus be argued that NPM entails an entirely new professional paradigm for public administrations based on management ideologies stressing result-oriented activities as well as a marked individual, instead of collective, accountability (Gow and Dufour 2000).

Today, one finds NPM reforms worldwide, but in very different shapes, degrees, and depths (for overviews, see Christensen and Lægreid 2001; Peters and Pierre 2001; Pollitt and Bouckaert 2011). The fact that NPM has become a paradigm does not mean that reforms have been homogeneous; there are notable national divergences that remain a puzzle to the literature (Lynn 2001, 19). There seem to be different trajectories of reform (Pollit and Bouckaert 2011). On the one side, we have the most reform-oriented countries such as Australia, New Zealand, and the United Kingdom, which are sometimes even referred to as the "NPM countries" (Ongaro 2012, 108). At the other side of the spectrum, examples of reluctance to NPM reforms would include France (Rouban 2008), Greece (Spanou 2008; Spanou and Sotiropoulos 2011), Spain (Parrado 2008), and Italy (Ongaro 2008). One can thus talk about clusters of countries (Ongaro 2012). Nevertheless, as experts in the administrations of Southern European countries have shown, the real picture in these Southern European countries has much greater nuance – a picture that cannot easily be summarized with simple terms such as "failures" or "laggards" (Ongaro 2008, 110; see also Bezes 2010; Gallego and Barzelay 2010; Ongaro 2012; Parrado 2008).

To sum up, the variation in NPM reforms between countries around the world is a relatively good case to test the reach of our institutional hypothesis. We should, however, as mentioned in the introduction, state that we are not making a normative argument that NPM reforms should be implemented; we are merely treating them as examples where there has been a pressure for reforms and therefore a good case for testing how adaptive the public sector of a given country is.

There is, unfortunately, a lack of reliable comparative measures and, more fundamentally, no clear consensus as to what precise features do constitute an NPM reform. In this chapter, we address these questions by focusing on one particular but paradigmatic NPM reform, namely the introduction of performance-related pay (PRP) in the public sector (Thompson 2007, 50). To start with, PRP systems imply a more individual treatment of employees and greater hierarchy since they aim at closer control of public employees' output. PRP systems are a core element of NPM because they exemplify a new component in rewarding systems, the emphasis being on job performance rather than on rank and educational attainment, which is not present in traditional public administration (Hood 1996). PRP systems thus represent a "symbolic break from the entitlement culture" (Risher 1999, 334) of "fixed increments that were awarded automatically" based on seniority that is characteristic of the traditional public administration (Freibert 1997; Willems, Janvier, and Henderickx 2006).

As the OECD remarks, "the adoption of performance-related pay in the public sector reflects the influence of the private sector culture of incentives and individual accountability on public administration" (OECD 2004, 4). In addition, scholars note the emblematic aspect of pay systems, since "pay programs are visible and powerful communicators of organizational goals, priorities and values" (Schuster and Zingheim 1992, xv). There is also one pragmatic reason for choosing PRP systems: unlike many other NPM reforms, there are both reliable cross-country indicators of the implementation of incentive systems as well as previous studies comparing the dissimilar adoption of pay systems (Dahlström and Lapuente 2010; Willems, Janvier, and Henderickx 2006). Consequently, we contend that PRP is one of the most feasible proxies for assessing the advancement of NPM reforms in a country.

PRP is also one of the most debated NPM reforms among practitioners and scholars alike. Even if precedents of individual performance ratings for public employees can be traced back in time to the late nineteenth century in the United States (Murphy and Cleveland 1995), it is during this current NPM era that they have gained momentum and, in particular, during the 1990s. As pointed out by both Radin (2000) and Heinrich (2003), the public sector in the 1990s was characterized by a demand for performance, which also led to a greater need of performance measures. The background to introducing PRP systems in numerous Western countries has been a context of economic and budgetary difficulties that has forced governments to search for mechanisms aimed at improving individual motivation and, as a result, overall government performance. Nevertheless, despite these similar pressures and the adoption, on paper, of PRP systems in most Western countries, "there are wide variations in the degree to which PRP is actually applied" and "only a handful of member countries can be considered to have an extended, formalized PRP policy (Denmark; Finland; Korea; New Zealand; Switzerland; the United Kingdom)" (OECD 2005, 10). This chapter aims to provide an account of these national variations.

Existing Explanations of NPM Reforms

During recent decades, public administration scholars have given NPM reforms much attention (Christensen and Lægreid 2001; Peters and Pierre 2001; Pollitt and Bouckaert 2011). The comparative literature on administrative reforms is dominated by case studies, however, and there are few case comparisons. Despite the systematic variation in the adoption of administrative reforms offering a unique chance for explanations, current research "too often consists of the accumulation of descriptive studies without an underlying analytic structure" (De Francesco 2012, 1279; Lynn 2001, 204). We thus know quite a bit about where and how NPM reforms have taken place, but less about why they happened (Lodge and Wegrich 2012). (There are, of course, several exceptions to this general characterization, such as Bennett's (1997); De Francesco's (2012); Drori, Jang and Meyer's (2006); Lee and Strang's (2006); Verhoest's (2010); and many others.)

The explanations for the adoption of NPM reforms that do exist have searched for causes of cross-country variations chiefly in three spheres: economic pressures, political impulse, and culture. Concerning economic explanations, scholars have highlighted demands from economic globalization that seem to push governments to undertake bolder administrative reforms (Farazmand 1999; Keller 1999; Thompson 2007). Reforms are not so much results of choices but the responses of governments under constant surveillance by global financial markets and increasing trade competition (De Francesco 2012; Dobbin, Simmons, and Garret 2007). In line with this claim, public sector reforms seem to be correlated with external pressures that are more intense in open economies and when countries suffer particularly stringent international pressures, such as the convergence criteria of the European Monetary Union (Cope, Leishman, and Starie 1997; Drori, Jang, and Meyer 2006; Thompson 2007). Economic pressures derived from financial crises may further contribute to the adoption of administrative reforms (Cassese 2003).

It has also been suggested that NPM reforms are the results of a neoliberal political agenda, and of the particular rule of right-wing governments (Ansell and Gingrich 2003; Bach 1999; Barlow et al. 1996; Deakin and Walsh 1996; Mascarehnas 1993; Rosta 2011). In this view, the ascension of a *New Right* ideology in the last two decades of the twentieth century has fostered public downsizing as well as the introduction of private sector-inspired managerial tools; the Thatcher and Reagan administrations in Britain and the United States "led the way" in public sector reforms (Lee and Strang 2006, 883; see also Halligan 1996). The NPM measures implemented in these two countries during the 1980s were definitely inspirational for many conservative parties worldwide. Following several scholars (Bach 1999; Barlow et al. 1996; Pollitt 1993), one should also expect that those countries that have been under right-wing governments for longer periods of time in recent decades would be the ones with more advanced NPM-minded reforms.

Finally, according to some of the most influential public administration studies (Peters 1997; Pollitt and Bouckaert 2011) and international organizations (OECD 2004), the spread of NPM seems to be associated with the prevailing values in the different administrative traditions. These values determine "the receptivity of the administrative system to change" (Peters 1992, 212) or act as a "filter" of externally induced reforms (Bouckaert 2007, 32). These values are in turn the result of long historical processes and thus exhibit a great ability to influence the path that administrations take, becoming almost a cultural 'soul' (Christensen and Lægreid 2012; Krasner 1988; Selznick 1957).

The literature focuses on the distinction between, on the one hand, the Anglo-Saxon tradition and, on the other, the *Rechtsstaat* tradition, covering fundamentally continental Europe and Scandinavia (Pierre 2011; Pollitt and Bouckaert 2011). The consensus is quite widespread and, generally speaking, NPM is seen as being a product of the Anglo-Saxon administrative tradition (Bouckaert 2007; Castles and Merrill 1989; Christensen and Lægreid 2012; Hood 1996; Pollit 1990; Verhoest 2010).

On the contrary, a *Rechtsstaat* administrative tradition is seen as being more hostile to NPM reforms, because it either involves egalitarian norms – as in Scandinavian countries – or creates closed civil service systems that are resistant to external pressures for reform

(Christensen and Lægreid 2012; Halligan 2001). In addition, public activity is more heavily regulated in the *Rechtsstaat* tradition than in the more pragmatic Anglo-Saxon tradition (Verhoest 2010). Pierre (2011, 676) provides an illuminating categorization of the features of the *Rechtsstaat* tradition vis-à-vis its counterparts in the Anglo-Saxon tradition that helps to explain the relatively lower reforming zeal of the former in comparison to the latter. *Rechtsstaat* emphasizes legality and equality instead of service and managerialism; legal security instead of efficiency; the citizen instead of the customer; group rights instead of individual rights; public law instead of common law; and upward accountability instead of the dual upward-as-well-as-downward accountability. As a result, one should expect the adoption of NPM reforms to happen at a significantly lower speed – if any – in these Latin European, continental, and Scandinavian countries (Peters 2001; Pollit and Bouckaert 2011; Verhoest 2010). And PRP systems should be less prevalent in career-based administrations, like Belgium, with informal contracts that emphasize loyalty and job security, which fits better with a traditional pay system based on seniority (Willems, Janvier, and Henderickx 2006).

Our Explanation: Divided We Reform

One of the most basic organizational questions concerns how much power the people at the top of an organization should have. The conventional answer, both regarding public and private organizations, has been "a lot." Individuals occupying the higher managerial echelons of an organization should enjoy an extensive margin of maneuver in order to appropriately steer the boat, especially when there are troubled waters ahead. Most organizational economists see discretion for managerial intervention as beneficial for the prospects of an organization because it allows quick responses to environmental changes (Foss, Foss, and Vázquez 2006).

As outlined in Chapter 2, the underlying theoretical framework of this organizational literature is the standard principal-agent theory, according to which the main source of organizational problems tends to be the agent (e.g., employee, subordinate). And the standard solution is an appropriate contract that minimizes the agent's informational advantage. The principal-agent theory mindset has permeated the literature on public organizations as well (Kettl 1993; Miller 1997; Moe 1984).

That is the reason why the concentration of political power in a few hands has been well received by many scholars.

As outlined earlier in this book, we disagree both that agents are the central source of organizational problems and that the solution can be written down in contracts. Instead, we follow scholars who have pointed out that the main problem for an efficient organization concerns trust and that this hampers the possibility for reforms (Levi 2005; Miller 1992; Miller and Falaschetti 2001). No organization can work without trust, but it is particularly important to note that it is not only the management of the organization that needs to trust the members; it is equally important that the members trust the management.

Performance-related pay, the subject of analysis in this chapter, provides an example of why this is a problem. It is widely held that PRP would increase productivity, but it often fails to deliver because employees suspect that the management would, *ex post*, manipulate the system to its advantage at the expense of the workers (Hays 1988; Lazear 1996; Miller 1992). The reason for this is that at period t, a manager can offer her employees a premium x for a concrete and measurable goal achieved, for example a reduction of crime rates in a certain neighborhood for a police inspector, or the number of items assembled in a factory line. However, the interaction between managers and employees can change once the latter start delivering their work. At period t+1, the manager knows employees' real marginal cost of effort functions and may therefore lower the PRP to x − y if she considers that the initial reward was too high in the light of the new data gathered on employees' effort functions (Falaschetti 2002, 163).

This means that organizations suffer a problem of time inconsistency similar to the problem that Kydland and Prescott (1977) and Weingast and Marshall (1988) detected in political economy: in period t+1 governments have incentives to renege on the promises given to economic agents in period t (Foss, Foss, and Vázquez 2006). The anticipation of an opportunistic intervention – by a manager against employees' interests or by a government against its citizens' interests – leads to a Pareto-suboptimal Nash Equilibrium (Miller 1992). Employees do not believe the manager will keep her promise and, as a result, they will not invest in, for example, new reforms. This is clearly a suboptimal outcome for all. Both counterparts in a potentially fruitful relationship would be better off if there was a credible guarantee that the *ex post* opportunistic intervention will not take place. As outlined in Chapter 2, our suggestion is that it is exactly this kind of lack of trust between managers and public employees that hinders reforms in the public sector.

How can organizations overcome this problem of managerial opportunism? On the one hand, we want managers who can actually manage, and who, in the words of Williamson (1996, 150), intervene "for good cause (to support expected net gains)." On the other, we want to minimize the managers' interventions "for bad (to support the subgoals of the interventor)" cause. The suggestion from organizational research contends that the chances for mutual trust in an organization are much higher when the ruler's power is balanced, very much in the way we described in Chapter 2 (Falaschetti and Miller 2002; Foss, Foss, and Vázquez 2006; Miller 1992). Groups with different interests should both be represented at the top in the organization.

Similar power sharing actually goes on in private sector organizations. For example, the separation of ownership and control typical of the American corporation is well known, but there is also other evidence that corporations with ownership separated from control seem to solve organizational problems of credibility better than those without checks and balances. Garvey and Gaston (1991) explore what types of firms introduce deferred compensation schemes. These schemes consist of paying employees less than their marginal products early in their careers and paying them more later in their careers. However, not all corporations that could install these schemes do so in practice. As Garvey and Gaston (1991) find, the more diffused the ownership of a firm is, the more likely it is that the firm will have deferred compensation schemes.

The problem of trust is probably an important aspect of an explanation of variation in PRP systems in the public sector, where "gain sharing" is a "radical ideal for government" (Risher 1999, 334). As the OECD (2005) notes, "...monitoring and measuring performance – especially the conduct of staff performance appraisals – is a difficult process. Experience indicates that the attempt to introduce highly formalised and detailed rating systems in public organisations was not successful, as it is very difficult to distinguish the average performance of the majority of employees who are working satisfactorily, no matter how complex and formal the criteria might be."

Performance assessment is even more challenging in the public sector than in private firms, since public activity invariably "requires a large element of managerial judgement" (OECD 2005). Consequently, the OECD considers, along the general lines of the organizational trust literature discussed here, that "certain conditions, such as transparency, clear promotion mechanisms and trust of top and middle management are essential before introducing a performance-oriented culture. PRP policies are counterproductive in an inadequate management framework, and may in such situations increase problems linked to trust and even lead to corruption and patronage." In sum, evaluators agree that, despite all their troubles, "the mechanics of a merit increase policy is the easy part to plan" while "the 'softer' side represents perhaps 90 percent of the problem" (Risher 1999, 336). It is probably the ability to solve the inherent problem of organizational trust, related to this softer side, that explains the difference between the success and failure in implementing a PRP system.

We argue that, similar to the credible corporations studied by Falaschetti and Miller (2001), the most effective public organizations in implementing PRP systems are those that address the issue of opportunism by means of separation of interests at the top, to ensure trust toward those agents whose long-term investments are essential for organizational success. The reason is that any government offering rewards to public employees in exchange for a given performance will certainly have opportunities *ex post* to modify the incentive system to his personal (or his party's) advantage – for instance, diverting part of the money to electorally more beneficial activities.

Consequently, as the OECD (2004) notes in its critical review of the failure of many PRP systems in Western countries, it is common to see "disappointed expectations of employees who have been promised money for improved performance and then find it is funded by means of smaller increases in base pay." Similarly to what happens in the private sector, PRP systems in the public sector necessarily create uncertainty among employees. The lack of trust in management is thus one of the most serious obstacles to the development of PRP systems. The OECD (2004, 7) thus warns that "PRP should be applied in an environment that maintains and supports a trust-based work relationship (...) with on-going dialogue, information sharing, negotiation, mutual respect, and transparency being prioritized." Other observers also state that performance appraisal systems in the public sector must produce a "higher level of commitment" and be designed in a "human-istic" way (Abrahamson 1997; Thompson 2007, 59). The "biggest hurdle" (Risher 1999, 341) is to build a consensus on the "beliefs" underlying the new pay program. Even in countries largely successful in the implementation of incentives for public employees such as the United Kingdom, high levels of dissatisfaction and stress have been reported, especially in the National Health Service and education (Horton 2000, 230).

Who are the equivalents of the owners in the public sector? Although in a democracy the ultimate owners are voters, we contend here that governments, and in particular ministers or cabinet members, are the *de facto* owners of public administrations and thus the ones potentially enjoying the fruits of opportunistic actions against public employees. Unlike private sector owners, members of government are not entitled to the residual produced by public employees but, as Miller and Hammond (1994) remark, there are many ways through which politicians benefit from the residual generated by the provision of public policies. And who are the managers in the public sector? In the complex structures of administrations, it is difficult to identify a precise measure of who a public manager is, and, given the existence of many cross-country and within-country differences, any decision will have a discretionary component. We, however, rely on previous work by public administration scholars who have identified the managerial ranks of the civil service (Pollitt and Bouckaert 2011). Managers of the administration are the senior civil servants or high officials, including, among others, positions such as permanent secretaries in the United Kingdom or *directores generales* in Spain – that is, those responsible for the day-to-day management of a public administration.

When there is no separation at all between ministers and managers, that is when ministers themselves, or their political appointees, manage the incentive system, we expect PRP systems or, for that matter, any promise of future reward, which is almost always an essential part of all reforms, to be less credible than when there exists a clearer separation of the interests of ministers and mandarins. In the latter case, since it is common knowledge that the manager is not fully responsive to all the demands of her minister and, for example, she values her reputation as a committed-to-employees, long-term man-ager, public employees will more likely find the manager's promises of future rewards credible.

Studying Variation in Performance-Related Pay in the Public Sector

The goal of the empirical analysis in this chapter is to test the hypothesis presented above, together with a set of alternative explanations. We will investigate whether countries where the careers of politicians and bureaucrats are separated implement PRP in the public sector more. As discussed above, we would interpret such a relationship as an indication that public employees are more willing to invest in public management reforms when they have good reasons to trust their managers, which we suggest is the case when politicians and bureaucrats have separated interests. The bulk of the analysis will be large-N cross-country comparisons, but we also provide illustrations from several countries, such as France, Sweden, and Spain.

We start the analysis in the next section by showing that there is indeed a strong bivariate correlation between the separation of careers of politicians and bureaucrats, on the one side, and the degree to which PRP is used in the public sector, on the other. We move on to a multivariate analysis, using an OLS estimator, including indicators of the alternative explanations discussed above. As both our main independent and our dependent variable are from the QoG Expert Survey, we also re-run our analysis with an indicator of the separation of careers from another source (Dahlström and Lapuente 2010). As a final step, we address a potential problem concerning sequencing. An objection to our results could be that both the separation of careers and the introduction of PRP reforms in the public sector are parts of a general NPM package. Therefore, we demonstrate that the institutions separating the careers of politicians and bureaucrats precede the introduction of PRP. We do this in two steps. First, we use an instrument variable technique, with an external regressor that captures the division between politicians and bureaucrats in a longer perspective (Charron, Dahlström, and Lapuente 2012). Second, we discuss the experiences in Sweden and Spain in more detail in order to show that the separation of careers indeed preceded the introduction of PRP in Sweden and that the within-country variation in Spain speaks in favor of our hypothesis.

We measure the degree of PRP in the public sector with the help of expert assessments from the QoG Expert Survey (Teorell, Dahlström, and Dahlberg 2011). This is thus our main dependent variable. It is measured on a scale from 1 to 7, and the exact wording of the question asked the experts is given in Table 2.2 in Chapter 2.

Table 6.1 *Descriptive statistics*

Variable	N	Mean	Std. dev.	Min	Max
Performance- related pay	107	2.95	0.94	1.23	5.62
Meritocratic recruitment	107	4.28	1.09	1.88	6.58
Minister/mandarin relations	25	0.52	0.50	0	1
Ln(GDP/cap)	178	8.48	1.31	5.42	11.06
Year open to trade	134	85.72	16.69	50	100
Year with center-right government	175	7.13	9.57	0	36
English legal origin	190	0.33	0.47	0	1
OECD	107	0.27	0.45	0	1
Bureaucratic history	30	0.47	0.51	0	1

Comment: Table 6.1 summarizes all variables. With the exception of the data on years with center-right government, the variables are available in the QoG standard dataset (Teorell et al. 2013) or the QoG Expert Survey (Teorell, Dahlström, and Dahlberg 2011).

On the independent side, we use two different indicators, the first one also from the QoG Expert Survey. It measures the level of meritocratic recruitment to the public sector on a scale from 1 to 7. Our second indicator of the separation of interests of politicians and bureaucrats is originally from Pollit and Bouckaert (2011) and is coded for twenty-five countries by Dahlström and Lapuente (2010). This is a dummy variable where 0 indicates that they are integrated, while 1 indicates separated careers.

We also include a number of political, economic, and cultural variables that previous research has suggested. On the economic side, we take GDP per capita (logged) from the World Bank and the years of openness to trade from Sachs and Warner (1995). We use the legal origin for common law countries as a proxy for the Anglo-Saxon administrative tradition. This is coded as a dummy variable, and data come from La Porta et al. (1999). On the political side, finally, we use the years of center-right government from 1975 to 2010. This is a cumulative variable where the party of the executive is coded, using data from Keefer (2010). With the exception of the years of center-right government, all control variables are available from the QoG dataset (Teorell et al. 2013). Table 6.1 summarizes the variables.

Separated Careers, Trust and PRP Reforms

We expect that public employees are willing to make investments in public management reforms to a larger extent if they have good reasons to trust their managers. On the basis of Miller (1992) and Falaschetti and Miller (2001), we assume this will occur more often if the careers of politicians and bureaucrats are separated. In the introduction and the theoretical section of this chapter, and in Chapter 2, we explain in more detail why. While this is quite a general claim, we have decided on a research strategy where we try this idea on a specific, but paradigmatic, reform in the public sector, namely the introduction of PRP. In order to empirically establish this relationship in its simplest form, and thus to see whether there is any substance to our idea, we start our empirical analysis by showing the bivariate correlation

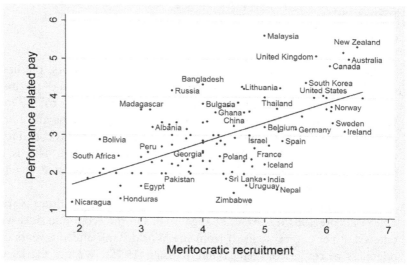

Figure 6.1 Correlation between performance-related pay in the public sector and meritocratic recruitment

Comment: The Y-axis shows the degree of performance-related pay in the public sector. The X-axis reports the extent to which the merits of the applicants decide who gets the job in the public sector, 1 (not at all) to 7 (a very large extent). Data cover 107 countries and come from the QoG Expert Survey (Teorell, Dahlström, and Dahlberg 2011).

between meritocratic recruitment, which is our preferred indicator of separation of careers, and PRP in the public sector.

On the independent side, we use a measure of the extent to which merit decides who gets a job in the public sector and, on the dependent side, we use an indicator of how closely linked salaries of public sector employees are to appraisals of their performance. Both are items from the QoG Expert Survey and are measured on a scale from 1 (hardly ever) to 7 (almost always). It should be noted that we also tried using an indicator of the level of politicization and the index of professionalization instead of the meritocracy indicator, and the results are substantially the same.

In Figure 6.1, we graphically show the correlation between meritocratic recruitment and performance-related pay. The comparison includes 107 countries. On the X-axis we report the degree of merit, and on the Y-axis we report the extent to which performance-related pay is used in the public sector. The bivariate relationship between the two variables is positive, strong, and statistically significant (R=0.61, p < 0.00), which is just what our theory suggests.

Although the correlation presented in Figure 6.1 does not include any control variables, and we thus run an obvious risk of omitted variable bias, we think that the results reported there are interesting. The reason is that meritocratic recruitment and PRP are not obviously connected to each other in any other way, while we present a theoretically grounded reason for why they should correlate. We can see how countries such as Australia, New Zealand, and the United Kingdom, known in the literature as "NPM countries" because of their reforming zeal, are precisely the countries at the top of the PRP scale (Ongaro 2012). For example, the British PRP system is, according to the OECD (2009, 2011), a particularly ambitious one. It not only involves bonuses for civil servants in the top category of the performance rating but also requires civil servants with unsatisfactory performance to set performance improvement plans, which are subsequently reviewed half a year later (OECD 2011).

Next to them in the top right corner of the graph is Canada, singled out by the OECD (2011, 141) for its innovative Performance Management Program. As mentioned in the theoretical section, one important difficulty in implementing PRP systems in the public sector is that, in the provision of different public services, they often depend on each other. The results tend to be more *team production* than individual

actions.[1] Consequently, performance appraisal in the public sector
should not only be a question of what particular activities public
employees carry out but also how they perform these activities in
interaction with other people (OECD 2009). The Canadian system of
performance appraisal is a forerunner in trying to capture this issue,
and its "performance ratings are based on what results were achieved
as well as how they were achieved" (OECD 2011, 141).

In the middle of the scale, and lower than most other European
countries, we find France. Several studies have actually noted a mechanism similar to the one presented here to understand the low levels of
PRP in the public sector in France. In general, France is considered a
"laggard" in the introduction of NPM reforms in human resources
(Thompson 2017, 51) and, as Figure 6.1 shows, has very limited performance payment. The OECD notes that France tends to use bonuses,
and not merit increments, as PRP (OECD 2004, 32), and thus that
"there is no real PRP system in France" (OECD 2003, France).

The lack of a clear delimitation between the careers of politicians
and civil servants actually helps us to understand the limited use of
PRP in the French public sector. To start with, as a 2004 report of a
French committee of enquiry into the cost and efficiency of public
services outlined, one of the main flaws of the performance appraisal
process in France is that "the adjustments made are not all based on an
objective appraisal process. Individual appraisals with systematic
annual interviews are by no means the rule. The opacity of the bonus
system and the lack of rigor in the methods for individual and collective staff appraisal, [which are not] based on explicit criteria, lessen
the legitimacy of bonus adjustments" (OECD 2004, 38). Likewise,
the OECD country report on the implementation of PRP in France
denounces its "lack of transparency," that it is "complex and obscure
for most civil servants," and, finally, that "bonuses are usually distributed according to other criteria than performance" (OECD 2003). In
addition, while the management of British PRP is delegated to autonomous agencies, pay setting is highly centralized in France (Thompson
2007). All this contributes to low credibility of the PRP system in
France and, according to our hypothesis, it thus explains why PRP is
used much less in France than in other European countries.

However, in order to handle the risk of having variables omitted
from the regression, we run a multivariate regression analysis, presented in model 1 in Table 6.2. In this model, we control for factors

that have been suggested to explain NPM reforms, of which PRP is one. Roughly, general explanations of the adoption of NPM reforms search for causes of cross-country variations in three spheres: administrative tradition, politics, and economics. According to these theories, NPM is a result of the Anglo-Saxon administrative tradition (Castles and Merrill 1989; Peters 1992; Pollit 1990; Pollitt and Bouckaert 2011), the rule of right-wing governments (Bach 1999; Barlow et al. 1996; Lee and Strang 2006; Pollitt, 1993), or economic development and globalization (Cope, Leishman, and Starie 1997, 448; Drori, Jang, and Meyer 2006, 209; Dobbin, Simmons, and Garret 2007; De Francesco 2012; Keller 1999; Thompson 2007). In addition to this, we include a control for OECD membership, as the OECD has actively pushed for NPM reforms generally and for performance-related pay specifically (OECD 2011; see De Francesco 2012 for a similar argument concerning regulatory impact assessment).

The main independent variable in the first model is the meritocratic recruitment variable from the QoG Expert Survey; the dependent variable is the PRP indicator from the same survey, while five controls for administrative tradition, economic openness and development, and the influence of center-right governments are included. What is most interesting for the purpose of the book is that meritocratic recruitment shows the expected positive sign and is highly statistically significant. Of the control variables, the English legal origin (our proxy for the Anglo-Saxon administrative tradition) and the log of GDP/capita have statistically significant effects in the expected direction, while years of openness to trade (our globalization measure) and OECD membership have no statistically significant effect. Perhaps most surprising is the statistically significant and negative effect of years of center-right government, which goes against our expectations. However, scholars have also pointed out that there are several examples of social democratic governments – for example in Sweden, New Zealand, and the Netherlands – that have implemented encompassing NPM reforms (Aberbach and Christensen 2001; De Vries and Yesilkagit 1999; Hood 1996; Yesilkagit and De Vries 2004). The negative and statistically significant coefficient might therefore be interpreted as a sign that social democratic governments are either more willing or more able to implement NPM reforms.

As our main independent measure and our dependent measures are from the same survey, we use another indicator on the independent

Table 6.2 *Meritocratic recruitment and performance-related pay in the public sector (OLS estimates)*

	(1)	(2)	(3)	(4)
Meritocratic recruitment	0.41***	–	0.78**	–
	(0.10)		(0.26)	
Minister/mandarin relations	–	1.25***	–	1.60***
		(0.38)		(0.46)
Ln(GDP/cap)	0.23*	-0.35	0.13	-0.194
	(0.117)	(0.88)	(0.84)	(0.944)
Years open to trade	-0.0072	0.0070	0.0096	0.0107
	(0.0076)	(0.021)	(0.018)	(0.0205)
Years with center-right government	-0.0173*	0.0094	-0.0047	0.0161
	(0.0093)	(0.018)	(0.016)	(0.0175)
English legal origin	0.37*	0.63	–	–
	(0.28)	(0.40)		
OECD	-0.35	–	–	–
	(0.28)			
Instrument variable	no	no	Yes	yes
Constant	0.010	5.68	-2.43	3.808
	(1.41)	(9.91)	(8.66)	(10.51)
N	94	23	28	22
R^2	0.40	0.64	0.54	0.645
adj. R^2	0.358	0.53	0.46	0.561

Comment: Entries in models 1 and 2 are OLS regression coefficients, while models 3 and 4 are two-stage OLS estimates (standard errors in parentheses). Models 3 and 4 use a measure of the state administration in the eighteenth century according to Ertman (1997) and coded by Charron, Dahlström, and Lapuente (2012). The dependent variable is the degree of performance-related pay in the public sector and comes from the QoG Expert Survey (Teorell, Dahlström, and Dahlberg 2011). OECD=Organization of Economic Co-operation and Development. The OECD variable is excluded from models 2–4 as all countries included in those analyses are OECD members. The English legal origin variable is excluded from models 3 and 4 because of a high correlation with the instrument (but see footnote 7 for a report of the results when the English origin variable is included). * $p < 0.10$, ** $p < 0.05$, *** $p < 0.01$

side in model 2, reported in the second column of Table 6.2. We do this in order to make sure that there is no underlying variable that affects the experts' assessments in both variables. We therefore use a coding of the relationship between the careers of politicians and bureaucrats based on Pollitt and Bouckaert (2011) and coded by Dahlström and Lapuente (2010). This variable captures whether the careers of politicians and bureaucrats are integrated or separated and is called minister/mandarin relations. We only have data on this variable for twenty-five OECD countries, however, which obviously strongly restricts the sample.

The minister/mandarin variable is a dummy variable, where 0 indicates that the careers of politicians and bureaucrats are integrated while 1 indicates that the careers are separated. We thus expect it to have a positive effect on the degree of PRP in the public sector. As reported in model 2 in Table 6.2, the minister/mandarin variable indeed has a strong, positive, and statistically significant effect even in this small sample. The effects of English legal origin, the log of GDP/capita variables, and years with center-right government reduce such that they are no longer statistically significant. The coefficient of the log of GDP/capita and years with center-right government are even opposite to what is reported in column 1. (The OECD control is excluded, as all countries in the sample are members.) Most important from the perspective of this book, however, is that our theory survives this test, which makes us more confident that the result in model 1 is not spurious.

We also re-ran all the models with another PRP indicator. We regressed our variables on a 4-degree indicator of PRP from OECD (2004), using an ologit estimator. These analyses confirm the results reported in columns 1 and 2 in Table 6.2 (the results are not shown in the table but are available on request).

We now turn to the time sequence of our main independent and dependent variables. One plausible objection to the analyses discussed above would be that both the introduction of PRP in the public sector and the separation of careers between politicians and bureaucrats are part of a larger NPM reform package. We take two steps to be able to disregard that possibility as much as possible. First, we instrument for meritocratic recruitment and minister/mandarin relations by using an external regressor. Institutions separating the interests of politicians and bureaucrats have been suggested to have deep historical roots, which in itself speaks against the possibility that both are part of the same reform package (Painter and Peters 2010; Pierre 1995a; Pollit and Bouckaert 2011). It also means that it might be possible to find an instrumental variable that picks up this historical experience and thus primarily affects PRP in the public sector today through the separation of interest mechanism. We use the same instrument as was used in Chapters 4 and 5, namely a measure of whether the administration was mainly bureaucratic or patrimonial in the eighteenth century according to Ertman (1997) and as coded by Charron, Dahlström, and Lapuente (2012).

Models 3 and 4 in Table 6.2 report the results when this instrument variable is used in a two-stage regression. In both models, the effect of the separation of careers indicators continues to be statistically significant, even though the sample is now very restricted, with only twenty-eight and twenty-two countries, respectively. The effect of the meritocratic recruitment variable in column 3 is almost doubled, while the effect of the minister/mandarin variable in column 4 increases by about 30 percent. As both the specification and the sample have changed, however, it is hard to say why this increase occurs.

While both of our indicators of separation of careers are statistically significant on the 0.01 level, the control variables are not. Still, it is important to note that we excluded the English legal origin control from models 3 and 4 because of its high correlation with our instrument variable. We describe in another paper, together with Nicholas Charron, that it is probable that the state infrastructure, including the relationship between politicians' and bureaucratics' careers, precedes the legal origin (Charron, Dahlström, and Lapuente 2012). We therefore think that it is justified to exclude the English legal origin control.

We, however, also tried including the English legal origin variable. The results point in the same direction when we do, but the effect of the meritocratic recruitment variable in the first of the models is reduced so that it falls just below standard thresholds for statistical significance, while the English legal origin variable is just above. In the second model, the effect of the minister/mandarin variable is significant on the 0.10 level while all other variables are not (results not shown but available on request).

The results from models 3 and 4 indicate that the separation of careers between politicians and bureaucrats has historical roots and that it is not a product of an NPM reform pressure. We therefore think that these results strengthen our interpretation that the separation of careers precedes the introduction of PRP, which makes it much less likely that they are both the outcome of some (unobserved) omitted variable.

In addition to quantitative tests, we now turn to a more detailed discussion of the sequencing and take a closer look at one country that introduced PRP systems in the public sector and one that was not able to do that. The two countries are Sweden and Spain. Sweden, indeed, has a long tradition of separation of careers between politicians and bureaucrats, which probably increases the capacity for reform. To the contrary, the Spanish case shows how a history of a lack of separation of careers precedes the relatively unsuccessful implementation of PRP systems and, for that matter, of many other reforms.

The relationship between politicians' and bureaucrats' careers is generally a product of long historical processes that were not introduced in recent decades (Pierre 1995a; Pollit and Bouckaert 2011). Sweden is one example. Swedish ministries are very small in comparative terms. They have been organized since 1997 in a single authority – the Government Offices (*Regeringskansliet*). In the Government Offices, there are today thirteen ministries with about 3,800 employees and, among them, a relatively small number of 173 political appointees (Dahlström and Pierre 2011). More importantly, the Government Offices almost exclusively focus on policymaking, with no direct involvement in policy implementation. The bulk of state activities, which in most countries take place in the ministries, are carried out in Sweden by semi-autonomous agencies. These agencies are not only organizationally separate from the ministries; the Swedish constitution indeed restricts the possibilities that ministers have to issue direct orders to the agencies (Instrument of Government; for a comparative perspective see van Thiel 2011).

The division between ministries and agencies is often considered the backbone of the Swedish administrative model and is sometimes referred to as a *dualistic* structure of the administration (Premfors 1991; Ruin 1991). This dualism clearly separates politicians from bureaucrats. The dualistic structure of the Swedish public administration has deep historical roots and was first introduced at the beginning of the eighteenth century. Andersson (2004) describes how the dualism has been discussed since then but writes that it still is a defining factor in how the public sector is organized in Sweden. It is especially important in this chapter to bear in mind that this delegation from politicians to agencies involves discretion in managing public employees' recruitment and pay (Pierre 2004).

Sweden long had a general and centralized grading and pay system that applied to the entire public sector. This began to change in 1985 when the Swedish Riksdag passed the Government's Personnel Policy Bill, making results and efficiency the top priority (Swedish Government Proposition 1984/85: 219). A series of decisions followed this bill and, between 1985 and 1989, Sweden abolished the salary grade scheme and implemented a performance appraisal system in the public sector. These dissensions were coupled to a number of other reforms whose common goal was to de-regulate and de-centralize pay policies for public employees (Riksdagens revisorer 2002). Pay is thus negotiated between individual public employees and their supervisors, and the "pay for performance is integrated in the yearly process of setting pay increases" (Willem, Janvier, and Henderickx 2006, 614).

As a result, Sweden is today considered to have a well-developed economic incentive system in the public sector with a close link between performance and pay (OECD 2011; Pollitt and Bouckaert 2011). Indeed, within the OECD context, seniority is still an important criteria for setting salaries for civil servants, but nowadays Sweden is "the exception" (Willem, Janvier, and Henderickx 2006, 616). After previously having a highly centralized pay system, currently, "individualism and flexibility in pay are only [of six OECD countries explored] truly adopted in Sweden" (Willem, Janvier, and Henderickx 2006, 617). Scholars emphasize that Sweden has experienced a remarkable change from traditional norms of equal pay to a more clearly performance-based system. In recent decades, Sweden has made "a clear movement away from centralized wage negotiation and fixed salary increases towards more flexible and individualized pay rates" (Wise 1993, 75). All in all, it is clear that the division between politicians' and bureaucrats' careers substantially pre-dates the introduction of PRP in the public sector.

Studies on the introduction of individualized salaries for Swedish public employees emphasize some of the mechanisms discussed here. Take the introduction of individualized pay for teachers in the 1990s, analyzed by Strath (2004). In the beginning, teacher unions opposed the proposal, fearing "subjectivity" of the local governments ultimately in charge of Swedish schools. In order to avoid "subjectivities," five-year agreements between employers and teachers unions were reached in which conditions were set on how the individualized pay would be conducted. The goal has been to "encourage(s) a dialogue between the teacher and the closest manager." This has been possible, to start with, because of the political independence of managers in the Swedish system, but, in addition, this dialogue is reinforced by the involvement of local union representatives "in making sure that the pay review is conducted in a fair manner." And in the few instances where it has not been possible, it has been due to a "lack of trust" among the different parties involved in the local educational system, including politicians (Strath 2004, 12).

The Spanish experience is rather different. There is much literature that places the systematic politicization of Spain's public administration, at the very least, with the collapse of the *Ancien Regime* after the Napoleonic invasion (1808). The public administration of the previous Absolutist regime was disrupted by the military invasion but, at the same time, a Bonaparte-like administration did not have time to take shape in Spain during the short French occupation (Jiménez-Asensio 1989. (For an extensive analysis of the Spanish Absolutist administration in the late eighteenth century, see De la Oliva and Gutiérrez Reñón 1968; Nieto 1976, 1986, 1996.) As early as 1810, an independent political regime started in the southern city of Cádiz, and the liberal Constitution of Cádiz was enacted in 1812. A new type of public administration then emerged in Spain based on an extensive use of spoils, known in Spain as the *cesantía system* (Jiménez-Asensio 1989; Parrado 2000).

Administrative scholars agree that one of the key requirements for candidates applying to the civil service was "electoral loyalty to a party, in particular to a certain stream within the party, and very especially to some political bosses" (Nieto 1996, 390–1). A decree issued in 1835 crudely shows how merit ranks second to political loyalty in the civil service: "may be removed those employees... who do not identify with the political or administrative course of the government or who, in spite of their good qualities as employees, do not have Minister's approval." Similarly, as one opposition MP denounced in the Spanish parliament in the late nineteenth century, it was not capacity but connections that seemed to matter. It was government loyalists who "obtain, without preparation or exams, the highest posts, with a reduction of the rights and aspirations of those who exhibit aptitude, zeal and competence" (quoted in Jiménez-Asensio 1989, 188).

Scholars have noted that this politicization also affected the credibility of organizational incentives at that time. Nieto (1976; 1996) describes that nineteenth-century civil servants' chief concern was the fact that the ambiguity of the spoils system had created a degree of "unsupportable anguish" among employees. In other words, public employees felt uncertain as to whether they would or would not be properly rewarded. In 1875, the well-known politician Lorenzo Domínguez described the problems created by the government's lack of credibility: "the employee knows that her application, assiduity, zeal, will be of little use, not only for promoting, but even for keeping her job"; and "she lives in a continuous state of alarm and start, fearing that some politician will require her post to compensate some relative, friend or protégée. The employee who notices, sees and fears all this, how is she going to work with zeal? Which kind of stimulus does she have?" (Domínguez 1875, 27). The public administrative literature on Spain thus shows that politicization was there long before any performance-related incentive systems and probably fatally affected the incentives of employees as early as in the nineteenth century.

If we move to the implementation of public management reforms today, Spain is seen as a country with a low level of reforms both in general (Ongaro 2008; Barzelay and Gallego 2010) and in terms of PRP for public employees (Dahlström and Lapuente 2010, 2011). At the same time, it must be noted that a few particular Spanish public agencies have undergone remarkable managerial reforms – even a managerial revolution. Parrado (2008) captures these differences in Spain:

This idea [i.e. all Spanish administrations as NPM 'laggards'] could be questioned by talking to and training senior civil servants and public managers of different government levels in Spain. It is not uncommon to witness that public managers working in identical or very similar services from different organisations or sites do not talk the same language. Some are performance oriented, work by results, practice merit payment and run their services in a managerial fashion while others are entrenched in the old bureaucratic culture less prone to change. Some would use the same language as their counterparts in the avant-garde countries of managerial reforms, while others would have severe difficulties to understand what is implied by each term of the managerial glossary.

This may be seen as an argument against the hypothesis presented in this chapter but, as we have argued elsewhere (Dahlström and Lapuente 2010), the existence of these within-country differences does not undermine our theoretical proposition. The reason why a few

Spanish agencies have been able to implement ambitious NPM reforms is that they do not suffer from the problems of politicization of the bureaucracy to the same extent as mainstream public bureaucracies. For instance, one of Spain's flagship agencies in NPM reforms – the Institute of National Social Security (INSS) – shows the characteristics of a separation of politicians' and bureaucrats' careers, given that the INSS is a "semi-autonomous public body" that enjoys "autonomy and functional disaggregation from the parent ministry" (Parrado 2008, 25). INSS's institutional configuration has probably played a decisive role in explaining its ability to reform, also within the field of performance-related pay (OECD 2005).

Conclusion

We started this chapter by asking why some countries do not reform their public administration, even under the most severe pressure. Now, nine years after the economic crisis began in 2008, one would expect public management reforms in Southern Europe. But we see almost no examples.

One reason for this, we think, is that public management reforms are unlikely when there are no good reasons for public employees to trust their managers, which is the case in Spain. Public employees will not make any extra effort if they are not certain that they will be rewarded. Previous research on private firms and other organizations has shown that when owners and managers are separated from each other employees have greater reason to trust their managers (Falaschetti and Miller 2001; Miller 1992). In line with this reasoning, we suggest that public employees will trust their managers more when the careers of these managers are separated from the careers of politicians, and thus that reforms in public management will be more likely in those cases.

It is important to note that our theory is not about what creates pressure for reform in the first place; it can be economic pressure, new ideas, or something else. What we describe are the organizational prerequisites for flexibility in government that make reforms less or more likely. We therefore chose a test case where there is no doubt that the pressure for public management reforms has been strong for decades. NPM has been high on the agenda since the 1980s, and one of its most paradigmatic components is performance-related pay. PRP reforms are also a new feature in the public sector, which, taken together, makes it a good case for testing our theory.

We have data for over one hundred countries in our most inclusive test, and the results have shown a strong positive correlation between meritocratic recruitment to the public sector and performance-related pay in the same, which is indeed what we would expect of the theory. This relationship also holds when we include a set of alternative explanations previously suggested in the literature. We also addressed a potential objection to our interpretation of the results. It could be claimed that both separation of careers and PRP reforms are parts of a more general reform package, and that the relationship is spurious. We therefore used an instrument variable technique to demonstrate that the separation of careers probably precedes PRP reforms in a larger sample, and we discussed the Swedish and Spanish cases in more detail to show the same sequencing in those two countries.

We interpret these empirical results as indicating that integration of politicians' and bureaucrats' careers hampers reform capacity in the public sector. If a more flexible government is desired, in Southern Europe for example, the close connections between politics and bureaucracy should probably first be untied.

7 | Conclusions

The Road to High Government Quality

We have tried to explain why there are good reasons to expect countries where careers of politicians and bureaucrats are separated to have fewer failures in government, corruption being one such example, to be more effective in public management and service delivery, and to be more prone to efficiency-enhancing reforms in the public sector. Generally, we argue that setting incentives right is more important than formal rules, laws, and auditing, and that career prospects are essential determinants of individual behavior in the political and bureaucratic sectors alike. If politicians and bureaucrats have different career incentives, they are more likely to mutually monitor each other, and more likely to have the courage to say no to corruption and wasteful spending. A separation of careers also contributes positively to effectiveness and reform initiatives, because it gears incentives away from short-sighted gains, toward professional and service-oriented goals.

This suggestion is rooted in a both academic and practically oriented discussions about how relations between politicians and bureaucrats should be organized that started as early as the late nineteenth century (Goodnow 1900; Northcote and Trevelyan 1853; Weber [1921] 1978; Wilson 1887). There is indeed an ongoing debate on these issues in political science and public administration, from which we have learned a lot, but we think these insights have had too little influence on the discussion of the quality of government (Aberbach, Putnam, and Rockman 1981; Grindle 2012; Hood and Lodge 2006; Lewis 2008; Miller 2000; Peters and Pierre 2004; Rauch and Evans 2000; Rothstein 2011).

The purpose of this book is therefore to identify how the relationship between politicians and bureaucrats is important for the quality of government, and test this suggestion empirically on a broad set of countries. We try to specify the causal paths through which we think career incentives influence societal development and in what areas effects should occur. As indicated above, we think that career incentives are fundamental, as they both influence day-to-day monitoring, management, and motivation in the public sector, and that the career incentives, in turn, are largely determined by the recruitment process. We therefore expect countries with a separated career structure to be less corrupt, have higher government effectiveness, and have more successful efficiency-enhancing reforms in the public sector.

In a series of quantitative tests, supported also by contemporary and historical case studies, we have seen how the effects of separation of careers are robust to the inclusion of controls from the different literatures that have previously analyzed corruption, government effectiveness, and administrative reforms. For example, irrespective of regime type, economic development, electoral system, political majority, legal origin, and administrative tradition, the degree of separation of careers in the state apparatus matters for understanding why some countries score higher than others on different indicators of government performance.

Not taking separation of careers into account when trying to understand country differences in quality of government could lead to biased conclusions and, centrally for those interested in reforms, also to wrong policy implications. For example, prevailing policy recommendations often concern political institutions, while, quite differently, the picture that emerges from our analyses is that the bureaucratic institutions are central to good government. There are separation of power systems that perform well, such as the United States, and others that perform more poorly, as in Latin America; there are majoritarian electoral systems seen as underpinning the rule of law and government effectiveness (Britain) and others where it is linked to divisive politics and bad performance (Jamaica); and there are countries with proportional electoral rules and coalition governments that function better in some regions (Northern Europe) than in others (Southern Europe).

In the light of the evidence presented in this book, the explanation for these puzzles lies in the fact that the nature of bureaucratic institutions is just as or even more important than the nature of the political institutions. What the high performing governments in the examples just listed have in common is a relatively high separation of careers in their state apparatuses. Policy processes in those countries are the result of the struggles, tensions, and forced collaboration between two factions, namely politicians and bureaucrats, that counterbalance each other. To the contrary, policies in low performing governments tend to be dominated, in some cases even monopolized, by one faction that can impose its first-best option at the expense of social welfare.

The next section in this chapter summarizes the theoretical arguments and empirical findings of the book. Following those insights, we will turn to a discussion of the broader theoretical implications of the results and pinpoint four discussions to which we think the book makes contributions: the research on the relationship between economic resources and institutional quality; the studies on the effects of democracy on good government; the scholarship on Weberian bureaucracies; and theories on managerial control of large organizations. Finally, we end the book with a reflection about potential policy implications of our findings.

Organizing Leviathan

We started the theoretical chapter by arguing that public administration has more to offer to the comparative literature in economics and political science than is normally acknowledged. Although the literature in economics, for example, has indeed taught us a lot about the fundamental relationship between intuitions and power elites, on the one hand, and economic and social well-being, on the other, it often fails to take the administration into account (two examples are Acemoglu and Robinson 2012; North, Wallis, and Weingast 2009).

We think, however, that not considering the administration and its organization is a misinterpretation of the dynamic leading to high government quality, and might lead to wrong policy implications. Take the situation in the Middle East, where foreign intervention in the region has been determined by the fact that "...policy makers and political scientists alike privileged democracy as the measure of politics" (Anderson 2006, 191). The existing scholarship has given – and still does give – preference to the establishment of democratic institutions (Mitchell 2003). Policy-makers, like US Secretary of State Condoleezza Rice, endorsed the view of democracy as "the ideal path for every nation" with all the means at their disposal (Rice 2005). The narrow focus on the top political layer of the Leviathan has, however, been costly and borne little fruit.

This focus has recently been criticized by scholars who are more familiar with the importance of bureaucratic structures as essential underpinnings of government effectiveness. Sheri Berman (2010) notes in a critical overview of the efforts to increase the quality of governance in Afghanistan that "...the central challenge" is "not democracy promotion... It is state building." Berman's view is in tune with that of scholars who have underlined the administrative foundations of good government, such as Miller (2000) and Greif (2008). Following the footsteps of these scholars, we argue that although all public officials may have opportunistic temptations by virtue of their privileged position, their incentives can be geared toward socially efficient actions depending on how their career incentives are organized.

But even though much of the modern comparative literature in political science and economics has not included political and bureaucratic relations in either their theoretical or their empirical models, the idea that this relationship has far-reaching consequences is certainly not new. As mentioned above, the discussion about how to organize political-bureaucratic relations is more than a century old, and many of the most influential authors in public administration, such as Goodnow (1900), Weber ([1921] 1978), and Wilson (1887), have been part of the debate. We build on these insights when we suggest that the relations between politicians and bureaucrats determine incentives for individuals in both groups.

More specifically, we propose that how individuals in these groups think about their future careers largely influences whom they are loyal to, and thus also what goals they are likely to prioritize. What's more, our idea, again building on insights from the public administration literature, is that the most important signal about future career perspectives comes from how recruitments are made. If, for example, bureaucrats are recruited on the basis of merit or because of political affiliation, their loyalty is directly affected. In the first case, it is more likely that they will be loyal to their professional peers, while in the second case it is more likely that they will be loyal to the politician who hired them. This loyalty in turn affects both incentives to monitor the other group and thus hit the fire alarm if someone engages in illegal activities, such as corruption, and the incentives to prioritize social and economic goals over power gains.

Separation of careers is therefore of fundamental importance. The book discusses several mechanisms through which the degree of separation of bureaucrats' and politicians' careers determines government performance. First, if a bureaucrat's professional future depends on the

will of her political boss, it may both induce a fear of questioning –
let alone reporting – suspected malfeasances on the part of her superiors
and encourage an administrative behavior geared toward pleasing certain political constituencies at the expense of impartial policy implementation and advice. In such a system, with only one channel of
accountability, monitoring will probably be low, and the actors in such
a system will count on it to be so. As illustrated by the Spanish cases
discussed in Chapter 1, politicians are not afraid of being questioned by
bureaucrats in a relatively integrated career system such as the Spanish.
They know they can control the bureaucrats, because they hired them.

By contrast, in a system with separated careers, the fact that the
professional fortunes of bureaucrats and their political superiors are
separated means, as Hugh Heclo (1977, 248) pointed out, "...there
are officials with an independent career status who could exercise their
right to say 'No'." Individuals in the contrasting group – either politicians or bureaucrats – will know this and thus anticipate that illegal,
or even shady, deals will probably be brought to light. A separation of
careers therefore creates an ongoing two-way monitoring mechanism,
embedded in the organization, which is probably superior to formal
monitoring because, first, formal monitoring is costly and therefore
rare, and, second, external auditors lack the insider knowledge that
you need when you work with an issue on a day-to-day basis, and will
therefore be less efficient.

This monitoring mechanism is not only important for hampering
corruption and other illegal activities, however. It is also significant
for government effectiveness in another sense. First, with separated
careers, the probability that bureaucrats "speak truth to power"
increases a great deal, which probably decreases wasteful, although
legal, government spending (Wildavsky 1987). Again we can think
about the Spanish examples presented earlier in the book, where badly
planned infrastructure and prestige projects, such as highways, airports, and high speed trains, were pushed through by shortsighted
leaders when the bureaucrats probably should have said no, but did
not dare to because they feared the consequences.

Separated careers also influence the priorities of managers and
employees in the public sector in their daily jobs. Management of the
public sector will probably be better in a system with separated careers,
because management decisions will not be biased by partisan considerations. In an integrated system, the public manager knows that her

future depends more on the political fortunes of her sponsor than on the fulfillment of some professional goals, and this will probably push her actions away from effectiveness toward opportunism. The public employees will be similarly affected. In a separated career system, it is important for the employee to work hard to effectively deliver service for the purpose of her future career, which again will gear the system toward higher government effectiveness, while being part of the right group is important in an integrated career system.

So far, we have tried to explain why we expected separated career systems to correlate with low corruption and high government effectiveness, but we also think there are reasons why countries can be trapped with these bad outcomes. One such reason, elaborated in this book, is that with an integrated career system reform of the public sector is much harder to implement. We take inspiration from organizational researchers who have pointed out that employees in large organizations often lack motivation for creative and innovative behavior (Miller 1992). The reason is that innovations can easily be taken over by the organization, and this process cannot be regulated in contracts or through a price mechanism. It is therefore risky for an employee to make a costly investment (in time and energy) when she does not know if she can keep the fruits of her work, or even know what her innovation will be used for. Miller (1992) showed that this problem is minimized in the private sector if incentives for managers and owners are separated. We suggest that something similar happens in the public sector if the careers of politicians (who in this model have the owner's characteristics) and bureaucratic managers are separated. The separation of careers might therefore contribute not only to a higher quality of government, as described above, but also to a public sector that is much more easily adapted to external changes. Integrated careers between politicians and bureaucrats might in contrast contribute to stagnation.

Although we have built our theoretical suggestion on well-known ideas in public administration, we depart from the mainstream interpretations in some important aspects. It has been claimed since the late 1990s that characteristics of a Weberian bureaucracy should reduce corruption and raise government effectiveness. The main idea in this line of research is that formal and informal rules and the protection of bureaucrats' positions would make the bureaucracy a strong constraint on opportunistic leaders (Du Gay 2000; Evans and Rauch 1999;

Rauch and Evans 2000). We think this view underestimates the multidimensionality of the bureaucratic structures around the world and we show both theoretically (Chapter 2) and empirically (Chapter 3) that a closed – that is, an institutionally highly protected bureaucracy – is not the same thing as a separated career system. And, while the former does not correlate with low corruption, high government effectiveness, and more efficiency-enhancing reforms, the latter does. A closed Weberian bureaucracy is therefore probably not the answer, while a separated career system might very well be.

In three chapters (4, 5, and 6) we put our theoretical suggestion to empirical tests. These tests are in many ways unique, as very few datasets are available that make cross-country comparisons between bureaucratic structures in about one hundred countries possible. On the independent side, we use data from the QoG Expert Survey (Teorell, Dahlström, and Dahlberg 2011) together with a board set of economic, political, cultural, and geographical control variables, mostly taken from the QoG Standard dataset (Teorell et al. 2013). On the dependent side, we use indicators of corruption, wasteful spending, public management, and public management reforms from several different sources. Each of Chapters 4, 5, and 6 corresponds to the theoretical suggestions about low corruption, high government effectiveness, and more efficiency-enhancing reforms in countries with separated career systems. The analyses show that, even after including several demanding controls, the separation of careers indicators we use perform in accordance with our theoretical expectations. In these chapters, we have also discussed several contemporary and historical cases in order to make correct interpretations of the regressions. All in all, the empirical analyses strengthen our confidence in the suggestion, and we therefore think it is justified to move on to a discussion of theoretical and policy implications.

Theoretical Implications

Indeed, in many of the analyses presented in this book, our suggestion carries more explanatory power than the dominant accounts in the literature. This, we believe, is because our variable captures what Hamilton (1788) referred to as an "ingredient" of the good executive, namely the presence of an institution dividing the incentives of agents working within the government that acts to avoid abuses. As we have mentioned, our focus on staff policy follows the classic approach in public administration and the reformers their works inspired. As Rohr (2009, xiii) notes, "...no aspect of administration was more important for the Progressives than civil service reform." Goodnow (1900) was one of the clearest advocates of separating politics and administration with a claim similar to the one presented here. No matter how well intentioned, political interference in administrative matters is "...likely to produce evil rather than good (...) an inefficient administration in that it makes administrative officers feel that what is demanded of them is not so much work that will improve their own department, as compliance with the behest of the political party" (Goodnow 1900, 82–3). Thus, on the one hand, our book can be seen as providing evidence from a new field for the hypothesis that the greatest progress has taken place in countries that have separated politics and bureaucracy.

On the other hand, Goodnow (1900), as well as in the usual interpretation of the work of other classical scholars (Weber [1921] 1978; Wilson 1887), understood the separation of politics and bureaucracy as a separation of the career paths of politicians and bureaucrats – along the lines of what we argue here – and as a separation of the activities of politicians and bureaucrats. This latter aspect has in fact driven many administrative reforms in Western countries. The emphasis has been on separating what politicians and bureaucrats do while often leaving career aspects aside. Think, for instance, of the strict division of tasks enshrined in local governments belonging to the Napoleonic administrative tradition between elected officials – who monopolize policy decision-making – and administrative officers – who merely overview the legal aspects of those decisions and face many limitations to engaging in substantive policy discussion (see Mouritzen and Svara 2002 for a classification of municipals along these lines). Even if the legal checks by administrative officers are impeccable, administrators lack the opportunity to make a more substantive evaluation of how the policy was decided by politicians: was it truly impartial or was it devised to benefit some entrenched interests? Isolating politicians and bureaucrats may indeed prevent, instead of facilitate, the abilities of civil servants to monitor politicians and vice versa (see Heclo 1977 for a similar point). Such separations may consequently create opportunities for factions to emerge in both the political and administrative spheres.

In general, we believe that our argument on the importance of the separation of careers may contribute to different research agendas across the social sciences. We would particularly like to highlight here how this argument may help to address four puzzles in the literature concerning: (i) money and institutions; (ii) democracy and good government; (iii) Weberian bureaucracies and the quality of government; and (iv) control of large organizations.

Money and Institutions

Among the most pressing issues in the discussion about quality of government is how to go from partial to impartial (Rothstein and Teorell 2008), from "limited" to "open" access order (North, Weingast, and Wallis 2009, 2), or away from "extractive" to "inclusive" institutions (Acemoglu and Robinson 2012, 73). On the one hand, many scholars would argue that good institutions are mostly a consequence of rich economies or societal forces that are largely outside the scope of governmental action, see for instance Clark's (2007) attack on institutions in which he demystifies the institutional underpinnings of the industrial revolution, or the attempt to rescue modernization theory by Welzel and Inglehart (2008), who say that good institutions will ultimately be the result of economic development. As societies become richer, individuals care more about the quality of government.

On the other hand, other scholars claim that economic wealth, especially if it is the result of a windfall, such as natural resources or cheap credit, actually leads to poorer institutions, an idea known as the "paradox of plenty" (Karl 1997). An abundance of resources exacerbates political moral hazard because there is a larger pool from which to extract.

The argument in this book is in line with arguments of authors who consider that the institutions shaping the incentives of rulers explain these opposite effects that resources have on quality of government (see among others Fernandez-Villaverde, Garicano, and Santos 2013; Mehlum, Moene, and Torvik 2006; Roldan 2013). Natural resources yield positive effects in countries with "producer-friendly" institutions – such as Australia, Canada, the United States, or Norway – but deleterious effects in countries with "grabber-friendly" institutions – such as Sierra Leone, Angola, the Sudan, or Venezuela (Mehlum, Moene, and Torvik 2006, 1121). Similarly, the financial booms enjoyed by many

European countries after the creation of the euro had negative effects in the countries, such as Greece, Italy, or Portugal, that had poorer initial institutions (Roldan 2013).

This literature has nevertheless not answered which particular characteristic it is that turns good into bad – or producer-friendly into grabber-friendly – institutions. There is general agreement among economists, for example captured in the concept of bad equilibrium in Murphy, Shleifer, and Vishny (1993), as well as among political scientists, see the concepts of "vicious" versus "virtuous cycles" in Rothstein and Uslaner (2005, 67), that political systems can get trapped in either a high quality of government equilibrium or in a low quality one. What force drives them toward one equilibrium and not the other is far from clear in the existing literature. We have proposed one such force: A close alignment of politicians' and bureaucrats' incentives leads governments toward the pole of bad government, and a separation of those interests drives governments to the pole of good government.

Democracy and Good Government

Another long-lasting academic debate regards the ability of democratic institutions to produce quality of government. Following a long literature on accountability, one should expect that rulers subject to democratic accountability have stronger incentives to improve government performance than rulers who are not accountable to their citizens (Adserà, Boix, and Payne 2003; Barro 1973; Besley and Case 1995; Ferejohn 1986; Przeworski et al. 2000). This is also a prevailing view outside academia and has fueled both recommendations of international organizations for achieving good government and the political discourses justifying the imposition – even by military force – of democratic institutions in different regions of the world.

However, the picture that emerges from the multiple cross-national studies exploring the relationship between levels of democracy and proxies for government performance is less clear-cut than expected (Harris-White and White 1996; Montinola and Jackman 2002; Sung 2004). Some democracies do actually perform worse than some authoritarian regimes, although there is no consensus about the reasons for their underperformance. It might be that some democracies lack proper bottom-up mechanisms to control abuses (Bäck and

Hadenius 2008), credible political parties (Keefer 2007), or a critical mass of citizens preferring long-term investments rather than short-sighted consumption goods (Charron and Lapuente 2010). Conversely, democracies that score high in civil and political liberties (Bäck and Hadenius 2008), that are old (Keefer 2007), or that are wealthy (Charron and Lapuente 2010) exhibit a high quality of government.

This book has provided a further factor to help our understanding of the remarkable differences of government performance across democracies, namely the alignment of politicians' and bureaucrats' incentives. The empirical analyses we have undertaken in this book have shown that, regardless of how high a democracy scores in civil and political liberties, how many years it has or how rich it is, democracies that operate with a politicized administration perform poorly while those that work with a merit-based administration enjoy high levels of quality of government. In simple words, regimes ruled by politicians who are accountable to their citizens require bureaucrats who are not accountable to their political masters.

Furthermore, the factor introduced in this book could also contribute to an understanding of the curvilinear relationship between levels of democracy and levels of quality of government, as it opens up the possibility of an interaction between the organization of the administration and democratization over time. It is possible that the full effect of the mutual monitoring system between politicians and bureaucrats is only achieved in democratic regimes. As one of the analyses in Chapter 4 pointed out, there seems to be an interactive effect between democracy and the separation of careers, and thus between the basic nature of the political system and the basic nature of its administration. A state run by political masters who are democratically accountable to citizens in combination with an administration populated by bureaucrats who are democratically unaccountable to their political masters leads to the highest levels of government performance.

This interaction warrants further research, given its potentially great implications. Coleman and Ferejohn (1986, 25) ask for "...gaining a fuller understanding of the likely performance of democratic institutions" in order to establish the arbitrariness of different types of collective decision-making. We consider that our study contributes to an understanding of the performance of democracies by providing a mechanism that helps to disentangle what Pasquino (2008, 7) referred

to as the "...intimate connection between democracy and populism."
Following the historical experience of American checks and balances,
many political philosophers have defended the existence of strong
constitutional limitations on the rule of the majority, such as the ones
famously advocated by William Riker in *Liberalism against Populism*
(1982). According to Riker (1982), these limitations prevent the arbitrary wishes of the majority from instantly becoming law. To prevent
this potential tyranny of the majority, a democracy needs to tie the
hands of the representatives of the people via creating separate institutions that share political powers (Neustadt 1991) or with a combination of horizontal and vertical divisions of political powers (Pasquino
2008), such as in a "market-preserving federalism" (Weingast 1995).
To prevent the accumulation of power in a single large organization,
we should thus create several sub-organizations.

Nevertheless, the good performance of many democracies that lack
such constitutional constraints questions the importance of dividing
political power into different institutions. Think of the accumulation of
power in the ruling parties of Westminster parliamentarian systems,
and think also of the highly centralized polities in the Scandinavian
countries. Despite their outstanding concentration of political power in
a single party or governing coalition, these countries systematically top
most rankings of good government democracies. Populist impulses,
such as any favorable treatment of the members of the electoral majority at the expense of long-term social welfare, are stopped in these
polities, we would argue, because of the counterbalancing role played
by their highly meritocratic administrations. A, let's say, British or
Danish, newly appointed minister walks into her department either
alone or surrounded by less than a dozen party fellows – and unable to
alter the career paths of the thousands of members of her workforce.
These will dutifully follow all the commands issued by their minister –
but only as long as the commands do not hinder their professional
reputation, and thus their future career prospects. It is the prevalence
of those professional norms in Westminster and Nordic democracies –
and any others with a clear separation of politicians' and bureaucrats'
careers – that prevents the most arbitrary wishes of the majority from
becoming law. Not only this, but the professional norms of non-
politically dependent bureaucrats may be a more effective and flexible
limit to the tyranny of the majority than unavoidably rigid constitutional constraints.

Weberian Bureaucracies and the Quality of Government

A third theoretical discussion this book engages in concerns whether a Weberian bureaucracy is a necessary condition for good government, as a large strand of the literature on public administration has stated for over a century (from Weber [1921] 1978 to Evans and Rauch 1999), or, to the contrary, whether there is a "problem of bureaucracy," that is, a protected workforce that is "...inefficient, wasteful and, seemingly, out of control" (Johnson and Libecap 1994, 3). The latter view is based on the public choice assumption of budget-maximizing bureaucrats who can exploit their privileged, and well-protected, positions to extract rents from the population at large (Niskanen 1971, 41, and ch 4). Since a Weberian bureaucracy represents the removal of competitive market forces from government activities, we should expect bureaucrats to enjoy their monopolistic position. This view has not only been championed by public choice scholars, however; many politicians have considered that a bureaucracy with no direct political accountability subverted their programs (Johnson and Libecap 1994, 1). Likewise, it has been argued that a bureaucracy where officials are directly accountable to their political masters "...may not necessarily have negative consequences for the overall management of organizations or the administration of the state" (Grindle 2012, 23).

We thus have two relatively clear sides in the discussion of administrative structures and quality of government: on the one hand, a pro-Weberian front urging for strong protection of the bureaucracy and, on the other, an anti-Weberian front that demands a more accountable bureaucracy, responsive to their political masters and/or to competitive forces. The former demands an isolated bureaucracy, the latter a bureaucracy embedded in political and/or market forces.

We consider that a great deal of the disagreement between these opposite views of Weberian bureaucracy has to do with an underlying one-dimensional understanding of public administrations. Johnson and Libecap (1994, 7) justly complain about the usual treatment among many social scientists of bureaucracy as a "single unitary entity." Since bureaucracies have been seen as relatively uniform organizations, regardless of whether they are populated by patronage appointments or meritocratic ones, it is difficult to extract conclusions about their efficiency. Classifying them on a continuum from discretionary at-will appointments, on the one extreme, to highly regulated civil service regulations, on the other, has allowed insightful studies of bureaucracies – from Johnson and Libecap (1994) to Grindle (2012), to name two highly influential ones. Yet not acknowledging the two-dimensionality of a Weberian bureaucracy suggested in this book prevents previous studies from reaching stable conclusions on the effectiveness of bureaucracies. Because, if we accept that there is not only one, but two, independent dimensions underlying a Weberian bureaucracy – one regarding formal rules and the other career incentives – we are in a better position to understand the dual effects of Weberian bureaucracies on performance. As we have shown in several tests, the dimension related to bureaucratic incentives seems to exert a significant and robust positive effect on good government, while the dimension related to bureaucratic rules does not seem to share these virtues.

We can see this duality in the evaluations of bureaucracies with the example of Brazil. On the one hand, if we compare Brazil with its neighbors, we will find that it ranks high in meritocracy, both in previous studies (Grindle 2012, 149) and in ours. This may explain the relatively good performance of the Brazilian government in comparison with other Latin American countries – consider, for instance, Venezuela, Bolivia, Nicaragua – in control of corruption, government effectiveness, and the likelihood of administrative reforms. (It is, however, important to note that the performance of Brazil in these aspects is well below not only the OECD, but also other emerging economies such as Chile.)

On the other hand, Brazil occupies a top position in the second dimension – the presence of bureaucratic rules – as can be seen in our data. For instance, it is a world leader in the existence of special employment laws protecting public employees (see Chapter 3). It is Brazil's position in this second dimension, and not so much in the first dimension, that could be driving the well-known criticism of Brazilian bureaucracy. Grindle (2012) recalls the old joke about the lion that escaped the zoo and took refuge in a ministerial building where it survived eating bureaucrats without being discovered, until the day that the lion killed the employee who brought the morning coffee. It was only then that people noticed it. According to the accounts of many international observers on inefficiencies and waste in Brazilian bureaucracy, this joke about the lion may still be a fair characterization. For instance, in "How the Bureaucrats Rob the Taxpayer,"

The Economist (16-06-2012) notes that the mayor of Sao Paolo, Gilberto Kassab, ironically acknowledged that right after leaving office he would apply for a job in the garages of the city's municipal assembly, where an overprotected civil service receives salaries up to twelve times those of their counterparts in the private sector. Likewise, a year after, *The Economist* (28-09-2013), in "The Land of the Setting Sun," criticized the pensions of some high-ranked officials that can amount to up to ten times the national average salary. Not only are pensions in the public sector very generous, but the existence of special privileges for civil servants also allows them to retire much earlier. It is thus not uncommon that many teachers retire at the age of fifty. This may help explain why pensions and transfers to inactive public employees amounted to up to 45 percent of the overall Brazilian government payroll in 2002 (Iacoviello and Rodríguez-Gustá 2006). Scholars also note the high rigidity of the Brazilian civil service – which is recognized at constitutional level (Marconi, 2002) – and the margin of maneuver for simultaneously improving its merit and its flexibility (Longo 2007).

Grindle (2012) uses the view of the Brazilian bureaucracy in the lion joke as an example of the difficulties in judging the consequences of a merit-based bureaucracy: Brazil may be merit-based, but this does not mean that it has rid itself of inefficiencies. It has simply created others. This is also the underlying view in the highly cited studies by Johnson and Libecap (1994) and Heclo (1977). Merit-based systems solve some poignant problems of patronage, but they generate other problems of bureaucracy. In contrast, our interpretation is that what explains the waste and inefficiencies reported in the Brazilian civil service, or for that matter in some highly regulated American agencies, such as those noted by Moe and Caldwell (1994), or in the Napoleonic countries depicted here, is not the adoption of merit but the adoption of (stringent) civil service rules. In other words, it is not so much a problem of bureaucracy as a problem of bureaucratic rules.

The two dimensions do not need to go hand in hand. The clearest example would be the *managerial administrations* that we find in countries so culturally and geographically remote as, for instance, New Zealand and Sweden. They show that a combination between meritocratic incentives and an absence of cumbersome bureaucratic rules is not only possible but also desirable, given the fact that these countries systematically top all standard indicators of quality of government. In the data presented in this book, Sweden does, for example, end up among the top five in our indicators of separation of careers and in the bottom half of bureaucratic regulations, and this is also in accordance with previous evaluations of the high degree of separation of careers between politicians and bureaucrats (Dahlström and Pierre 2011; Pierre 1995; Pollitt and Bouckaert 2011). There thus seems to be an agreement that meritocratic recruitment is possible without strict rules and, as the Swedish case shows, more private-like recruitment processes such as screening CVs and job interviews. The cases of New Zealand and Sweden may be examples of the "mobility-contingent professionalism" defended by Teodoro (2010). On the one hand, institutions perform better if run by professionals. On the other, professionals does not mean insiders – that is, internally recruited managers in the way closed Weberian bureaucracies work. As a matter of fact, public managers with a diagonal career path are more likely to become policy innovators and exhibit better outcomes than executives promoted from within (Teodoro 2009, 2014). If public employees are not flexible, if they are not mobile, they cannot be true professionals, since, in essence, professionalism is the degree to which you are free to practice your field without restrictions (Misner 1963).

Control of Large Organizations

Finally, the book has some implications for the debate on organizational theory, particularly in corporate governance. Our work follows insight from the work of classic organizational theorists, such as Barnard (1938), Thompson (1965), and Miller (1992), on the intrinsic lack of motivation for creative and innovative behavior in large organizations. As it is impossible to write perfect contracts and the absence of price mechanisms makes any creative initiative an extremely risky adventure for those occupying middle- and low-level positions, an employee that makes a costly effort to increase productivity can never be sure that her superior will not use it opportunistically. In other words, how can the entrepreneurial employee trust that her newly discovered method for more efficient service delivery will not be either appropriated by her superior or be used to increase employees' workload?

Launching new initiatives is thus difficult in all large organizations, and particularly in public bureaucracies where the existence of economic incentives for employees is subject to numerous constraints, given the inherent tension between the interests of superiors and subordinates. As a matter of fact, Weber foresaw this organizational problem: "...historical reality involves a continuous, though for the most part latent, conflict between chiefs and their administrative staffs for appropriation and expropriation in relation to one another" (Weber [1921] 1978, 264). Yet this insight has chiefly been ignored by contemporary agency theory (Perrow 1990; Kiser and Baer 2005). These scholars have instead been concerned with the *agent* (e.g., the employee) as the main source of organizational inefficiency, overlooking the moral hazard of the *principal* (e.g., the employer). Re-discovering Weber's insight, influential political scientists – first and foremost, Gary Miller (1992), but also Margaret Levi (2005) – have remarked during the latest two decades on the importance of the trustworthiness of the principals (the political officials in our study) in the eyes of their agents (here, public employees).

The implications of this shift in the principal-agent framework, from an emphasis on the problems generated by an agent who exploits her informational advantages to greater weight on the trust problems created by powerful principals who can expropriate agents' work, has notable normative implications. For instance, from the standard perspective, organizations that separate ownership and day-to-day control, such as the American corporation, have previously been seen as an anomaly, because they violate the golden rule that there should be an alignment between the incentives of the principal and those of the agent. This, in different variations, has actually been the prevailing view among many scholars that are fairly critical of the problems the American corporation creates (Baumol 1959; Berle and Means [1932] 1968; Marris 1964). Still, following Miller's (1992) work, aligning the incentives of day to day managers with those of the owners encourages the former to act opportunistically in relations with their subordinates – who, in turn, mistrust their superiors. The separation of ownership and control characteristic of the American corporation may thus not be seen as a liability but quite the opposite: the key to its worldwide success. Likewise, we have argued that states need a similar separation between political owners – even if temporary, as they are in a democracy – and bureaucratic managers. If the career prospects of politicians and bureaucrats respond to two different channels of accountability – the political party and professional peers, respectively – they will create a trustworthy working environment that will stimulate, instead of inhibit, rank and file employees' efficiency-enhancing initiatives.

Acemoglu and Robinson (2012) argue that economic entrepreneurship is extremely difficult in a society where political power is highly concentrated. Since the ruler can always change the rules of the game unilaterally, she lacks credibility in the eyes of potentially entrepreneurial individuals, who, instead, may prefer to devote their time and effort to less productive, and very probably less risky, activities. In a similar vein, we have claimed here that employees' entrepreneurship will also be difficult in organizations where powers are concentrated in hands that share a common fate. If the career incentives of top political officials, such as cabinet ministers, and middle range managers are perfectly aligned, employees may naturally believe that those at the top of the organization will appropriate initiatives. Conversely, if there are two groups of individuals (politicians and bureaucrats) checking and counterbalancing each other, employees may feel more impelled to craft and launch creative solutions for any kind of organizational problem.

Finally, Chapter 6 shows how the career structure, and the trust that follows from it, influences the ability for public management reforms, and is thus also important for understanding why we see reforms in some public administrations and not in others. The factor presented in this book is almost absent in the extensive literature on New Public Management reforms but, as indicated by the discussion above and the empirical results in Chapter 6, it might be very important (for overviews of NPM research see Christensen and Lægreid 2011; Peters and Pierre 2001; Pollitt and Bouckaert 2011). In failing to take the prerequisites for reform into account, the NPM literature risks missing a key determinant.

The Not-So-Obvious Path to a Good Administration

Good government is crucial for sustaining rich, egalitarian, healthy, and happy societies (Holmberg, Rothstein, and Nasiritousi 2009). Consequently, many reforms to improve government performance have been promoted worldwide by international actors. The results of these reform efforts have not always been satisfactory, however. Think of Latin America, where seven countries were already recorded in 1954 to have the legal foundations of a career civil service system, and, in the 2000s, these civil service reforms *de jure* covered most countries (Grindle 2012, 144). Despite these continued efforts for reform, and with some relative exceptions such as Brazil and Chile (Iacoviello and Zuvanic 2005), "the reality of the region is one of states with a weak capacity to execute public policies" (Zuvanic, Iacoviello, and Rodríguez Gusta 2010, 148). In the view of most scholars, the prevalence of highly politicized bureaucracies in most of the region is to blame for this (Prats 2003). The relationship between politicians and bureaucrats – of an almost total dependence of the latter on the former – represents the "weakest link" in Latin American state structures (Zuvanic, Iacoviello, and Rodríguez Gusta 2010, 147). Or take sub-Saharan Africa, where the outcome of more than three decades of donor-funded public management reforms has been that the quality of public service institutions "...remains poor, seriously undermining governments' capacity to provide public goods and services to the majority of the poor" (Srivastava and Larizza 2012, 2). A major reason why reforms have failed seems to be that they have not seriously taken into account "the incentives that drive politicians and civil servants" (2; Scott 2011, Srivastava and Larizza 2012).

The failure of governance reforms is not a monopoly in the developing world. There are well-documented cases in OECD countries, where an extensive politicization of state and para-state institutions has been blamed for explaining the abandonment of the reform process after the adoption of common currency in the euro zone periphery (Fernández-Villaverde, Garicano, and Santos 2013). Even after several years with sluggish economies, the peripheral countries seem unable to implement in-depth administrative reforms. Greece is a case in point. Despite that the Memoranda attached to the loan from the IMF and EMU members granted to Greece included public service reforms, observers note that the "...pace of the reforms is slow, delays are observed and an implementation gap can be noticed" (Ladi 2012, 28).

All in all, there is a disappointment with public sector reforms that, based on the experience of successful countries, try to reproduce their best practices in institutional contexts that are not suitable, as the World Bank (2012) has recently acknowledged. Unfortunately, the two major – and very different – scholarships working on comparative institutions have not helped to understand why these reforms have failed.

Comparative political economy has been geared toward input-side institutions, neglecting bureaucratic institutions. While the incentives for achieving good policy-making seem to have been extensively studied, we lack symmetric studies on the incentives to have good policy implementation. This superficial view of the state could explain the discomforting absence of policy implications from this literature. For instance, the outstandingly encompassing description of the differences between growth-promoting and growth-inhibiting governments in *Why Nations Fail* by Acemoglu and Robinson (2012) sharply contrasts with its scarce discussion on policy implications. Likewise, the most explored variables in the dense body of cross-country quantitative studies on the determinants of quality of government have not led to precise policy implications. For instance, in the light of this literature, it is still far from clear which electoral system or which political regime we should recommend to a newly created country in order to maximize its chances of achieving a high quality of government.

In turn, the public administration literature has largely focused on either the political control of bureaucracy – a favorite theme for American scholars (Bendor, Glazer, and Hammond 2001; Calvert et al. 1987; Epstein and O'Halloran 1994; Huber and Shipan 2002; Knott and Hammond 2003; McCubbins, Noll, and Weingast 1987) – or on the things that explain the different types of bureaucracies and administrative reform trajectories – a major concern for comparative scholars (Christensen and Lægreid 2001; Hood and Lodge 2006; Peters 2002; Pollit and Bouckaert 2011). Nevertheless, with few exceptions – such as Lewis (2008, and with Krause and Douglas 2006) and Teodoro's (2009, 2011) studies of American bureaucracy, or Evans and Rauch's analyses of emerging countries (1999, 2000) – the effects of types of bureaucracies have largely been overlooked.

An explanation for that neglect may be the underlying assumption in the scholarship that there is a fundamental politico-administrative trade-off between the flexibility and direct accountability of discretionary at-will personnel systems and the risk of political patronage they create. Conversely, tying the hands of politicians with civil service regulations may prevent politicization, but this comes at the cost of rigid rules. In simple words, if we want to gain merit, we must renounce flexibility and, consequently, efficiency. If, in contrast, we want to discipline, democratize, and properly reward (or punish) the civil service, we will open the door for political opportunism.

In the light of this trade-off, reform efforts to strengthen the quality of government have mainly aimed at implementing new rules in attempts to achieve bureaucracy with Weberian characteristics. In opposition to the existence of a fundamental trade-off, this book argues that the two bureaucratic dimensions, the degree of merit and the level of closed Weberianism, are independent and therefore do not need to correlate. There are countries that have been able to achieve both merit-based professional careers in the administration and an open bureaucratic structure. This combination between flexibility and professionalism is key to understanding why the countries classified as *managerial administrations*– such as the Scandinavian countries, Canada, Australia, or New Zealand – top almost all available comparative rankings of quality of government. Likewise, we can also have the many bureaucratic rules together with a highly politicized civil service.

A mistake from earlier reforms has been to focus on closed Weberian institutions, from which this book can trace no positive effects, and largely neglect the incentives created by career perspectives, but this might begin to change. In a large-scale project to assist public sector reforms in the twenty-first century, the OECD considered that a major challenge is to "...make human resource management and employment provisions in the public service more flexible but without undermining human resource rules that prevent patronage and corruption" (OECD 2011, 12). This book has shown that this is possible, but at the same time warns that it is likely only in countries that have separated the career incentives of politicians and bureaucrats. Public employees can be recruited and promoted and can work under conditions similar to those of their private sector counterparts, and still be rewarded according to professional and not political criteria. This requires both that politicians do not get involved in recruiting and promoting bureaucrats and that, also crucially, bureaucrats do not become politicians either. The bureaucratization of politics may be as equally pernicious for quality of government as the politicization of the bureaucracy because in both cases we witness an integration of the professional fates of two distinctive factions into one single faction.

Notes

1 Why Relations between Politicians and Bureaucrats Matter

1 Original transcript "Feliz Navidad, amiguito del alma. . . .te quiero un huevo" Conversation retrieved (October 31, 2013) from: www.elpais.com/especial/caso-gurtel/.

2 Theory

1 Early exponents of this hypothesis on the importance of government (for *good* or for *bad*) for economic prosperity would be the scholars generally seen as new institutionalist economists (e.g., Buchanan and Tullock 1962; North 1981, 1990; North and Thomas 1973). Yet it has been during the last two decades that we have witnessed an explosion of empirical work offering support for this institutionalist view of economic growth (Acemoglu, Johnson, and Robinson 2001, 2005; Dollar and Kray 2003; Hall and Jones 1999; Knack and Keefer 1995; De Long and Shleifer 1993; Mauro 1995). It is obviously not without debate: while probably most would agree that "Institutions Rule" (Rodrik, Subramanian, and Trebbi, 2004), others are more skeptical, ranging between "Institutions Don't Rule" (Sachs 2003a) and "Institutions Matter, but not for Everything" (Sachs 2003b). The highly influential article asking "Do Institutions Cause Growth?" (Glaeser, La Porta, Lopez-de-Silanes, and Shleifer 2004) has so far received 1888 "responses" (i.e., citations in Google Scholar).

2 This is also obvious from the experiences of countless politicians disappointed by the narrow margin of maneuver that bureaucrats gave them to implement their wishes. British minister Barbara Castle stated this very clearly in her famous article in the *Sunday Times* (10-06-1973) with the revealing title of "Mandarin Power. An Attack on Civil Service Methods and How They Stifle True Political Decision." Her fellow minister Richard Crossman lamented in a furious entry in his diary on May 1968 that "the Department [i.e. the civil servants] takes over and does exactly what it likes" (Crossman 1977, 78). Or, as Spain's former Prime Minister (1983–1996) Felipe González famously put it, "sometimes you order an

204

aircraft to be built; and the aircraft is simply not built" (p.c. with a former collaborator, Joan Prats, 21-05-2005).

6 Reforms

1 Technically, a team production process is one in which at least two factors (not owned by a single individual) with interdependent productivities (i.e., the marginal product of each factor is a function of at least one other factor) are combined to produce some output (Alchian and Harold 1972; Falaschetti 2002).

References

Aberbach, J. D. & Christensen, T. (2001). Radical Reform in New Zealand: Crisis, Windows of Opportunity, and Rational Actors. *Public Administration* 79(2), 403–22.

Aberbach, J. D., Putnam, R. D. & Rockman, B. A. (1981). *Bureaucrats and Politicians in Western Democracies*. Cambridge, MA: Harvard University Press.

Abrahamson, E. (1997). The Emergence and Prevalence of Employee Management Rhetoric: The Effects of Long Waves, Labor Unions, and Turnover, 1875 to 1992. *Academy of Management Journal* 40(3), 491–533.

Acemoglu, D. & Robinson J. (2012). *Why Nations Fail: The Origins of Power, Prosperity, and Poverty*. Random House Digital Inc.

Acemoglu, D., Johnson, S. & Robinson, J. A. (2001). The Colonial Origins of Comparative Development: An Empirical Investigation. *American Economic Review* 91(5), 1369–1401.

(2005). Institutions as a Fundamental Cause of Long-Run Growth. *Handbook of Economic Growth*, 1, pp. 385–472.

Acemoglu, D., Verdier, T. & Robinson, J. A. (2004). Kleptocracy And Divide-and-Rule: A Model of Personal Rule. *Journal of the European Economic Association* 2(2–3), 162–92.

Ades, A & Di Tella, R. (1997). The New Economics of Corruption: A Survey and Some New Results. *Political Studies* 45(3), 496–515.

Ades, A. & Di Tella, R. (1999). Rents, Competition, and Corruption. *The American Economic Review* 89(4), 982–93.

Adserà, A., Boix, C. & Paine, M. (2003). Are You Being Served? Political Accountability and Quality of Government. *Journal of Law, Economics, & Organization* 19(2), 445–90.

Aghion, P., Algan, Y., Cahuc, P. & Shleifer, A. (2010). Regulation and Distrust. *Quarterly Journal of Economics* 125(3), 1015–49.

Alba, C. (2001). Bureaucratic Politics in Spain: A Long-Standing Tradition. In B. G. Peters and J. Pierre, eds., *Bureaucrats, Politicians and Administrative Reform*. London: Routledge, pp. 93–105.

Alchian, A. & Harold, D. (1972). Production, Information Costs, and Economic Organization. *American Economic Review* 62(5), 777–95.

206

Alesina, A. & Tabellini, G. (2007). Bureaucrats or Politicians? Part I: A Single Policy Task. *American Economic Review* **97**(1), 169–79.

Alesina, A., Baqir, R. & Easterly, W. (1999). Public Goods and Ethnic Divisions. *Quarterly Journal of Economics* **114**(4), 1243–84.

Anderson, L. (2006). Searching Where the Light Shines: Studying Democratization in the Middle East. *Annual Review of Politcal Science*, 9, 189–214.

Andersson, C. (2004). *Tudelad trots allt – dualismens överlevnad i den svenska staten 1718 1987*. Doctoral dissertation. Stockholm: Stockholm University, Department of Political Science.

Andrews, J. T. & Montinola, G. R. (2004). Veto Players and the Rule of Law in Emerging Democracies. *Comparative Political Studies* **37**(1), 55–87.

Ansell, C., & Gingrich, J. (2003). Reforming the Administrative State. In B. E. Cain, R. J. Dalton and S. E. Scarrow, eds., *Democracy Transformed? Expanding Political Opportunities in Advanced Industrial Semocracies*. New York, NY: Oxford University Press, pp. 164–91.

Argyris, C. (1960). *Understanding Organizational Behaviour*. Homewood, IL: Dorsey Press.

Arnold, P. E. (2003). Democracy and Corruption in the 19th Century United States: Parties, Spoils and Political Participation. In S. Tiihonen, ed., *The History of Corruption in Central Government, no: 7*. Washington, DC: IOS Press, pp. 197–212.

Auer, A., Demmke, C. & Poltet, R. (1996). *Civil Services in the Europe of Fifteen: Current Situation and Prospects*. Maastricht: European Institute of Public Administration.

Axelrod, Robert. (1984). *The Evolution of Cooperation*. New York, NY: Basic Books.

Bach, S. (1999). Changing Public Service Employment Relations. In S. Bach, L. Bordogna, G. Della Rocca and D. Winchester, eds., *Public Service Employment Relations in Europe, Transformation, Modernization and Inertia*. London: Routledge, pp. 1–17.

Baena, M. (1999). *Elites y conjuntos de poder en España (1939–1992)*. Madrid: Tecnos.

Bagues, M. F. & Esteve-Volart, B. (2008). Top Civil Service: Meritocracy or Nepotism? [Unpublished working paper]. Available at: www.iza.org/conference_files/TAM_08/bagues_m4229.pdf. [Retrieved 15 May 2013]

Baker, G., Gibbons, R. & Murphy, K. J. (2002). Relational Contracts and the Theory of the Firm. *The Quarterly Journal of Economics* **117**(1), 39–84.

Ballart, X. & Zapico E. (2010). Budget Reforms in Spain. In J. Wanna, L. Jensen and J. de Vries, eds., *The Reality of Budget Reform: Counting the Consequences in 11 Advanced Democracies*. Cheltenham: Edward Elgar, pp. 240–59.

Barberis, P. (2011). The Weberian legacy. *International Handbook on Civil Service Systems*, pp.13–30.

Barlow, J., Farnham, D., Horton, S. & Ridley, F. F. (1996). Comparing Public Managers. In D. Farnham, S. Horton, J. Barlow and A. Hondeghem, eds., *New Public Managers in Europe: Public Servants in Transition*. London: Macmillan Business, pp. 3–25.

Barnard, C. (1938). *The Functions of the Executive*. Cambridge, MA: Cambridge University Press.

Barro, R. (1973). The Control of Politicians: An Economic Model. *Public Choice* **14**(1), 19–42.

Barzelay, M & Gallego, R. (2010). The Comparative Historical Analysis of Public Management Policy Cycles in France, Italy, and Spain: Symposium Introduction. *Governance* **23**(2), 209–23.

Baumol, W. J. (1959). *Business Behavior, Value, and Growth*. New York: MacMillan.

BBC. 7-01-2014. Hundreds of Turkish Police Officers Dismissed.

BBC News. 26-07-2012. The White Elephants that Dragged Spain into the Red.

Becker, G. & Stigler, G. (1974). Law Enforcement. Malfeasance, and the Compensation of Enforces. *Journal of Legal Studies* **3**(1), 1–19.

Bekke, H. A. G. M., Perry, J. L. & Toonen, T. A. J. (1996). Introduction: Conceptualizing Civil Service Systems. In H. A. J. G. M. Bekke, J. L. Perry and T. A. J. Toonen, eds., *Civil Service Systems in a Comparative Perspective*. Bloomington, IN: Indiana University Press, pp. 1–12.

Bekke, H. A. G. M. & Van der Meer, F. M. (2000). *Civil Service Systems in Western Europe*. Cheltenham: Edward Elgar.

Bel i Queralt, G. (2010). La racionalización de las infraestructuras de transporte en España. *Cuadernos económicos de ICE* **80**, 211–28.

Beltrán Villalva, M. (2001). La Función Pública en el siglo XX. In A. Morales Moya, ed., *La Organización del Estado*. Madrid: *España Nuevo Milenio-Generalitat Valenciana*. Las Claves de la España del Siglo XX.

Bendor, J., Glazer, A. & Hammond, T. H. (2001). Theories of Delegation. *Annual Review of Political Science* **4**, 235–69.

Bennett, C. J. (1997). Understanding the Ripple Effects: The Cross-National Adoption of Policy Instruments for Bureaucratic Accountability. *Governance* **10**(3), 213–33.

Berle, A. A. & Means, G. C. (1968)[1932]. *The Modern Corporation and Private Property*. New York, NY: Harcourt, Brace & World.

Berman, S. (2010). From the Sun King to Karzai Lessons for State Building in Afghanistan. *Foreign Affairs*, March-April.

Bertelsmann Transformation Index 2012. Available at: www.bti-project.org/index/ [Retrieved 15 May 2013].

Besley, T. & Burgess, R. (2001). Political Agency, Government Responsiveness and the Role of the Media. *European Economic Review* 45(4–6), 629–40.

Besley, T & Case, A. (1995). Does Electoral Accountability Affect Economic Policy Choices? Evidence from Gubernatorial Term Limits. *Quarterly Journal of Economics* 110(3), 769–98.

Besley, T. & McLaren J. (1993). Taxes and Bribery: The Role of Wage Incentives. *The Economic Journal* 103(416), 119–41.

Bezes, P. (2010). Path-dependent and Path-breaking Changes in the French Administrative System: The Weight of Legacy Explanations. In M. Painter and G. B. Peters, eds., *Tradition and Public Administration*. New York, NY: Palgrave Macmillan, pp. 158–74.

Bezes, P & Lodge, M. (2007). *Historical Legacies and Dynamics of Institutional Change in Civil Service Systems*. London: Macmillan Publishers Limited.

Bezes, P. & Parrado, S. (2013). Trajectories of Administrative Reform: Institutions, Timing and Choices in France and Spain. *West European Politics*, 36(1), 22–50.

Blanchard, O. & Giavazzi, F. (2003). Macroeconomic Effects of Regulation and Deregulation in Goods and Labor Markets. *Quarterly Journal of Economics* 118(3), 879–907.

Boix, C. & Stokes, S. C. (2003). Endogenous Democratization. *World Politics* 55(4), 517–49.

Bouckaert, G. (2007). Cultural Characteristics from Public Management Reforms Worldwide. *Research in Public Policy Analysis and Management* 16(4), 29–64.

Bossaert, D., Demmke, C., Nomden, K., Polet, R. and Auer, A. (2001). *Civil Services in the Europe of Fifteen. Trends and New Developments*. Maastricht: European Institute of Public Administration.

Brehm, J. & Gates, S. (1997). *Working, Shirking and Sabotage*. Ann Arbor, MI: The University of Michigan Press.

Browne, C., Geiger, T. & Gutknecht, T. (2012). The Executive Opinion Survey: The Voice of the Business Community. In K. Schwab, ed., *The Global Competitiveness Report*. World Economic Forum.

Brunetti, A. & Weder, B. (2003). A Free Press is Bad News for Corruption. *Journal of Public Economy* 87(7–8), 1801–24.

Buchanan, J. M. & Tullock, G. (1962). *The Calculus of Consent: Logical Foundations of Constitutional Democracy*. Ann Arbor, MI: University of Michigan Press.

Bågenholm, A. (2015). "Corruption and Anti-corruption in 19th Century Sweden". Paper to be presented at the Conference on the History of Anticorruption in Amsterdam, 7–9 September, 2015.

Bäck, H. & Hadenius, A. (2008). Democracy and state capacity: exploring a J-shaped relationship. Governance, 21(1), pp. 1–24.

Bågenholm, A. (2015). "Corruption and Anti-corruption in 19th Century Sweden". Paper to be presented at the Conference on the History of Anticorruption in Amsterdam, 7-9 September, 2015.

Cadena SER 15-12-2014 "En AENA había orden 'de contactar con Correa desde que el PP ganó las elecciones'"

Cádiz Deleito, J. L. (1987). Notas sobre la carrera profesional del funcionario público. *Documentación administrativa* 210, 97–120.

Caldwell, L. K. (2000). Is Leviathan Manageable? *Public Administration Review* 60(1), 72–4.

Calvert, R., McCubbins, M. D. & Weingast, B. (1987). Congressional Influence over Policy Making: The Case of the FTC. In M. D. McCubbins and T. Sullivan, eds., *Congress: Structure and Policy.* New York, NY: Cambridge University Press, pp. 272–98.

Cassese, S. (2003). The Age of Administrative Reforms. In J. Hayward and A. Menon, eds., *Governing Europe.* Oxford: Oxford University Press, pp. 128–39.

Cassese, Sabino. (1993). Hypotheses on the Italian Administrative System. *West European Politics* 16(3), 316–28.

Castles, F. G. & Merrill, V. (1989). Towards a General Model of Public Policy Outcomes. *Journal of Theoretical Politics* 1(2), 177–212.

Cejudo, Guillermo M. (2006). *New Wine in Old Bottles: How New Democracies Deal with Inherited Bureaucratic Apparatuses. The Experiences of Mexico and Spain.* Mexico: Documentos de Trabajo del CIDE.

Chang, E. C. C & Golden, M. A. (2007). Electoral Systems, District Magnitude and Corruption. *British Journal of Political Science* 37(1), 115–37.

Chapman, R. A. & Greenaway, J. R. (1980). *The Dynamics of Administrative Reform.* London: Croom Helm.

Charron, N. & Lapuente, V. (2010). Does Democracy Produce Quality of Government? *European Journal of Political Research* 49(4), 443–70.

Charron, N., Dahlström, C. & Lapuente, V. (2012). No Law without a State. *Journal of Comparative Economics* 40(2), 176–93.

Chong, A., La Porta R., Lopez-de-Silanes, F. & Shleifer A. (2014). Letter Grading Government Efficiency. *Journal of the European Economic Association.* 12(2), 277–99

Christensen, T. & Lægreid, P, eds., (2001). *New Public Management. The Transformation of Ideas and Practice.* Aldershot: Ashgate.

Christensen, T. & Lægreid, P. (2010). *The Ashgate Research Companion to New Public Management.* Aldershot: Ashgate.

   (2012). Competing Principles of Agency Organization – The Reorganization of a Reform. *International Review of Administrative Sciences December* 78(4), 579–96.

Christensen, T. & Lægreid, P. (2007). *Transcending New Public Management. The Transformation of Public Sector Reforms*. Burlington: Ashgate Publishing Limited.

Christensen, T. and Lægreid, P. (2011). *The Ashgate Companion to New Public Management*. Burlington: Ashgate Publishing Limited.

Ciccone, A. & Papaioannou, E. (2006). Red Tape and Delayed Entry. *Centre for Economic Policy Research Discussion Paper 5996*. London: Centre for Economic Policy.

Clark, G. (2007). *A Farewell to Alms: A Brief Economic History of the World*. New Jersey, NJ: Princeton University Press.

Coleman, J. & Ferejohn, J. (1986). Democracy and Social Choice. *Ethics* 97(1), 6–25.

Collier, P. (2009). *Wars, Guns, and Votes: Democracy in Dangerous Places*. New York, NY: Harper Collins.

Cope, S., Leishman, F. & Starie, P. (1997). Globalization, New Public Management and the Enabling State: Futures of Police Management. *International Journal of Public Sector Management* 10(6), 444–60.

Coppedge, M. (1994). *Strong Parties and Lame Ducks: Presidential Partyarchy and Factionalism in Venezuela*. Stanford, CA: Stanford University Press.

Crespo M. & Fernando, L. (2003). *Mitos y Ritos de la Administración Española*. Madrid: Instituto Nacional de Administración Pública.

Crossman, R. (1977). *The Diaries of a Cabinet Minister, Volume HI: Secretary of State for Social Services 1968–70*. London: Hamish Hamilton and Jonathan Cape.

Dahl, R. (1947). The Science of Public Administration: Three Problems, *Public Administration Review* 7(1), 1–11.

Dahlberg, S., Dahlström, C., Sundin, P. & Teorell, J. (2013). The Quality of Government Expert Survey 2008–2011: A Report. *QoG Working Paper Series 2013:15*. Gothenburg: Gothenburg University, The Quality of Government Institute.

Dahlström, C. (2012). Political and Administration. In B.G. Peters and J. Pierre, eds., *The SAGE Handbook of Public Administration*. London: SAGE Publications Ltd, pp. 361–67.

Dahlström, C. & Lapuente, V. (2015). Democratic and Professional Accountability. In C. Dahlström and L. Wängnerud, eds., *Elites, Institutions and the Quality of Government*. London: Palgrave Macmillan.

Dahlström, C. & Lapuente, V. (2010). Explaining Cross-Country Differences in the Adoption of Performance-Related Pay in the Public Sector. *Journal of Public Administration Research and Theory* 23(4), 577–600.

(2011). Has New Public Management a Trust Problem? In J-M. Eymeri-Douzans and J. Pierre, eds., *Administrative Reforms and Democratic Governance*, London, Routledge, pp. 27–40.

(2012). Weberian Bureaucracy and Corruption Prevention. In S. Holmberg and B. Rothstein, eds., *Good Government. The Relevance of Political Science.* Cheltenham: Edward Elgar, pp. 150–73.

Dahlström, C. & Pierre, J. (2011). Steering the Swedish State. Politicization as a Coordinating Strategy. In C. Dahlström, B.G. Peters and J. Pierre, eds., *Steering from the Centre: Strengthening Political Control in Western Democracies.* Toronto: University of Toronto Press, pp. 3–26.

Dahlström, C., Lapuente, V. & Teorell, J. (2012a). The Merit of Meritocratization Politics, Bureaucracy, and the Institutional Deterrents of Corruption. *Political Research Quarterly* 65(3), 656–68.

Dahlström, C., Lapuente, V. and Teorell, J. (2012b). Public Administrations around the World. In S. Holmberg and B. Rothstein, eds., *Good Government. The Relevance of Political Science.* Cheltenham: Edward Elgar, pp. 40–67.

de Cervantes Saavedra, M. (1833) [1615]. *El Ingenioso hidalgo don Quijote de la Mancha.* Madrid: Mariano Arévalo.

De Francesco, F. (2012). Diffusion of Regulatory Impact Analysis among OECD and EU Member States. *Comparative Political Studies,* 45(10), 1277–1305.

De la Oliva, A. & Gutiérrez-Reñón, A. (1968). Los Cuerpos de Funcionarios. *Documentación Administrativa* 124.

De Long, J. B. & Shleifer, A. (1993). Princes and Merchants: European City Growth before the Industrial Revolution. *The Journal of Law and Economics* 36(2), 671–702.

De Vries, J. & Yesilkagit, A.K. (1999). Core Executive and Party Politics: Privatisation in The Netherlands. *West European Politics* 22(1), 115–37.

Deakin, N. & Walsh, K. (1996). The Enabling State: The Role of Markets and Contracts. *Public Administration* 74(1), 33–47.

Demetriades, P. O. & Mamuneas T. (2000). Intertemporal Output and Employment Effects of Public Infrastructure Capital: Evidence from 12 OECD Economies. *The Economic Journal* 110(465), 687–712.

Demmke, C. (2010). Civil Services in the EU of 27 – Reform Outcomes and the Future of the Civil Service. *EIPASCOPE* 2010/2.

Demmke, C., and Moilanen, T. (2010). *Civil Services in the EU of 27: Reform Outcomes and the Future of the Civil Service.* Frankfurt am Main: Peter Lang.

Demsetz, H. (1967). Towards a Theory of Property Rights. *American Economic Review* 57(2), 61–70.

Di Tella, R. & Schargrodsky, E. (2003). The Role of Wages and Auditing during a Crackdown on Corruption in the City of Buenos Aires. *Journal of Law and Economy* 46(1), 269–92.

Dierickx, G. (2004). Politicization in the Belgian Civil Service. In B.G. Peters J. and J. Pierre, eds., *Politicization of the Civil Service in Comparative Perspective. The Quest for Control.* London: Routledge, pp. 178–205.

Djankov, S., Glaeser, E., La Porta, R., Lopez-de-Silanes, F. & Shleifer, A. (2003). The New Comparative Economics. *Journal of Comparative Economics* 31(4), 595–619.

Djankov, S., La Porta R., Lopez-de-Silanes F. & Shleifer A. (2002). The Regulation of Entry. *Quarterly Journal of Economics* 117(1), 1–37. (2003). Courts: The Lex Mundi Project. *Quarterly Journal of Economics* 118(2), 453–517.

Djankov, S., La Porta, R., Lopez-de-Silanes, F. & Shleifer, A. (2010). Disclosure by Politicians. *American Economic Journal: Applied Economics* 2(2), 179–209.

Dobbin, F., Simmons, B. A. & Garrett, G. (2007). The Global Diffusion of Public Policies: Social Construction, Coercion, Competition, or Learning? *Annual Review of Sociology* 33, 449–72.

Dollar, D. & Kraay, A. (2003). Institutions, Trade, and Growth. *Journal of Monetary Economics*, 50(1), 133–62.

Dollar, D., Fisman, R. & Gatti, R. (2001). Are Women Really the Fairer Sex? Corruption and Women in Government. *Journal of Economic Behavior and Organization* 46(4), 423–29.

Dominguez, J. I., ed., (1997). *Technopols: Ideas and Leaders in Freeing Politics and Markets in Latin America in the 1990s.* Pennsylvania, PA: Penn State University Press.

Domínguez, L. (1875). *La Cuestión de los Empleados Públicos en España,* Biblioteca Nacional de España.

Drori, G. S., Jang, Y. S. & Meyer, J. W. (2006). Sources of Rationalized Governance: Cross-national Longitudinal Analyses, 1985–2002. *Administrative Science Quarterly* 51(2), 205–29.

Du Gay, P. (2000). *In Praise of Bureaucracy,* London: Sage.

Dunleavy, P. & Hood, C. (1994). From Old Public Administration to New Public Management. *Public Money and Management* 14(3), 9–16.

East, J. P. (1965). *Council-manager Government: The Political Thought of Its Founder, Richard S. Childs.* Chapel Hill: University of North Carolina Press.

Easterly, W. & Levine, R. (1997). Africa's Growth Tragedy: Policies and Ethnic Divisions. *Quarterly Journal of Economcs* 112(4), 1203–50.

El Confidencial. 18-10-2013. Interior liquida al comisario de Policía que investigaba los papeles de Bárcenas.

El País. 12-12-2000. Gil suspende y expedienta al interventor de Marbella. 10-10-2006. El interventor y el ex secretario de Marbella cobraron un plus temporal durante 12 años.

27-06-2009. Las guerras internas de Estepona desvelaron la corrupción municipal.

07-04-2010. Un voluminoso sumario de 50.000 páginas en 291 tomos.

18-04-2010. Corrupción a la Sombra del Poder.

08-01-2011. Ciudad de la Cultura... y de los excesos.

02–06-2011. El vasto patrimonio del cabecilla.

12-11-2011. Monumento a la incoherencia.

13-02-2013. Otro aeropuerto sin aviones.

17-02-2013. Un funcionario de Estepona pide amparo por supuesto acoso laboral.

30-05-2013a. Viajes Gurtel: de Disney a Laponia.

30-05-2013b. La Comunidad de Madrid fraccionaba contratas para la red Gürtel y eludir la ley.

17-06-2013. El exedil Peñas reafirma que Correa presumía de ser el amo en Valencia.

23-06-2013. Relojes de 2.000 euros a la cúpula del PP.

26-07-2013. Los visitadores de la trama Gürtel.

06–08-2013. López Viejo cobró una mordida del 10% por cada acto que montó Gürtel.

08–09-2013. La derrota debilita a Botella.

23-09-2013. Una quiebra evitable.

4-10-2013. Marbella era la 'corrupción generalizada'.

22-11-2013. Los inspectores: 'Con Cemex se ha cruzado una línea roja.

06–12-2013. Montoro acusa a los directores de Hacienda dimitidos de ser socialistas.

10–12-2013. El director de Hacienda asegura que no pide el carné político a nadie.

06-03-2015. "As the case goes to trial, who's who in the Gürtel investigation"

14-02-2016. "Volvería a denunciar el caso Gürtel. Porque no tengo hijos"

El Periodico. 08–12-2013. Els rescats de les infraestructures fantasma, a 'Salvados'.

El Periodista Digital. 02–10-2009. El PSOE o Enchufes Estepona S.A. Available at: www.periodistadigital.com/politica/partidos-politicos/2009/10/02/el-psoe-o-enchufes-estepona-s-a.shtml. [Retrieved 03 Nov 2013].

Epstein, D. & O'Halloran, S. (1994). Administrative Procedures, Information, and Agency Discretion. *American Journal of Political Science* **38**(3), 697–722.

Ertman, T. (1997). *The Birth of Leviathan: Building States and Regimes in Medieval and Early Modern Europe.* Cambridge, MA: Cambridge University Press.

Evans, P. (1995). *Embedded Autonomy: States and Industrial Transformation.* Princeton, NJ: Princeton University Press.

Evans, P & Rauch, J. (1999). Bureaucracy and Growth: A Cross-National Analysis of the Effects of 'Weberian' State Structures on Economic Growth. *American Sociological Review* 64(5), 748–65.

Fageda, X. (2013). El despilfarro del AVE. *El País* 08-01-2013. Available at: http://politica.elpais.com/politica/2013/01/08/actualidad/1357672895_538712.html [Retrieved 08 January 2014].

Falaschetti, D. (2002). Golden Parachutes: Credible Commitments or Evidence of Shirking? *Journal of Corporate Finance* 8(2), 159–78.

Falaschetti, D. & Miller, G. J. (2001). Constraining Leviathan: Moral Hazard and Credible Commitment in Institutional Design. *Journal of Theoretical Politics* 13(4), 389–411.

Farazmand, A. (1999). Globalization and Public Administration. *Public Administration Review* 59(6), 509–22.

Feldbaek, O. (2000). The Historical Role of the Nordic Countries in Europe. *European Review* 8(1): 123–28.

Ferejohn, J. (1986). Incumbent Performance and Electoral Control. *Public Choice* 50(1): 5–25.

Fernandez-Villaverde, J., Garicano, L. & Santos, T. (2013). Political Credit Cycles: The Case of the Euro Zone. NBER Working Paper No. 18899. Cambridge, MA: National Bureau of Economic Research.

Ferraro, A. (2011). A Splendid Ruined Reform: The Creation and Destruction of a Civil Service in Argentina. In A. Massey, ed., *International Handbook on Civil Service Systems*. Cheltenham: Edward Elgar, pp. 152–77.

Financial Times. 15-05-2013. Spain's Ghost Highway. Available at: http://blogs.ft.com/photo-diary/2013/05/spains-ghost-highway/?Authorised=false [Retrieved 08 January 2014].

Finer, H. (1932). *The Theory and Practice of Modern Government*. London: Methuen.

Finnemore, M. (1996). *National Interests in International Society*. New York, NY: Cambridge University Press.

Fischer, W. & Lundgren, P. (1975). The Recruitment of Administrative Personnel. In C. Tilly, ed., *The Formation of National States in Western Europe*. Princeton, NJ: Princeton University Press, pp. 456–561.

Fisman, R. & Sarria-Allende, V. (2004). *Regulation of Entry and the Distortion of Industrial Organization*. NBER Working Paper No. 10929. Cambridge, MA: National Bureau of Economic Research.

Fleischer, J. (2011). In C. Dahlström, G. B. Peters and J. Pierre, eds., *Steering from the Centre. Strengthening Political Control in Western Democracies*. Toronto: University of Toronto Press, pp. 54–79.

Folke, O., Hirano, S. & Snyder, J. M. (2011). Patronage and Elections in U.S. States. *American Political Science Review* 105(3), pp. 567–85.

Foss, K., Foss, N. J. & Vázquez, X. H. (2006). 'Tying the Manager's Hands': Constraining Opportunistic Managerial Intervention. *Cambridge Journal of Economics* 30(5), 797–818.

Frant, H. (1993). Rules and Governance in the Public Sector: The Case of Civil Service. *American Journal of Political Science* 37(4), 990–1007.

Freedom House. (2013). *Freedom of the World and Freedom of the Press.* published online [Retrieved 15 May 2013].

Freibert, A. (1997). Public Pay Programs in OECD Countries. In H. Risher and C. Fay, eds., *New Strategies for Public Pay: Rethinking Government Compensation Programs,* San Francisco, CA: Jossey-Bass, pp. 294–311.

Frisk Jensen, M. (2008). *Korruption og embedsetik – danske embedsmænds korruption i perioden 1800 – 1866.* Doctoral dissertation. Aalborg: Aalborg University, Department of History.

Frisk-Jensen, M. & Mungiu-Pippidi, A. (2011). Becoming Denmark: Understanding Good Governance Historical Achievers. In M. Frisk-Jensen and A. Mungiu-Pippidi, eds., *The Development of Good Governance.* Available at: www.againstcorruption.eu/uploads/norad/Becoming-Denmark-Historical-Lessons-Learned.pdf. [Retrieved 12 Jan 2014].

Fry, G. K. (2000). The British Civil Service System. In H.A.G.M. Bekke and F. M. Van der Meer. *Civil Service Systems in Western Europe.* Cheltenham: Edward Elgar, pp. 12–35.

Fukuyama, F. (2011). *The Origins of Political Order: from Prehuman Times to the French Revolution.* New York, NY: Farrar: Straus & Giroux.

  (2013). What Is Governance? *Governance* 26(3), pp. 347–68.

  (2012). The Strange Absence of the State in Political Science. *The American Interest's blog,* 2 October 2. Available at: http://blogs.the-american-interest.com/fukuyama/2012/10/02/the-strange-absence-of-the-state-in-political-science/ [Retrieved 15 December 2013].

Gailmard, S. & Patty J. (2007). Slackers and Zealots: Civil Service, Policy Discretion, and Bureaucratic Expertise. *American Journal of Political Science* 51(4): 873–89.

  (2012). *Learning While Governing: Expertise and Accountability in the Executive Branch.* University of Chicago Press.

Gallego, R. (2003). Public Management Policy Making in Spain, 1982–1996: Policy Entrepreneurship and (in) Opportunity Windows. *International Public Management Journal,* 6(3), 283–307.

Gallego, R. & Barzelay, M. (2010). Public Management Policymaking in Spain: The Politics of Legislative Reform of Administrative structures, 1991–1997. *Governance* 23(2), 277–96.

Garvey, G. & Gaston, N. (1991). Delegation, the Role of Managerial Discretion as a Bonding Device, and the Enforcement of Implicit Contracts.

In T. B. Fomby. *Advances in Econometrics 9*. Greenwich, CT: JAI Press Inc, pp. 87–119.

Gaus, J. M. (1936). The Responsibility of Public Administration. In J. M. Gaus, L. D. White and M. E. Dimock, eds., *The Frontiers of Public Administration*. Chicago, IL: University of Chicago Press, pp. 26–44.

Geddes, B. (1994). *Politician's Dilemma: Building State Capacity in Latin America, vol. 25*. Berkeley, CA: University of California Press.

Gelb, A. (1988). *Oil Windfalls: Blessing or Curse?* New York, NY: Oxford University Press.

Gennaioli, N, La Porta R., Lopez-de-Silanes F. & Shleifer A. (2013). Human Capital and Regional Development. *Quarterly Journal of Economics* **128**(1), 105–64.

Gerring J. & Thacker S. (2004). Political Institutions and Corruption: The Role of Unitarism and Parliamentarism. *British Journal of Political Science* **34**(2), 295–330.

Gerring J. & Thacker, S. (2005). Do Neoliberal Policies Deter Political Corruption? *International Organization* **59**(1), 233–54.

Glaeser, E. L., La Porta, R., Lopez-de-Silanes, F. & Shleifer, A. (2004). Do Institutions Cause Growth? *Journal of Economic Growth* **9**(3), 271–303.

Golden, M. A. (2000). Political Patronage, Bureaucracy and Corruption in Postwar Italy, Annual Meeting of the *APSA 2000 Annual Meeting Paper*. Washington, DC.

(2003). Electoral Connections: The Effects of the Personal Vote on Political Patronage, Bureaucracy and Legislation in Postwar Italy. *British Journal of Political Science*, **33**(02), 189–212.

González De Lara, Y., Greif, A. & Jha, S. (2008). The Administrative Foundations of Self-enforcing Constitutions. *American Economic Review* **98**(2), 105–9.

Goodnow, F. J. (1900). *Politics and Administration*. New York, NY: Macmillan.

Gow, J. I. & Dufour, C. (2000). Is the New Public Management a Paradigm? Does It Matter? *International Review of Administrative Sciences* **66**(4), 573–97.

Greenaway, J. (2004). Celebrating Northcote/Trevelyan: Dispelling the Myths. *Public Policy and Administration* **19**(1), 1–14.

Greif, A. (2008). The Impact of Administrative Power on Political and Economic Development: Toward a Political Economy of Implementation. In E. Helpman, ed., *Institutions' Economic Performance*. London: Harvard University Press, pp. 17–63.

Grindle, M. S. (1977). *Bureaucrats, Politicians, and Peasants in Mexico: A Case Study in Public Policy*. Berkeley, CA: University of California Press.

(2012) *Jobs for the Boys: Patronage and the State in Comparative Perspective*. Cambridge, MA: Harvard University Press.

Grønnegaard Christensen, J. (2004). Political Responsiveness in a Merit Bureaucracy: Denmark. In B.G. Peters and J. Pierre, eds., *Politicization of the Civil Service in Comparative Perspective*. London: Routledge, pp. 14–40.

Grzymala-Busse, A. (2007). *Rebuilding Leviathan: Party Competition And State Exploitation in Post-Communist Democracies*. Cambridge: Cambridge University Press.

Hall, R. E. & Jones, C.I. (1999). Why do Some Countries Produce so Much More Output per Worker than Others? *The Quarterly Journal of Economics* 114(1), 83–116.

Hall, R. H. (1963). The Concept of Bureaucracy: An Empirical Assessment. *American Journal of Sociology* 69, 32–40.

Halligan, J. (1996). Learning from Experience in Australian Reform: Balancing Principle and Pragmatism. In J. P. Olsen and G. B. Peters, eds., *Lessons from Experience: Experiential Learning in Administrative Reforms in Eight Democracies*. Stockholm: Scandinavian University Press, pp. 71–112.

(2001). Politicians, Bureaucrats and Public Sector Reform in Australia and New Zeeland. In G. B. Peters and J. Pierre, eds., *Politicians, Bureaucrats and Administrative Reform*. New York, NY: Routledge, pp. 157–68.

Hamilton, A. (1788). *Federalist No. 70 The Executive Department Further Considered*. The Federalist Papers.

Harling, P. (1995). Rethinking "Old Corruption." *Past & Present* 147(1), 127–58.

(1996). *The Waning of Old Corruption: The Politics of Economical Reform in Britain, 1779–1846*. Oxford: Clarendon Press.

Harris-White, B. & White, G., eds., (1996). *Liberalization and New Forms of Corruption*. Brighton: Institute of Development Studies.

Havro, G. & Santiso, J. (2008). To Benefit from Plenty: Lessons from Chile and Norway. *OECD Policy Brief No. 37*.

Hawkins, K., Rosas G. & Johnson M. (2011). The Misiones of the Chávez Government. In D. Smilde and D. Hellinger, eds., *Venezuelas Bolivarian Democracy: Participation, Politics, and Culture Under Chávez*, pp. 186–218. Duke University Press.

Hayek, F. A. (1960). *The Constitution of Liberty*. Chicago, IL: University of Chicago Press.

Hays, L. (1988). All Eyes on Du Pont's Incentive-Pay Plan. *Wall Street Journal* 1: A1.

Heady, F. (1996). Configurations of Civil Service Systems. In A. J. G. M. Bekke, J. L. Perry and T. A. J. Toonen, eds., *Civil Service Systems in Comparative Perspective*. Bloomington, IN: Indiana University Press, pp. 207–26.

(2001). *Public Administration, a Comparative Perspective*. Sixth edition. CRC Press.

Heclo, H. (1977). *A Government of Strangers*. Washington, DC: The Brookings Institution.

Heinrich, C. J. (2003). Measuring Public Sector Performance and Effectiveness. In G. B. Peters and J. Pierre, eds., *The SAGE Handbook of Public Administration*. London: SAGE Publications, pp. 25–37.

Helpman, E., Melitz, M. J. & Rubinstein, Y. (2008). Estimating Trade Flows: Trading Partners and Trading Volumes. *Quarterly Journal of Economics* 123(2), 441–87.

Henisz, W. J. (2000). The Institutional Environment for Economic Growth. *Economics and Politics* 12(1), 1–31.

Hollyer, J. (2011). Patronage or Merit? Civil Service Boards in US Cities. Working paper, Yale University, MacMillan Center for International and Area Studies.

Holmberg, S., Rothstein, B. and Nasiritousi, N. (2009). Quality of Government: What You Get. *Annual Review of Political Science* 12, 135–61.

Holmstrom, B. (1982). Moral Hazard in Teams. *The Bell Journal of Economics* 13(2), 324–40.

Hood, C. (1991). A Public Management for All Seasons? *Public Administration* 69(1), 3–19.

(1996). Exploring Variations in Public Management Reforms of the 1990s. In H. A. G. M. Bekke, J. L. Perry and T. A. Toonen, eds., *Civil Service Systems in Comparative Perspective*. Bloomington, IN: Indiana University Press, pp. 268–87.

(2000). Paradoxes of Public-sector Managerialism, Old Public Management and Public Service Bargains. *International Public Management Journal* 3(1), 1–22.

(2002). Control, Bargains, and Cheating: The Politics of Public Service Reform. *Journal of Public Administration Research and Theory* 12(3), 309–32.

(2007). What Happens When Transparency Meets Blame-Avoidance? *Public Management Review* 9(2), 191–210.

Hood, C. & Lodge, M. (2006). *The Politics of Public Service Bargains Reward, Competency, Loyalty - and Blame*. Oxford: Oxford University Press.

Hood, C. & Peters, G. B. (2004). The Middle Aging of New Public Management: Into the Age of Paradox? *Journal of Public Administration Research and Theory* 14(3) 267–82.

Hoogenboom, A. (1961). *Outlawing the Spoils: A History of the Civil Service Reform Movement, 1865–1883*. Urbana, IL: University of Illinois Press.

Hopkin, J. and Blyth, M. (2012). What can Okun Teach Polanyi? Efficiency, Regulation and Equality in the OECD. *Review of International Political Economy* 19(1), 1–33.

Hopkin, J., Lapuente, V & Möller, L. (2013). Varieties of Statism. Economic Regulation and Economic Redistribution in Southern Europe. Paper presented at the 20th International Conference of Europeanists (CES), Amsterdam, June 2013.

Horton, S. (2000). Competency Management in the British Civil Service. *International Journal of Public Sector Management* 13(4), 354–68.

(2011). Contrasting Anglo-American and Continental European civil service systems. In Andrew Massey, ed., *International Handbook on Civil Service Systems*, Cheltenham, Glos: Edward Elgar, pp. 31–54.

Howard, D. (1998.) The French Strikes of 1995 and their Political Aftermath. *Government and Opposition* 33(2), 199–220.

Huber, J. D. & Shipan, C.R. (2002). *Deliberate Discretion: The Institutional Foundations of Bureaucratic Autonomy*. New York, NY: Cambridge University Press.

Hyden, Goran. (2010). Where Administrative Traditions and Alien: Implications for Reform in Africa. In M. Painter and B.G. Peters, eds., *Tradition and Public Administration*. Basingstoke: Palgrave Macmillan, pp. 69–83.

Iacoviello, M. & Rodríguez-Gustá, A. (2006). Síntesis del Diagnóstico. Caso Brasil. In K. Echebarría, *Informe sobre la situación del servicio civil en América Latina*. Banco Interamericano de Desarrollo, Diálogo Regional de Política, Departamento de Integración y Programas Regionales, Departamento de Desarrollo Sostenible.

Iacoviello, M. & Zuvanic L. (2005). Diagnóstico Institucional de los Servicios Civiles de América Latina. Informe Final Diálogo Regional de Política, BID. Paper presented at the V Reunión de la Red de Gestión y Transparencia de la Política Pública, Washington, DC, 17–18.

Iglesias, F., ed., (2007). *Urbanismo y democracia. Alternativas para evitar la corrupción*, Madrid: Fundación Alternativas.

Instrument of Government, chapter 7, §2

International Country Risk Guide. (2013). Available at: www.prsgroup.com/ICRG.aspx. [Retrieved 15 May 2013].

Jiménez-Asensio, R. (1989). *Políticas de selección en la Función Pública española (1808–1978)*. Madrid: Instituto Nacional de Administración Pública (INAP).

Johnson, R. N. & Libecap, G. D. (1994). *The Federal Civil Service System and the Problem of Bureaucracy: Economics and Politics of Institutional Change*. Chicago, IL: University of Chicago Press.

Jones, P. (2013). History Matters: New Evidence on the Long Run Impact of Colonial Rule on Institutions. *Journal of Comparative Economics* 41(1), 181–200.

Karl, T. L. (1986). Petroleum and Political Pacts: The Transition to Democracy. In P. C. Schmitter and L. Whitehead, eds., *Transitions from Authoritarian Rule: Latin America*. Baltimore: The Johns Hopkins University Press, pp. 196–219.

(1997). *The Paradox of Plenty: Oil Booms and Petro-states*. Chicago, IL: University of California Press.

Kaufman, H. (1960). *The Forest Ranger: A Study in Administrative Behavior*. London: Routledge.

Kaufmann, D., Kraay, A. & Mastruzzi, M. (2010). The Worldwide Governance Indicators. Methodology and Analytic Issues. The World Bank Policy Research Working Paper No. 5430. The World Bank: The World Bank Group.

Keefer, P. (2002). The Political Economy of Public Spending Decisions in the Dominican Republic: Credibility, Clientelism and Political Institutions. Report prepared for the Public Expenditure and Institutional Review, The Dominican Republic. The World Bank.

(2007). Clientelism, Credibility, and the Policy Choices of Young Democracies. *American Journal of Political Science* 51(4), 804–21.

(2009). *Database of Political Institutions: Changes and Variable Definitions. Development Research Group*. Washington, DC: The World Bank: Development Research Group.

(2010). *Database of Political Institutions: Changes and Variable Definitions*. Washington, DC: The World Bank: Development Research Group.

Keefer, P. & Vlaicu, R. (2008). Democracy, Credibility, and Clientelism. *Journal of Law, Economics, and Organization* 24(2), 371–406.

Keller, B. (1999). Germany: Negotiated Change, Modernization and the Challenge of Unification. In S. Bach, L. O. Bordogna, G. Della Rocca and D. Winchester, eds., *Public Service Employment Relations in Europe, Transformation, Modernization and Inertia*. London: Routledge, pp. 56–93.

Kelman, S. (1987). *Making Public Policy: A Hopeful View of American Government*. New York, NY: Basic Books.

Kettl, D. F. (1993). *Sharing Power: Public Governance and Private Markets*. Washington, DC: Brookings Institution.

(2000). *The Global Public Management Revolution: A Report on the Transformation of Governance*. Washington, DC: Brookings Institution's Press.

Kickert, W. (2007). Public Management Reforms in Countries with a Napoleonic State Model: France, Italy and Spain. In C. Pollitt, S. Van Thiel and V. Homburg, eds., *New Public Management in Europe. Adaptation and Alternatives*. London: Palgrave MacMillan, pp. 26–51.

(2011). Distinctiveness of Administrative Feform in Greece, Italy, Portugal and Spain. Common Characteristics of Context, Administrations and Reforms. *Public Administration* **89**(3), 801–18.

Kiser, E. & Baer, J. (2005). The Bureaucratisation of States: Toward an Analytical Weberianism. In J. Adams, E. Clemens and A. S. Orloff, eds., *The Making and Unmaking of Modernity: Politics and Processes in Historical Sociology*. Durham: Duke University Press, pp. 224–48.

Kitschelt, H. & Wilkinson, S. I. eds., (2007). *Patrons, Clients and Policies: Patterns of Democratic Accountability and Political Competition*. Cambridge, MA: Cambridge University Press.

Klapper, L., Laeven, L. & Rajan, R. (2006). Entry Regulation as a Barrier to Entrepreneurship. *Journal of Financial Economics* **82**(3), 591–629.

Klein, B., Crawford, R.T. G & Alchian, A. A. (1978). Vertical Integration, Appropriable Rents, and the Competitive Contracting Process. *Journal of Law and Economics* **21**(2), 297–326.

Knack, S, & and Keefer, P. (1995). Institutions and Economic Performance: Cross-country Tests using Alternative Institutional Measures. *Economics & Politics* **7**(3), 207–27.

Knott, J. H. (2011). Federalist No. 10: Are Factions the Problem in Creating Democratic Accountability in the Public Interest? *Public Administration Review* **71**(Issue Supplement), 29–36.

Knott, J. H. & Hammond, T. H. (2003). Formal Theory and Public Administration. In G. B. Peters and J. Pierre, eds., *Handbook of Public Administration*. London: SAGE Publications, pp. 138–49.

Knott, J. H. & Miller, G. J. (2008). When Ambition Checks Ambition Bureaucratic Trustees and the Separation of Powers. *The American Review of Public Administration* **38**(4), 387–411.

Knudsen, T. (2006). *Fra enevælde til folkestyre. Dansk demokratihistorie indtil 1973*. Copenhagen: Akademisk Forlag.

Kopecký, P. & Mair, P. (2012). Party Patronage as an Organizational Resource. In P. Kopecký, P. Mair and M. Spirova, eds., *Party Patronage and Party Government in European Democracies*. Oxford University Press.

Kopecký, P. & Scherlis, G. (2008). Party patronage in contemporary Europe. *European Review* **16**(3), 355–71.

Krasner, S. D. (1988). Sovereignty an Institutional Perspective. *Comparative Political Studies* **21**(1), 66–94.

Krause, G. A., Lewis, D. E. & Douglas, J. W. (2006). Political Appointments, Civil Service Systems, and Bureaucratic Competence: Organizational Balancing and Executive Branch Revenue Forecasts in the American States. *American Journal of Political Science* **50**(3), 770–87.

Kuhlmann, S. & Bogumil,J. (2007). Public Servants at Sub-national and Local Levels of Government: A British-German-French Comparison. In J. Raadschelders, T. Toonen and F. M. Van der Meer, eds., *Comparative Civil Service Systems in the 21st Century*. Houndmills: Palgrave Macmillan, pp. 137–51.

Kunicova, J. & Rose-Ackerman S. (2005). Electoral Rules and Constitutional Structure as Constraints on Corruption. *British Journal of Political Science* 35(4), 573–606.

Kydland, F. E. & Prescott, E. C. (1977). Rules Rather than Discretion: The Time Inconsistency of Optimal Plans. *Journal of Political Economy* 85(3), 473–91.

La Información 15-09-2015 "Maite Carol, el origen del 'caso Pretoria': 'Me dije: me iré a vender barras de pan, pero no me callo'"

La Porta, R., Lopez-deSilanes, F., & Shleifer, A. (2008). The Economic Consequences of legal Origins. *Journal of Economic Literature* 46(2), 285–332.

La Porta, R, Lopez-de-Silanes, F., Shleifer, A. & Vishny, R. (1997). Legal Determinants of External Finance. *Journal of Finance* 52(3), 1131–50.

La Porta, R, Lopez-de-Silanes, F., Shleifer, A. & Vishny, R. (1998). Law and Finance. *Journal of Political Economy* 106(6), 1113–55.

La Porta, R., Lopez-de-Silanes, F., Shleifer, A. & Vishny, R. (1999). The Quality of Government. *Journal of Law, Economics and Organization* 15(1), 222–79.

Ladi, S. (2012). The Eurozone Crisis and Austerity Politics: A Trigger for Administrative Reform in Greece? Hellenic Observatory Papers on Greece and Southeast. Paper No. 57. London: London School of Economics.

Lægreid, P. (2001). Administrative Reforms in Scandinavia–Testing the Cooperative Model. In B. C. Nolan, ed., *Public Sector Reform. An International Perspective*. London: Palgrave Macmillan, pp. 66–82.

Lægreid, P. & Pedersen, O. K., eds., (1996). *Integration og decentralisering. Personale og forvaltning i Skandinavien*. Copenhagen: Jurist- og økonomforbundet.

Lægreid, P. & Recascino Wise, L. (2007). Reforming Human Resource Management in Civil Service systems. In J. C. N. Raadschelders, T. A. J. Toonen and F. M. Van der Meer, eds., *The Civil Service in the 21st Century: Comparative Perspectives*. Basingstoke: Palgrave Macmillan, pp. 169–82.

Lafontaine, F. & Sivadasan, J. (2007). *The Microeconomic Implications of Input Market Regulations: Cross-Country Evidence from within the Firm*. Ross School of Business Paper No. 1069. University of Michigan, Ann Arbor, MI.

Landes, D. S. (1998). *The Wealth and Poverty of Nations: Why Some Countries Are So Rich and Some So Poor.* New York, NY: W.W. Norton & Company.

Lapuente, V. (2007). *A Political Economy Approach to Bureaucracies.* Doctoral dissertation. Oxford: University of Oxford.

Lapuente, V. (2010). A Tale of Two Cities. Bureaucratization in Mayor-Council and Council-Manager Municipalities. *Local Government Studies* 36(6), 739–57.

Lapuente, V. & Nistotskaya, M. (2009). To the Short-Sighted Victor Belong the Spoils: Politics and Merit Adoption. *Governance* 22(3), 431–58.

Lazear, E. (1996). Performance Pay and Productivity. NBER Working Paper Series *1996: 5672.* Cambridge, MA: National Bureau of Economic Research.

Lederman, D., Norman, L. & Soares R. R. (2005). Accountability and Corruption: Political Institutions Matter. *Economy and Politics* 17(1), 1–35.

Lee, C. K. & Strang, D. (2006). The International Diffusion of Public-sector Downsizing: Network Emulation and Theory-driven Learning. *International Organization* 60(4), 883–909.

Leslie, W. J. (1987). *The World Bank and Structural Adjustment in Developing Countries: The Case of Zaire.* Boulder, CO: Lynne Rienner Publishers.

Levi, M. (2005). Inducing Preferences within Organizations. In I. Katznelson and B. R. Weingast, eds., *Preferences and Situations: Points of Intersection Between Historical and Rational Choice Institutionalism.* New York, NY: Russell SAGE Foundation, pp. 219–46.

Levine, R. (2005). Law, Endowments and Property Rights. *Journal of Economic Perspectives* 19(3), 61–88.

Lewis, C. W & Catron, B. L. (1996). Professional standards and ethics. *Handbook of Public Administration* 2, 699–712.

Lewis, D. E. (2008). *The Politics of Presidential Appointments: Political Control and Bureaucratic Performance.* Princeton, NJ: Princeton University Press.

Lindert P. H. (2006). The Welfare State is the Wrong Target: A Reply to Bergh. *Economic Journal Watch* 3(2), 236–50.

Lipset, S. M. (1960). *Political Man: The Social Basis of Modern Politics.* New York, NY: Doubleday.

Lodge, M. & Hood, C. (2012). Into an Age of Multiple Austerities? Public Management and Public Service Bargains across OECD Countries. *Governance* 25(1), 79–101.

Lodge, M. & Wegrich, K. (2012). Public Administration and Executive Politics: Perennial Questions in Changing Contexts. *Public Policy and Administration* 27(3), 212–29.

Longo, F. (2007). *Mérito e flexibilidade: a gestão das pessoas no serviço público*. São Paulo: Edições Fundap.

Lynn, L. E. J. (2001). The Myth of the Bureaucratic Paradigm: What Traditional Public Administration Really Stood For. *Public Administration Review* 61(2), 144–60.

(2001). Globalization and Administrative Reform: What Is Happening in Theory? *Public Management Review* 3(2), 191–208.

Lyrintzis, C. (1984). Political Parties in Post-junta Greece: A Case of Bureaucratic Clientelism? *West European Politics* 7(2), 99–118.

Madison, J. (1787). Federalist No. 10: The Same Subject Continued: The Union as a Safeguard Against Domestic Faction and Insurrection. *New York Daily Advertiser*. November 22, 1787.

(1788). The Federalist No. 51: The Structure of the Government Must Furnish the Proper Checks and Balances between the Different Departments. *Independent Journal* 6.

Mahoney, P. G. (2001). The Common Law and Economic Growth: Hayek Might Be Right. *Journal of Legal Studies* 30(2), 503–25.

March, J. G. & Olson, J. P. (1983). Organizing Political Life: What Administrative Reorganization Tells Us about Government. *American Political Science Review* 77(2), 281–96.

Marconi, N. (2002). *Diagnóstico do Sistema de Serviço Civil do Governo Federal no Brasil*. Washington, DC: Banco InterAmericano de Desarrollo.

Marris, R. (1964). *The Economic Theory of Managerial Capitalism*. Glencoe, IL: Free Press of Glencoe.

Marsden, D. (1997). Public Service Pay Reforms in European Countries. *Transfer*, 3(1), 62–85.

Mascarenhas, R. C. (1993). Building an Enterprise Culture in the Public Sector: Reform of the Public Sector in Australia, Britain, and New Zealand. *Public Administration Review* 53(4), 319–28.

Massey, A. ed. (2011). *International Handbook on Civil Service Systems*. Cheltenham: Edward Elgar.

Mauro, P. (1995). Corruption and Growth. *Quarterly Journal of Economics* 110(3), 681–712.

McCubbins, M. D., Noll, R. G. & Weingast, B. R. (1987). Administrative Procedures as Instruments of Political Control. *Journal of Law, Economics, & Organization* 3(2), 243–77.

McMillan, J. & Zoido, P. (2004). How to Subvert Democracy: Montesinos in Peru. *Journal of Economic Perspectives* 18(4), 69–92.

Mehlum, H., Moene, K. & Torvik, R. (2006a). Cursed by Resources or Institutions? *The World Economy* 29(8), 1117–31.

Mehlum, H., Moene, K. & Torvik, K. (2006b). Institutions and the Resource Curse. *The Economic Journal* 116(508), 1–20.

Meiniger, M-C. (2000). The Development and Current Features of the French Civil Service System. In H. A. G. M. Bekke and F. M. Van der Meer, eds., *Civil Service Systems in Western Europe*, Bodmin, Cornwall: MPG Books Ltd.

Meyer, R. & Hammerschmid, G. (2006). Public Management Reform: An Identity Project. *Public Policy and Administration* 21(1): 99–115.

Meyer-Sahling, J-H. (2010). In Search of the Shadow of the Past: Legacy Explanations and Administrative Reform in Post-Communist East Central Europe. In M. Painter and G. B. Peters, eds., *Tradition and Public Administration*. Basingstoke: Palgrave Macmillan, pp. 203–14.

Meyer-Sahling, J-H. & Veen, T. (2012). Governing the Post-Communist State: Government Alternation and Senior Civil Service Politicisation in Central and Eastern Europe. *East European Politics* 28(1), 4–22.

Micco, A. & Pagés, C. (2006). *The Economic Effects of Employment Protection: Evidence from International Industry-Level Data*. Institute for the Study of Labor Discussion Paper No. 2433. Bonn: Institute for the Study of Labor.

Miller, G. J. (1992). *Managerial Dilemmas: The Political Economy of Hierarchy*. Cambridge, MA: Cambridge University Press.

   (1997). The Impact of Economics on Contemporary Political Science. *Journal of Economic Literature* 35(3), 1173–1204.

Miller, G. (2000). Above Politics: Credible Commitment and Efficiency in the Design of Public Agencies. *Journal of Public Administration Research and Theory* 10(2), 289–328.

   (2005). The Political Evolution of Principal-Agent Models. *Annual Review of Political Science* 8(1), 203–25.

Miller, G. J. & Hammond, T. H. (1994). Why Politics Is More Fundamental than Economics. *Journal of Theoretical Politics* 6(1), 5–26.

Miller, G. J. and Whitford, A. B. (2002). Trust and Incentives in Principal-agent Negotiations. *Journal of Theoretical Politics*, 14(2), 231–67.

Miller, G. J. and Whitford, A. B. (2016). *Above Politics. Bureaucratic Discretion and Credible Commitment*. Cambridge: Cambridge University Press.

Mills, C. W. (1956). *The Power Elite*. Oxford: Oxford University Press.

Misner, G. (1963). Mobility and the Establishment of a Career System in Police Personnel Administration. *Journal of Criminal Law, Criminology, and Police Science* 54(4), 529–39.

Mitchell T. (2003). The Middle East in the Past and Future of Social Science. UCIAS Ed. Vol. 3. The Politics of Knowledge: Area Studies and Disciplines. Available at: http://repositories.cdlib.org/uciaspubs/editedvolumes/3/3/.

Moe, T. & Caldwell, M. (1994). The Institutional Foundations of Democratic Government: A Comparison of Presidential and Parliamentary Systems. *Journal of Institutional and Theoretical Economics* 150(1), 171–95.

Moe, T. M. (1984). The New Economics of Organization. *American Journal of Political Science* 28(4), 739–77.

(1990). Political Institutions: The Neglected Side of the Story. *Journal of Law, Economics, and Organization* 6, 213–53.

(1997). The Positive Theory of Public Bureaucracy. In D. Mueller, eds., *Perspectives on Public Choice: a Handbook*. New York, NY: Cambridge University Press, pp. 455–80.

Molinas, C. (2013). *Qué hacer con España*. Barcelona: Ediciones Destino.

Montero, D. (2009). *La casta. El increíble chollo de ser político en España*. 4th edn. Madrid: La Esfera de los Libros.

Montinola G. R. & Jackman, R. W. (2002). Sources of Corruption: A Cross-country Study. *British Journal of Political Science* 32(1), 147–70.

Morris, S. D. (2009). *Political Corruption in Mexico: The Impact of Democratization*. Boulder, CO: Lynne Rienner Publishers.

Mouritzen, M. P. E. & Svara, J. H. (2002). *Leadership at the Apex: Politicians and Adminstration in Western Local Governments*. Pittsburgh, PA: University of Pittsburgh Press.

Murnighan, K. J., Malhotra, D. & Weber, M. J. (2004). Paradoxes of Trust: Empirical and Theoretical Departures from a Traditional Model. In R. M. Kramer and K. S. Cook, eds., *Trust and Distrust Across Organizational Contexts: Dilemmas and Approaches*. New York, NY: Russell SAGE Foundation, pp. 293–326.

Murphy, K. R. & Cleveland, J. (1995). *Understanding Performance Appraisal: Social, Organizational, and Goal-based Perspectives*. London: SAGE Publications Inc.

Murphy, K., Shleifer A. & Vishny, R. (1993). Why is Rent-seeking so Costly to Growth? *The American Economic Review* 83(2), 409–14.

Nelson, M. (1982). A Short Ironic History of American National Bureaucracy. *Journal of Politics* 44(3), 747–78.

Neustadt, R. E. (1991). *Presidential Power and the Modern Presidents: The Politics of Leadership from Roosevelt to Reagan*. Simon and Schuster.

Nieto, A. (1976). *La burocracia. El pensamiento burocrático*. Madrid: Instituto de Estudios Administrativos.

(1986). *Concepciones burocráticas y reformas funcionariales. AAVV Estudios históricos sobre Administración y Derecho Administrativo*. Madrid: INAP.

(1996). *La nueva organización del desgobierno*. Madrid: Ed. Ariel.

Nilsson, T. (2000). Ämbetsmannen I själva verket – rekrytering och avance-mang I en moderniserad stat 1809–1880. Score rapportserie 2000:5.

Stockholm: Stockholm University, Stockholms centrum för forskning om offentlig sektor.

Niskanen, W. (1971). *Bureaucracy and Representative Government*. Chicago, IL: Aldine Atherton.

North, D. C. (1981). *Structure and Change in Economic History*. New York, NY: Norton & Co.

North, D. C (1990). *Institutions, Institutional Change, and Economic Performance*. New York, NY: Cambridge University Press.

North, D. C. & Thomas, R. P. (1973). *The Rise of the Western World: A New Economic History*. New York, NY: Cambridge University Press.

North, D. C. and B. R. Weingast, (1989). Constitutions and Commitment: The Evolution of Institutions Governing Public Choice in Seventeenth Century England. *Journal of Economic History* 49(4).

North, D.C, Wallis, J. J. & Weingast, B. (2009). *Violence and Social Orders. Violence and Social Orders: A Conceptual Framework for Interpreting Recorded Human History*. New York, NY: Cambridge University Press.

Northcote, S. & Trevelyan, C. (1853). *Report on the Organisation of the Permanent Civil Service*. London: House of Commons.

O'Gorman, F. (2001). Patronage and the Reform of the State in England, 1700–1860. In S. Piattoni, ed., *Clientelism, Interests, and Democratic Representation: The European Experience in Historical and Comparative Perspective*. Cambridge, MA: Cambridge University press, pp. 54–76.

OECD. (1995). *Governance in Transition: Public Management Reforms in OECD Countries*. Paris: OECD.

OECD Public Governance Review. (2012). Greece: Reform of Social Welfare Programmes. Available at: www.oecd-ilibrary.org/governance/greece-social-welfare-programmes_9789264196490-en;jsessionid=3kumbubinbs7e.x-oecd-live-02 [Retrieved 17 December 2013].

(2003). Country Reports on Performance-related Pay from France, Germany, the UK and Sweden. [Unclassified document].

(2004). Performance-related Pay Policies for Government Employees: Main Trends in OECD Member Countries. [Unclassified document].

(2005). Performance-related Pay policies for Government Employees: Main Trends in OECD Member Countries. [Unclassified document]. Available at: http://www.oecd-ilibrary.org/governance/performance-related-pay-policies-for-government-employees_9789264007550-en [Retrieved 15 May 2013].

(2008). *The State of the Public Service*. Paris: OECD.

(2009). *Gender, Institutions and Development Database.* Available at: http://stats.oecd.org/Index.aspx?DatasetCode=GID2 [Retrieved 15 May 2013].

(2009). *Government at a Glance.* Paris: OECD Publishing.

(2011). *Public Servants as Partners for Growth. Toward a Stronger, Leaner and More Equitable Workforce.* Paris: OECD Publishing.

Olsen, J. P. (2003). Towards a European Administrative Space? *Journal of European Public Policy* 10(4), 506–31.

(2005). Maybe it is Time to Rediscover Bureaucracy. *Journal of Public Administration Research and Theory* 16(1), 1–24.

(2008). The Ups and Downs of Bureaucratic Organization. *Annual Review of Political Science* 11(14), 13–37.

Olson, M. (1965). *The Logic of Collective Action: Public Goods and the Theory of Groups.* Vol. 124. London: Harvard University Press.

(1982). *The Rise and Decline of Nations. Economic Growth, Stagflation and Social Rigidities.* London: Yale University Press.

(1993). Dictatorship, Democracy, and Development. *American Political Science Review* 87(3), 567–76.

(2000). *Power and Prosperity: Outgrowing Communist and Capitalist Dictatorships.* New York, NY: Basic Books.

Ongaro, E. (2008). Introduction: The Reform of Public Management in France, Greece, Italy, Portugal and Spain. *International Journal of Public Sector Management* 21(2), 101–17.

(2010). The Napoleonic Administrative Tradition and Public Management Reform in France, Greece, Italy and Portugal. In M. Painter and B. G. Peters, eds., *Tradition and Public Administration.* Basingstoke: Palgrave MacMillan, pp. 174–90.

(2011). The Role of Politics and Institutions in the Italian Administrative Reform Trajectory. *Public Administration* 89(3), 738–55.

(2012). From Reluctant to Compelled Reformers? Reflections on Three Decades of Public Management Reform in France, Greece, Italy, Portugal, and Spain. In J. Diamond and J. Liddle, eds., *Emerging and Potential Trends in Public Management: An Age of Austerity (Critical Perspectives on International Public Sector Management, Volume 1)*, Bingley: Emerald Group Publishing Ltd, pp. 105–27.

Osborne, D. & Gaebler, T. (1992). *Reinventing Government: How the Entrepreneurial Spirit Is Transforming Government.* Reading, MA: Addison Wesley Public Company.

Page, E. C. (2012). Comparative and International Public Administration. In G. Peters, and J. Pierre, eds., *The Sage Handbook of Public Administration.* London: SAGE Publications Ltd, pp. 507–10.

Page, E. C. & Wright, V., eds., (1999). *Bureaucratic Elites in Western European States: A Comparative Analysis of Top Officials.* Oxford: Oxford University Press.

Painter, M. & Peters. B. G. (2010). Administrative Traditions in Comparative Perspective: Families, Groups and Hybrids. In M. Painter and G. B. Peters, eds., *Tradition and Public Administration.* Basingstoke: Palgrave Macmillan, pp. 19–30.

Panizza, U. (2001). Electoral Rules, Political Systems, and Institutional Quality. *Economics and Politics* 13(3), 311–42.

Panozzo, F. (2000). Management by Decree. Paradoxes in the Reform of the Italian Public Sector. *Scandinavian Journal of Management* 16(4), 357–73.

Parrado, S. (2000). The Development and Current Features of the Spanish Civil Service System. In H. A. G. M. Bekke and F. M. Van der Meer, eds., *Civil Services Systems in Western Europe.* London: Edward Elgar, pp. 247–74.

(2004). Politicization of the Spanish Civil Service: Continuity in 1982 and 1996. In G. B. Peters and J. Pierre, eds., *Politicization of the Civil Service in Comparative Perspective. The Quest for Control.* London: Routledge, pp. 227–56.

(2008). Failed Policies but Institutional Innovation through "Layering" and 'Diffusion' in Spanish Central Administration. *International Journal of Public Sector Management* 21(2), 230–52.

(2012). Rewards for High Public Offices in Spain (1990–2009). In M. Brans and G. B. Peters, eds., *Rewards for High Public Office in Europe and North America.* London: Routledge, pp. 111–24.

Pasquino, G. (2008). *Populism and Democracy. Twenty-First Century Populism. The Spectre of Western Democracy.* Basingstoke: Palgrave MacMillan, 15–29.

Peltzman, Sam. (1976). Toward a More General Theory of Regulation. *Journal of Law and Economics* 19(2), 211–40.

Pérez Boga, R. Riña a Garrotazos. *El País.* 11–12-2013.

Perrow, C. (1990). Economic Theories of Organization. In S. Zukin and P. Dimaggio, eds., *Structures of Capital.* New York, NY: Cambridge University Press, pp. 121–52.

Persson, T. & Tabellini, G. (2003). *The Economic Effects of Constitutions. Munich Lectures in Economics.* London: The MIT Press.

Persson, T., Roland, G. & Tabellini, G. (2000). Comparative Politics and Public Finance. *Journal of Political Economy* 108(6), 1121–61.

Persson, T., Tabellini, G. & Trebbi, F. (2003). Electoral Rules and Corruption. *Journal of the European Economic Association* 1(4), 958–89.

Peters, B. G. & Pierre, J. (2012). *The SAGE Handbook of Public Administration.* London: SAGE Publications.

Peters, B. G. (2002). *Politics of Bureaucracy*. London: Routledge.

(2008). The Napoleonic Tradition, *International Journal of Public Sector Management* **21**(2), 118–32.

Peters, B. G. (1992). Government Reorganization: A Theoretical Analysis. *International Political Science Review/Revue internationale de science politique* **13**(2), 199–217.

(1997). Policy Transfers between Governments: The Case of Administrative Reforms. *West European Politics* **20**(4), 71–88.

(2001). *The Future of Governing: Four Emerging Models*. Lawrence, KS: University Press of Kansas.

Peters, B. G. & Pierre, J. (2001). Civil Servants and Politicians: The Changing Balance. In G. B. Peters and J. Pierre, eds., *Politicians, Bureaucrats and Administrative Reform*. London: Routledge, pp. 1–10.

(2001). Developments in Intergovernmental Relations: Towards Multilevel Governance. *Policy and Politics* **29**(2), 131–36.

(2004). Politicization of the Civil Service: Concepts, Causes, Consequences. In B. G. Peters and J. Pierre, eds., *Politicization of the Civil Service in Comparative Perspective*. London: Routledge, pp. 1–13.

Petersson, O. & Söderlind, D. (1993). *Förvaltningspolitik*. Stockholm: C.E. Fritzes AB.

Piattoni, S. (2001). *Clientelism, Interests, and Democratic Representation: The European Experience in Historical and Comparative Perspective*. New York, NY: Cambridge University Press.

Pierre, J. (1993). Legitimacy, Institutional Change, and the Politics of Public Administration in Sweden. *International Political Science Review* **14**(4), 387–401.

(1995a). A Framework of Comparative Public Administration. In J. Pierre, ed., *Bureaucracy in the Modern State*. London: Edward Elgar, pp. 205–18.

(1995b). Governing the Welfare State: Public Administration, the State and Society in Sweden. In J. Pierre, ed., *Bureaucracy in the Modern State*. London: Edward Elgar, pp. 140–60.

(2004). Politicization of the Swedish Civil Service: A Necessary Evil – Or Just Evil? In B. G. Peters, and J. Pierre, eds., *Politicization of the Civil Service in Comparative Perspective*. London: Routledge, pp. 1–13.

(2011). Stealth Economy? Economic Theory and the Politics of Administrative Reform. *Administration & Society* **43**(6), 672–92.

Pinotti P. (2012). Trust, Regulation, and Market Failures. *Review of Economics and Statistics* **94**(3), 650–58.

Pollit, C. (1990). Performance Indicators: Root and Branch. In M. Cave, M. Kogan and R. Smith, eds., *Output and Performance Measurements in Government: The State of the Art*. London: Jessica Kingsley, pp. 167–78.

Pollitt, C. (1993). *Managerialism and the Public Service*. Oxford: Blackwell.
Pollitt, C. & Bouckaert, G. (2011). *Public Management Reform: A Comparative Analysis - New Public Management, Governance, and the Neo-Weberian State*: 3rd edition. Oxford: Oxford University Press.
Prats, J. (1984). Administración Pública y Transición Democrática. Pensamiento Iberoamericano **5b**, 445–62.
Prats, J. in Catalá, J. (2003). *Reinventar la burocracia y construir la nueva gerencia pública*. Spain: Virtual Library of the Instituto Internacional de Gobernabilidad de Cataluña.
Interview with Joan Prats at Institut Internacional de Gobernabilitat de Catalunya, 21 May 2005, Barcelona.
Premfors, R. (1991). The "Swedish Model" and Public Sector Reform. *West European Politics* **14**(3), 83–95.
Przeworski, A., Alvarez, M., Cheibub, J. & Limongi, F. (2000). *Democracy and Development: Political Institutions and Well-being in the World, 1950–1990*. Cambridge, MA: Cambridge University Press.
Público 12-01-2011, "400 millones de euros para un proyecto vacío"
27-02-2011, "Las estaciones fantasma del AVE"
30-12-2013.El SUP acusa a Interior de 'politizar' las unidades anticorrupción.
Raadschelders, J., Toonen, T. and Van der Meer, F. (2015). Civil Service Systems and the Challenges of the 21st Century. In F. Van der Meer, T. Toonen, and J. Raadschelders, eds., *Comparative Civil Service Systems in the 21st Century*. London: Palgrave Macmillan, pp. 1–14.
Radin, B. A. (2000). The Government Performance and Results Act and the Tradition of Federal Management Reform: Square Pegs in Round Holes? *Journal of Public Administration Research and Theory* **10**(1), 111–35.
Rauch, J. & Evans, P. (2000). Bureaucratic Structure and Bureaucratic Performance in Less Developed Countries. *Journal of Public Economics* **75**(1), 49–71.
Rice C. (2005). Remarks at the American University in Cairo, June 20. Available at: www.state.gov/secretary/rm/2005/48328.htm.
Riker, W. H. (1982). *Liberalism against Populism*. San Francisco: W. H. Freeman.
Riksdagens revisorer. (2002). *Statens personalpolitik. En uppföljning av 1985 års personalpolitiska beslut. 2001/02:12*. Stockholm: Riksdagens revisorer.
Riley, J. G. (2001). Silver Signals: Twenty-five Years of Screening and Signaling. *Journal of Economic Literature* **39**(2), 432–78.
Risher, H. (1999). Are Public Employers Ready for a "New Pay" Program? *Public Personnel Management* **28**(3), 323–43.

Robinson, J. A. & Torvik, R. (2005). White Elephants. *Journal of Public Economics* **89**(2), 197–210.

Robinson, J. A., Torvik, R. & Verdier, T. (2006). Political Foundations of the Resource Curse. *Journal of Development Economics* **79**(2), 447–68.

Rodrik, D., Subramanian, A. & Trebbi, F. (2004). Institutions Rule: The Primacy of Institutions over Geography and Integration in Economic Development. *Journal of Economic Growth* **9**(2), 131–65.

Roeder, P. G. (2001). *Ethnolinguistic Fractionalization (ELF) Indices, 1961 and 1985.* February 16. Available at: http://weber.ucsd.edu/~proeder/elf.htm [Retrieved 15 May 2013].

Rohr, J. (2009). Introduction. In F. J. Goodnow, ed., *Politics and Administration: A Study in Government*, 5th edition. Transaction Publishers.

Roldan, A. (2013). Financial Windfalls and Institutional Deterioration: Evidence from the EMU. Working Paper. London: Mimeo, London School of Economics.

Root, H. (1989). Tying the King's Hands: Royal Fiscal Policy during the Old Regime. *Rationality and Society* **1**(2), 240–59.

Rosenbloom, D. (1971). *Federal Service and the Consitution: The Development of the Public Employment Relationship.* Ithaca: Cornell University Press.

Rosta, M. (2011). *What Makes a New Public Management Reform Successful? An Institutional Analysis.* Research Paper. Budapest: Corvinus University of Budapest.

Rothstein, B. (1998). *Just Institutions Matter: The Moral and Political Logic of the Universal Welfare State.* Cambridge, MA: Cambridge University Press.

(2009). Creating Political Legitimacy Electoral Democracy versus Quality of Government. *American Behavioral Scientist* **53**(3), 311–30.

(2011). *The Quality of Government: Corruption, Social Trust and Inequality in International Perspective.* Chicago, IL: University of Chicago Press.

Rothstein, B. & Teorell, J. (2008). What Is Quality of Government: A Theory of Impartial Political Institutions. *Governance* **21**(2), 165–90.

(2012). Defining and Measuring Quality of Government. In B. Rothstein and S. Holmberg, eds., *Good Government, The Relevance of Political Science.* Cheltenham: Edward Elgar Publishing Limited, pp. 13–39.

Rothstein, B. & Teorell J. (2015). Getting to Sweden, Part II: Breaking with Corruption in the Nineteenth Century. *Scandinavian Political Studies* **38**(3), 238–54.

Rothstein, B. & Uslaner, E. (2005). All for All: Equality, Corruption, and Social Trust. *World Politics* **58**(1), 41–72.

Rouban, L. (2004). Politicization of the Civil Service in France: From Structural to Strategic Politicization. In B. G. Peters and J. Pierre, eds.,

Politicization of the Civil Service in Comparative Perspective. London: Routledge, pp. 81–100.

(2008). Reform without Doctrine: Public Management in France. *The International Journal of Public Sector Management* **21**(2), 133–49.

(2012) Politicization of the Civil Service. In B. G. Peters and J. Pierre, eds., *Handbook of Public Administration.* London: SAGE Publications Ltd, pp. 380–91.

Rubinstein, W. D. (1983). The End of Old Corruption in Britain, 1780–1860. *Past & Present* **101**, 55–86.

Rugge, F. (2003). Administrative Tradition in Western Europe. In B. G. Peters and J. Pierre, eds., *Handbook of Public Administration*, London: SAGE Publications Ltd, pp. 177–91.

Ruhil, A. V. S. (2003). Urban Armageddon or Politics as Usual? The Case of Municipal Civil Service Reform. *American Journal of Political Science* **47**(1), 159–70.

Ruhil, A. V. S. & Camões, P. J. (2003). What Lies Beneath: The Political Roots of State Merit Systems. *Journal of Public Administration Research and Theory* **13**(1), 27–42.

Ruin, O. (1991). The Duality of the Swedish Central Administration: Ministeries and Central Agencies. In A. Farzmand, ed., *Handbook of Comparative and Developmental Public Administration.* Basel: Marcel Dekker.

Sachs, J. D. & Warner, A. M. (1995). Economic Reform and the Process of Global Integration. *Brookings Papers on Economic Activity* **26**(1), 1–118.

Sachs, J. D. (2003a). Institutions Don't Rule: Direct Effects of Geography on Per Capita Income. NBER Working Paper No. 9490. Cambridge, MA: National Bureau of Economic Research.

Sachs, J. D. (2003b). Institutions Matter, but not for Everything. *Finance and Development* **40**(2), 38–41.

(2001). The Curse of Natural Resources. *European Economic Review* **45** (4–6), 827–38.

Sahlin-Andersson, K. (2001). National, International and Transnational Construction of New Public Management. In T. Christensen and P. Lægreid, eds., *New Public Management: The Transformation of Ideas and Practice.* Aldershot: Ashgate, pp. 43–72.

Salvados (2013a), El denominador común de las infraestructuras es que el contribuyente es el que sale perdiendo La Sexta TV 08–12-2013. Available at: www.lasexta.com/programas/salvados/noticias/%E2%80% 9Cel-denominador-comun-infraestructuras-que-contribuyente-que-sale-perdiendo%E2%80%9D_2013120800123.html [Retrieved 08 Jan 2014].

(2013b), En el negocio de las autopistas de peaje un 50% de lo que facturas va al bolsillo La Sexta TV 08–12-2013. Available at: www.lasexta.com/programas/salvados/noticias/%E2%80%9Cen-negocio-autopistas-peaje-que-facturas-bolsillo%E2%80%9D_2013120800124.html [Retrieved 08 Jan 2014].

Sánchez-Cuenca, I. (2009). Estado de Derecha, *El País*. 02–08-2009.

Sandholtz, W. & Gray, M. M. (2003). International Integration and National Corruption. *International Organization* 57(4), 761–800.

Sandholtz W. & Koetzle W. A. (2000). Accounting for Corruption: Economic Structure, Democracy, and Trade. *International Studies Quarterly* 44(1), 31–50.

Santiso, J. (2011). Peligro de 'exitomanía. *El País*. 2011-04-24.

Saura, P. (2013). La Crisis en la Agencia Tributaria. *El País*. 26-11-2013.

Sausman, C. & Locke, R. (2004). The British civil service:examining the question of politicization. In B. G. Peters and J. Pierre, eds., *Politicization of the Civil Service in Comparative Perspective*. London: Routledge, pp. 101–24.

Schaffer, B. (1973). *The Administrative Factor: Papers in Organization, Politics and Development*. London: Frank Cass Publishers.

Schelling, T. (1960). *The Strategy of Conflict*. Oxford: Oxford University Press.

Schneider, B. R. (2004). *Business Politics and the State in Twentieth-century Latin America*. New York, NY. Cambridge University Press.

Schultz, D. A. & Maranto, R. (1998). *The Politics of Civil Service Reform*. New York, NY: Peter Lang.

Schuster, C. (2014). *When the Victor Cannot Claim the Spoils: Patronage Control and Bureaucratic. Professionalization in Latin America*. Paper presented at the 64th Annual Conference of the Political Science Association, 14–16 April 2014, Manchester, United Kingdom.

Schuster, J. & Zingheim, P. (1992). *The New Pay. Linking Employee and Organizational Performance*, New York, NY: Impressum Lexington Books.

Schwab, K. (2012). *The Global Competitiveness Report*. Geneva: World Economic Forum.

Scott, Z. (2011). *Evaluation of Public Sector Governance Reforms 2001–2011. Literature Review*. Oxford. Oxford Policy Management.

Selznick, P. (1957). *Leadership in Administration: A Sociological Interpretation*. West Sussex: University of California Press.

Shleifer A. (2010). Efficient Regulation. NBER Working Paper No. 15651. Cambridge, MA: National Bureau of Economic Research.

Silberman, B. (1993). *Cages of Reason: The Rise of the Rational State in France, Japan, the United states, and Great Britain*. Chicago, IL: Chicago University Press.

Sjölund, M. (1989). *Statens Lönepolitik 1966–1988*. Doctoral Dissertation. Uppsala: Uppsala University, Department of Government.

Sotiropoulos, D. A. (1999). A Description of the Greek Higher Civil Service. In Page, E. C. and Wright, V, eds., *Bureaucratic Elites in Western European States: A Comparative Analysis of Top Officials*. Oxford: Oxford University Press, pp. 13–31.

   (2004). Two Faces of Politicization of the Civil Service: The Case of Contemporary Greece. In G. B. Peters and J. Pierre, eds., *Politicization of the Civil Service in Comparative Perspective. The Quest for Control*. London: Routledge, pp. 257–282.

Sovey, A. & Green D. (2011). Instrumental Variables Estimation in Political Science: A Readers' Guide. *American Journal of Political Science* 55(1), 188–200.

Spanou, C. (1996). Penelope's Suitors: Administrative Modernization and Party Competition in Greece. *West European Politics* 19(1), 97–124.

   (2008). State Reform in Greece: Responding to Old and New Challenges. *The International Journal of Public Sector Management* 21(2), 150–73.

Spanou, C. & Sotiropoulos, D. (2011). The Odyssey of Administrative Reform in Greece, 1981–2009: A Tale of Two Reform Paths. *Public Administration* 89(3), 723–37.

Srivastava, V. & Larizza, M. (2012). Working with the Grain for Reforming the Public Service: A Live Example from Sierra Leone. World Bank Policy Research Working Paper No. 6152.

Statskontoret. (1997). *Staten i omvandling. 1997:15*. Solna: Statskontoret.

Stigler, G. J. (1971). The Theory of Economic Regulation. *The Bell Journal of Economics and Management Science* 2(1), 3–21.

Stock, J., Wright, J. & Yogo, M. (2002). A Survey of Weak Instruments and Weak Identification in Generalized Method of Moments. *Journal of Business and Economic Statistics* 20, 518–29.

Strath, A. (2004). *Teacher Policy Reforms in Sweden: The Case of IndividuAlised Pay. International Institute for Educational Planning*. Paris: UNESCO.

Suay, J. (1987). La reforma de la Función Pública. *Su impacto sobre la burocracia española. Revista Española de Derecho Administrativo* 56, 511–28.

Suleiman, E. A. (2003). *Dismantling Democratic States*. Princeton, NJ: Princeton University Press.

Sundell, A. (2014). Are Formal Examinations the most Meritocratic Way to recruit Civil Servants? Not in all Countries. *Public Administration* 92(2), 440–57.

(2015). *Public Administration and Corruption*. Gothenburg: Department of Political Science, University of Gothenburg.

Sung, H. E. (2003). Fairer Sex or Fairer System? Gender and Corruption Revisited. *Social Forces* 82(2), 703–23.

(2004). Democracy and Political Corruption: A Cross-National Comparison. *Crime, Law and Social Change* 41(2), 179–93.

Svara, J. H. (1998). The Politics–Administration Dichotomy Model as Aberration. *Public Administration Review* 58(1), 51–8.

Svensson, J. (2005). Eight Questions about Corruption. *The Journal of Economic Perspectives* 19(3), 19–42.

Swamy, A. V., Knack, S., Lee, Y. & Azfar O. (2001). Gender and Corruption. *Journal of Development Economics* 64(1), 25–55.

Swedish Government proposition 1984/85: 219.

Tabellini, G. (2008). Presidential Address Institutions and Culture. *Journal of the European Economic Association* 6(2–3), 255–94.

Teaford, J. C. (1983). *The Unheralded Triumph: City Government in America, 1870–1900*. Baltimore, MD: Johns Hopkins University Press.

(1993). *The Twentieth-Century American City*. Baltimore, MD: Johns Hopkins University Press.

Teodoro, M. (2009). Bureaucratic Job Mobility and the Diffusion of Innovations. *American Journal of Political Science* 53 (1), 175–89.

(2010).Contingent Professionalism: Bureaucratic Mobility and the Adoption of Water Conservation Rates. *Journal of Public Administration Research and Theory*: 20(2), 437–59.

(2011). *Bureaucratic Ambition: Careers, Motives, and the Innovative Administrator*. Baltimore: Johns Hopkins University Press.

(2014). When professionals lead: Executive Management, Normative Isomorphism, and Policy Implementation. *Journal of Public Administration Research and Theory* 24(4), 983–1004.

Teorell, J. & Rothstein, B. (2015). Getting to Sweden, Part I: War and Malfeance, 1720–1850. *Scandinavian Political Studies* 38(3), 217–37.

Teorell, J., Dahlström, C. & Dahlberg, S. (2011). *The Quality of Government Expert Survey Dataset*. University of Gothenburg: The Quality of Government Institute. Available at: www.qog.pol.gu.se.

Teorell, J., Charron, N., Dahlberg, S., Holmberg, S., Rothstein, B., Sundin, P. & Svensson, R. (2013). The Quality of Government Dataset, version 15 May 13. University of Gothenburg: The Quality of Government Institute. Available at: www.qog.pol.gu.se.

Tepper, B. J. & Taylor, E. C. (2003). Relationships among Supervisors and Subordinates, Procedural Justice Perceptions and Organizational Citizenship Behaviours. *Academy of Management Journal* 46(1), 97–105.

The Bertelsmann Stiftung's Transformation Index 2012 (BTI). Available at: www.bti-project.org/index/. [Retrieved 15 May 2013].

The Economist. 18-02-2012. Venezuela's Oil Industry. Spilling Over.

16-06-2012. How the Bureaucrats Rob the Taxpayer.

28-09-2013. The Land of the Setting Sun.

The Guardian. 8-04-2006. Marbella, Where Corruption and Bad Taste Thrive.

07–08-2013. Yours for €100m: Spanish Airport, Mint Condition, One Careless Owner.

The New York Times. 18-07-2012. In Spain, a Symbol of Ruin at an Airport to Nowhere.

08–09-2013. Madrid and Istanbul Respond Differently to Rejection by Olympics.

07-01-2014. Purge of Police Said to be Move by Turkey to Disrupt Graft Inquiry.

The Wall Street Journal 11–12-2015 "Upstart in Spanish Election Gets Help From Blogging Professor."

The Worldwide Governance Indicators (WGI). Available at: http://info.worldbank.org/governance/wgi/index.aspx#home [Retrieved 15 May 2013].

Thompson, J. R. (2007). Labor-management Relations and Partnerships: Were They Reinvented? In G. B. Peters and J. Pierre, eds., *The Handbook of Public Administration.* London: SAGE Publications, pp. 49–62.

Thompson, V. A. (1965) Bureaucracy and Innovation. *Administrative Science Quarterly* 10(1), 1–20.

Tolbert, P. S. & Zucker, L. G. (1983). Institutional Sources of Change in the Formal Structure of Organizations: The Diffusion of Civil Service Reform, 1889–1935. *Administrative Science Quarterly* 28(1), 22–39.

Transparency International. (2013). *Corruption Perception Index 2013.* Available at: www.transparency.org/research/cpi/overview.

Treisman, D. (2000). *Decentralization and the Quality of Government.* Working paper. Department of Political Science University of California, Los Angeles.

(2007). What Have We Learned about the Causes of Corruption from Ten Years of Cross-National Empirical Research? *Annual Review of Political Science* 10, 211–44.

Tsebelis, G. (1995). Decision Making in Political Systems: Veto Players in Presidentialism, Parliamentarism, Multicameralism and Multipartidism. *British Journal of Political Science* 25(3), 289–325.

Tullock, G. (1965). *The Politics of Bureaucracy.* Washington, DC: Public Affairs Press.

Tullock G. (1967). Welfare Costs of Tariffs, Monopolies, and Theft. *Western Economic Journal* 5(3), 224–32.

UNESCO. (2010). Institute for Statistics. Available at: www.uis.unesco.org [Retrieved 15 May 2013].

United Nations Statistics Divisions. (2013). Available at: http://unstats.un.org/unsd/snaama/dnlList.asp [Retrieved 15 May 2013].

Uslaner, E. M. (2008). *Corruption, Inequality, and the Rule of Law: The Bulging Pocket Makes the Easy Life.* Cambridge, MA: Cambridge University Press.

Vandenabeele, W., Scheepers, S. & Hondeghem, A. (2006). Public Service Motivation in an International Comparative Perspective: The UK and Germany. *Public Policy and Administration* 21(1), 13–31.

Van der Meer, F. M., Steen, T. and Wille, A. (2007). Western European Civil Service Systems. A Comparative Analysis. In J. C. N. Raadschelders, T. A. J. Toonen and F. M. Van der Meer, eds., *Civil Service in the 21st Century.* Basingstoke: Palgrave Macmillan. pp. 34–49.

Van Rijckeghem, C. and Weder, B. (2001). Bureaucratic Corruption and the Rate of Temptation: Do Wages in the Civil Service Affect Corruption, and by How Much? *Journal of Development Economics* 65(2), 307–31.

Van Riper, P. P. (1958). *History of the United States Civil Service.* Evanston, IL: Row Peterson.

Van Thiel, S. (2011). Comparing Agencies across Countries. In S. Van Thiel, K. Verhoest, G. Bouckaert and P. Laegreid, eds., *Government Agencies. Practices and Lessons from 30 countries.* Basingstoke: Palgrave Macmillan, pp. 18–26.

Verhoest, K. (2010). The Influence of Culture on NPM. In T. Christensen and P. Laegreid, eds., *The Ashgate Research Compendium to New Public Management.* Farnham: Ashgate, pp. 47–65.

Villoria, M. (1999). El papel de la burocracia en la transición y consolidación de la democracia española: primera aproximación. *Revista Española de Ciencia Política* 1(1), 97–125.

Voz Populi 09-04-2016. 17 minutos que dejaron helado al Congreso: "Espasa rechazó hacer un libro sobre mi historia por miedo"

Wade, R. (1990). *Governing the Market.* Princeton, NJ: Princeton University Press.

Weber, M. (1978)[1921]. *Economy and Society,* edited by G. Roth and C. Wittich.Berkeley, CA: University of California Press.

(1998) [1948]. *Essays in Sociology.* London: Routledge.

Weingast, B. & Marshall, W. J. (1988). The Industrial Organization of Congress; Or, Why Legislatures, like Firms, are not Organized as Markets. *The Journal of Political Economy* 96(1), 132–63.

Weingast, B. R. (1995). Economic Role of Political Institutions: Market-Preserving Federalism and Economic Development. *The Journal of Law, Economics & Organization* 11, 1.

Welzel, C. & Inglehart, R. (2008). The Role of Ordinary People in Democratization. *Journal of Democracy* 19(1), 126–40.

Wiarda, H. (1968). *Dictatorship and Development: The Methods of Control in Trujillo's. Dominican Republic.* Gainsville, FL: University of Florida Press.

Wildavsky, A. (1987). *Speaking Truth to Power: The Art and Craft of Policy Analysis.* New Brunswick, NJ: Transaction Books.

Willems, I., Janvier, R. & Henderickx, E. (2006). New Pay in European Civil Services: Is the Psychological Contract Changing? *International Journal of Public Sector Management* 19(6), 609–21.

Williamson, O. E. (1975). *Markets and Hierarchies: Analysis and Antitrust Implications.* New York, NY: Free Press.

  (1985). *The Economic Institutions of Capitalism.* New York, NY: Free Press.

  (1996). *The Mechanisms of Governance.* Oxford: Oxford University Press on Demand.

Wilson, W. (1887). Study of Administration. *Political Science Quarterly* 2(2), 197–222.

Wise, L. R. (1993). Whither Solidarity? Transitions in Swedish Public-Sector Pay Policy. *British Journal of Industrial Relations* 31(1), 75–95.

Woloch, I. (1994). *The New Regime: Transformations of the French Civic Order, 1789–1820s.* New York and London: Norton.

World Bank. (1997). *World Development Report 1997: The Changing Role of the State.* Oxford: Oxford University Press.

  (2011). *World Development Indicators 2011.* Available at: http://data.worldbank.org/data-catalog/world-development-indicators [Retrieved 15 May 2013].

  (2012). *The World Bank's Approach to Public Sector Management 2011–2012: Better Results from Public Sector Institutions.* Washington, DC: The World Bank.

  (2013). *World Development Indicators.* Available at: http://data.worldbank.org/data-catalog/world-development-indicators [Retrieved 15 May 2013].

Wunder, B. (1995). The Influences of the Napoleonic "Model" of Administration on the Administrative Organization of Other Countries. *Cahier d'Histoire de l'Administration*, No. 4, IIAS, Brussels.

Wängnerud, L. (2008). Quality of Government and Women's Representation - Mapping Out the Theoretical Terrain. QoG Working Paper Series 2008:5. Gothenburg: Gothenburg University, The Quality of Government Institute.

Yesilkagit, K. (2010). The Future of Administrative Tradition: Tradition as Ideas and Structure. In M. Painter and G. B. Peters, eds., *Tradition and Public Administration*. New York, NY: Palgrave Macmillan, pp. 145–57.

Yesilkagit, K. & De Vries, J. (2004). Reform Styles of Political and Administrative Elites in Majoritarian and Consensus Democracies: Public Management Reforms in New Zealand and the Netherlands. *Public Administration* 82(4), 951–74.

Young, C. & Turner, T. (1985). *The Rise and Decline of the Zairian State*. Madison, WI: University of Wisconsin Press.

Ziller, J. (2003). The Continental System of Administrative Legality. In B.G. Peters and J. Pierre, eds., *Handbook of Public Administration*. London: Sage, pp. 260–8.

Zuvanic, L., Iacoviello, M. & Rodríguez, G. A. (2010). The Weakest Link: The Bureaucracy and Civil Service Systems in Latin America. In C. Scartascini, E. Stein and M. Tommasi, eds., *How Democracy Works: Political Institutions, Actors, and Arenas in Latin American Policymaking*. Washington, DC: Inter-American Development Bank, pp. 147–176.

Index

Note: data sources are listed at 'quality of government, measuring, datasets', tables and figures at 'tables and figures', but discussion the content is indexed under subject headings such as 'effectiveness, separation of careers as key factor, testing the thesis'; 'corruption, separation of careers as protection against, testing the thesis'; Weberian closed bureaucracy, testing the reality

242